A Feast of Reason

A Feast of Reason:

The Civil War Journal of James Madison Hall

By Karen Gerhardt Fort

State House Press

Abilene, Texas

Library of Congress Cataloging-in-Publication Data

Fort, Karen Gerhardt
A Feast Of Reason
Karen Gerhardt Fort
p. cm.
Includes Bibliographical references and index.
ISBN 978-1-933337-70-8 (pbk. alk. paper)
ISBN- 1-933337-70-2 (pbk. alk. paper)

1. History/United States/Civil War Period (1850-1877) 2. History/United States/
State & Local/Southwest(AZ, NM, OK, TX) 3. History/Military/General

This paper meets the requirements of ANSI/NISO, Z39.48-1992(permanence of paper)

Binding materials have been chosen for durability
I. Title.
"Cataloging-in-Publication Data available from the Library of Congress"

Manufactured in the United States

First Printing

State House Press
1 McMurry University # 637
Abilene, Texas 79697-0001
325-793-4686

Printed in the United States of America
Distributed by Texas A&M University Press Consortium
800-826-8911
www.tamupress.com

ISBN-13: 978-1-933337-70-8
ISBN-10: 1-933337-70-2

Book Design by Rosenbohm Graphic Design

Publishing Offices McMurry University

Table of Contents

List of Illustrations

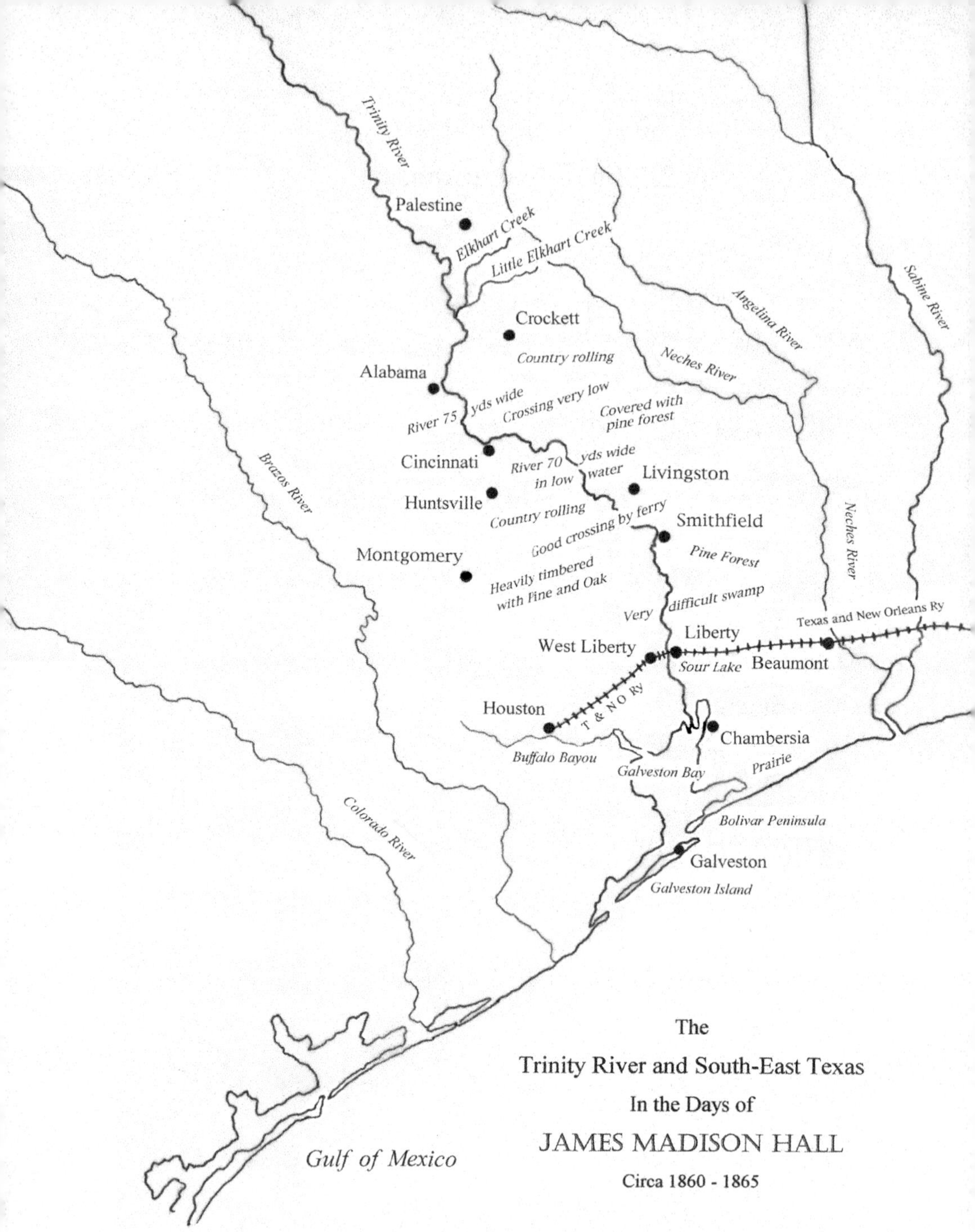

The

Trinity River and South-East Texas

In the Days of

JAMES MADISON HALL

Circa 1860 - 1865

Showing Principal Towns and Landings,
with notations about the Environs from the
Map of Texas and Part of New Mexico
Issued by the
U. S. Army Corps of Topographical Engineers,
1857

Map drawn by Tom A. Fort

Foreword

My introduction to the journal of James Madison Hall occurred in the mid-1990s when I was conducting research for a documentary film about the Texas home front during the Civil War. At the Sam Houston Regional Library in Liberty, librarian Darlene Mott showed me a typed copy of Hall's daily journal entries for the years 1860-1866, which provided details for my research. That led to further exploration of the people and places in Hall's world and the certainty that James Hall's story needed to be shared with others.

Hall's original journal is held by the Archives and Manuscripts Department at the Dolph Briscoe Center for American History at the University of Texas at Austin. A typed copy was given to the Sam Houston Regional Library by Robert L. Hall of Anahuac, great-nephew of James Hall, and by Robert Hall's son James H. and daughter-in-law Pattie Hall on October 14, 1975. A copy was also given to the Houston County Library in Crockett. I obtained a microfilm copy of the handwritten journal from the M. D. Anderson Library at the University of Houston. By comparing the handwritten journal with the typescript, I was able to clarify puzzling nineteenth century words and passages in the typescript and to create an accurate rendering of the journal. The handwritten journal, therefore, is the basis for all the material, quoted or summarized, herein.

During the work week, Hall wrote down notes about his activities in the margins and on blank pages of small books. For example, notes for 1862 were written in a small hardware catalogue from Tufts & Colley, Commission Merchants, in New York City. Hall may have acquired the undated catalogue during his trip to New York with his father in August 1860, but Tufts & Colley also had an office in Galveston, which Hall visited on occasion. The catalogue I saw was rather small with handwritten notes in the margins and on blank pages. On Sundays, Hall compiled his notes and wrote full entries in a large journal left over from his days as district clerk for Houston County. His copperplate handwriting is elegant and easy to read.

The handwritten journal showed that Hall often underlined words for emphasis. He also capitalized nouns, but not the word "negro," both common practices in the nineteenth century. He referred to "mill" in the singular and plural. There were two mills on the property, one at a higher elevation on Elkhart Creek than the other. The "upper" mill, as he identified it, collected water in the millpond that was occasionally allowed to drain downhill in order to fill the millpond for the "lower" mill on Elkhart Creek. The grinding of corn and wheat, with two pairs of millstones, occurred at the "lower" mill, and Hall built a home nearby.

Hall's few spelling errors were consistent, i.e., "stoped" for "stopped," and he separated "to day," but I have used it as one word. I have limited the use of [*sic*], meaning "thus in the original," for the sake of simplicity, except where the notation was needed for clarity. At times, Hall corrected his own misspellings, i.e., "changable" became "changeable," which the reader will easily follow. I have retained his spelling and capitalization, underlining and quotation marks, dashes and abbreviations. He often strung phrases together in long sentences or used only a word or two, indicating that he was in a hurry or that he had little to write about; where necessary for clarity, I have inserted commas or semicolons in brackets. Finally, I have summarized entries that were general in nature or repetitious, and for continuity I both described and concluded events that took place over several days or weeks. No important information has been omitted.

Due to a series of fires, the Houston County records that would have been enlightening in regard to Hall's frequent legal matters are lost. Articles in *The Houston Weekly Telegraph,* however, described the circumstances surrounding Hall's killing of Isaac Peacock and the two trials that followed, one in 1859 and one in 1860. Hall and his family also spent part of the war years in Liberty, where Hall served twice as mayor, but many Liberty County records were destroyed in a courthouse fire in 1874. Fortunately, newspapers from Crockett, Liberty, Houston, and Galveston have filled in details.

In the end, I came to know James Madison Hall, his family, and his world very well. A generous man, he opened his home to friends and strangers. He took in young Fanny Fitzsimmons and raised her as his own child. After his death, Margaret Hall honored his commitment by continuing to care for Fanny. Hall's relationship with Bill Hicks, as both slave and freedman, is remarkable. Hall taught the black man how to operate the gristmill and left Hicks to run it when he returned to Liberty in 1865. After the war, Bill Hicks remained with the Hall family as a paid employee. Hall once punished a "negro" caught stealing, but he also thrashed a white neighbor for beating a "negro." James Hall epitomized the Southern philosophy noted by English visitor Lieutenant Colonel Arthur J. L. Fremantle in 1863: "But they ["fellow travelers" in Texas, who did not "deny instances of cruelty"] say a man who is known to illtreat his negroes is hated by all the rest of the community." Hall did not mistreat his slaves and indeed worked alongside them during emergencies. He made no excuses for unruly Confederate soldiers, and he even praised Union troops for their treatment of Southerners. His "feast of reason" was to take the middle ground, to strive for a balance of justice, integrity, and fairness, and to place the needs of his family and the slaves dependent upon him above everything else.

Although a Confederate in sympathies, Hall was no political firebrand. Forty-two years old when the Civil War began in 1861, and responsible for a young wife and a baby daughter, as well as several slaves, he did not march off to war, but served the Confederacy as a provost marshal and deputy tax collector in Liberty and as a miller (a vital job exempted from conscription) in Houston County. However, like many Southerners, he became disillusioned with the Confederate government and the war effort. His modified philosophy toward the war, recorded in his journal entry for Monday, August 3, 1863, states, "Be it remembered that I voted for T. J. Chambers for Governor, because I am opposed to all those who advocate Military necessity as paramount to the Constitution and laws of the land."

Hall's unexpected death at the age of forty-seven was a tragedy to his wife and children, who needed him more than ever, and to the South, which needed strong, resourceful, reasonable men like James Madison Hall to rebuild and guide its war-weary people toward a brighter future.

Acknowledgments

This book would never have been possible without the generous help of the Hall family. Vickie P. Everhart, a descendant of Sam and Nellie Sharp, provided richly detailed genealogical data that explained and consolidated many disparate facts. She provided copies of depositions by Ida Mae Sharp Halyard, another descendant of Sam and Nellie Sharp, and Esther Hall Biggers, a descendant of Horace Oscar "Toby" Hall, which proved immensely important. Time and again, Mrs. Everhart answered my questions, forwarded information, and offered encouragement. The late Angelia Moore, a descendant of John A. and Margaret Hall McLemore, followed an historical trail that led back to my own hometown of Waco and to Oakwood Cemetery, where two of my grandparents are buried. Mrs. Moore found Cornelia Hall's tombstone there and traced the poetry carved into the marble, which she shared with me. I am deeply indebted to both of these ladies.

The late Eliza H. Bishop, Crockett historian, and Mary Ann Edwards of Austin, a descendant of the Aldrich family, provided important information, especially about photographs, at a critical time. Librarians, in my opinion, deserve a special place in heaven. Darlene Mott, Librarian, introduced me to the diary of James Madison Hall and helped me to locate hard-to-find materials at the Sam Houston Regional Library in Liberty. Her colleague, Archives Processor Sandra M. Burrell, searched out details like an archeologist and always found the right gem. Another colleague, Lisa Meisch, Archivist/Museum Curator, worked with me long distance to fill in missing and very necessary information. I am more grateful to each of them than I can say.

Bill Simmons at the Texas State Library and Archives Commission in Austin fielded questions and found important documentation. Lanita J. Clay, genealogist at the Texas Heritage Museum Historical Research Center, Hill College, Hillsboro, provided military histories. Nancy Davis and Melissa Almaraz of the McAllen Memorial Library in McAllen made microfilm copies of newspapers available through interlibrary loan. Stephanie Malmros, head of Archives and Manuscripts at the Dolph Briscoe Center for American History in Austin, confirmed that the original diaries of James Madison Hall and his father Joshua James Hall were kept there. Archivist Betsy Tyson at the Texas Medical Association Library in Austin greatly aided my research. I offer special thanks to Esteban Lomas, who always made the archives room at The Museum of South Texas History in Edinburg available so that I could review the microfilm at length.

Numerous individuals benefited my quest for information in unique ways, offering their insight, wisdom, and direction. Larry N. Jones, Associate Curator Emeritus, Agriculture Collection, Smithsonian Institution, enthusiastically helped with the finer points of nineteenth century technical terms. Jane Pidgeon at Conner Prairie Living History Museum (now Conner Prairie Interactive History Park), Fishers, Indiana, clarified details relative to weaving on a foot-powered loom. Curator Susan Cook provided additional data. Mason Maddox, miller at the Colvin Run Mill Historic Site, Great Falls, Virginia, explained the process of nineteenth century grist milling. Daniel Seifu, miller at Homestead Heritage Craft Village, Waco, Texas, explained historic milling terms used by Hall. Gary Kronk shared his vast knowledge of historic comets, with emphasis on the Civil War (Tebbutt) Comet of 1861. Gerard Mittelstaedt, former Director of the McAllen Memorial Library (now retired), found definitions of obscure terminology. Mark Klym, Information Specialist at the Wildlife Science, Research and Diversity Program, Texas Parks and Wildlife Department, identified a duck described by Hall, who did not recognize it.

Closer to home, Thomas A. Fort assisted with online and library research, reviewed the manuscript, researched and drew the map, and suggested excellent editorial and historical corrections. Historian and author Joseph E. Chance, Ph.D., now retired from the University of Texas–Pan American (now the University of Texas–Rio Grande Valley), reviewed the manuscript and made important suggestions for its improvement. Laurier B. McDonald searched census records on his personal computer using software unavailable to me. These three gentlemen, Southerners and Texans, soared above and beyond all expectations.

Leanna Cowan, Director of the Alvarado Public Library, helped me to locate information about James and Ann Wrigley. In Crockett, Barbara Wooten and Rhonda Jordan, members of the Texas Historical Commission, provided valuable assistance in my search for Bill Hicks. R. C. (Chris) von

Doenhoff, P.C., Attorney at Law, responded to my inquiry about the location of several photographs. Dorothy Harrison, Director, and Frances Welsh, Volunteer, at the Houston County Museum suggested new trails to follow regarding Hall's Bluff. I can never thank these generous people enough.

Throughout the years of research, many others answered questions, helped locate information, and clarified puzzling details. I regret that I cannot name them all, but I am intensely grateful for their help in bringing the world of James Madison Hall to life.

Any errors are my own.

As always, I am grateful to my son Richard Britton for his unconditional love; to my brothers Berry M. Gerhardt and Dana C. Gerhardt for their loyalty and encouragement; and to my dear friend Lianne E. Mercer for her uncanny ability to lift my spirits. And to my husband Thomas A. Fort, whose kindness, understanding, and love are a heaven-sent blessing, I offer the deepest thanks my heart and my voice can express.

James Madison Hall

Introduction

On Wednesday, April 12, 1865, after a nine-day journey from his home near Crockett, Texas, James Madison Hall and his companions on John Carr's flatboat reached Liberty at one o'clock in the afternoon. After they tied up "above the railroad bridge," Hall left the banks of the Trinity River and strode toward town, eager to find old friends.

That same afternoon in Virginia, in accordance with the terms of surrender agreed upon by generals Robert E. Lee and Ulysses S. Grant on April 9, Confederate General John B. Gordon surrendered the Army of Northern Virginia to Union General Joshua Chamberlain, ending the War Between the States east of the Mississippi River. West of the Mississippi, hostilities continued until June 2, when Confederate General Edmund Kirby Smith accepted the terms of surrender offered by Union General E. R. S. Canby.

Just as the nation began a long, painful transition toward social, cultural, and political reunification, Hall made his own adjustments to new realities. On that day, he exchanged a lifestyle based on agriculture for one tied to commerce, unaware that he represented an emerging South recognizable today.

Joshua James Hall

Born in Maryland on February 22, 1819, to Elizabeth (maiden name unknown) and Joshua James Hall (1790-1871), James was sixteen years old when he arrived in Texas with his father. In his journal entry for December 31, 1863, James wrote that he had lived in Texas for twenty-eight years, making the year of his arrival 1835.

During the preceding years, James and his widower father lived first in Natchez, Mississippi, and then Vicksburg, where Joshua owned a general mercantile store. They remained in Vicksburg about ten years, during which time Joshua married and divorced Virginia A. Hall. By 1833, father and son moved to New Orleans, where a yellow fever epidemic created a great need for coffins. Joshua was an expert craftsman, and the money he made building coffins financed a westward move to Texas.[1]

After residing a short time in what is now Montgomery County, the Hall men settled in Houston County in 1839, where several of their relatives already lived. Two years before, when the Republic of Texas created Houston County, settler Andrew E. Gossett of Tennessee donated land for a county seat. He and his father, Elijah Gossett, named the town for their Tennessee neighbor David Crockett, who camped in the area on his way to San Antonio and the Battle of the Alamo.[2]

Andrew Edwards Gossett

Incorporated on December 29, 1837, Crockett quickly became a crossroads for pioneers moving into north and central Texas, as well as a market town for local farmers and plantation owners. Joshua Hall bought 23,654 acres of the Ramón de la Garza Eleven League Grant, establishing his plantation on Elkhart Creek about twelve miles northwest of Crockett in the northern area of Section 16, near the present dam for the Little Elkhart Reservoir. (The Hall family cemetery lies in the middle of Section 16.) The Hall homestead has been described in family records as a one and one-half story house with a central passage and two large fireplaces. Where the Trinity River met the westernmost boundary of his property, Joshua constructed a steamboat landing, store, and warehouse for the shipment of cotton downstream to Liberty and the port at Galveston, and the delivery of goods brought upstream to Houston County planters and Crockett merchants. Young James helped his father in the store, buying and selling goods, learning accounting procedures, organizing shipments up and down the Trinity River, and making a positive reputation for himself. The village of Hall's Bluff sprang up at the landing and attracted enough settlers to support a post office from 1852 until the mid-1860s. After the Houston and Great Northern Railroad reached Crockett in 1872, Hall's Bluff declined, virtually disappearing by the 1960s.[3]

In 1841, at age twenty-two, James married eighteen-year-old Cornelia Amanda Bracken (1823-1894). Cornelia was the daughter of James R. Bracken. According to Houston County historian Armistead Albert Aldrich, the Bracken family settled on land northeast of Crockett in 1839. The senior Bracken served as a justice of the peace. His sons Ben and Charley fought in the war with Mexico and in the Civil War.[4] At times, Cornelia's younger brothers James H. B. and Madison H. Bracken lived with James and Cornelia. Their daughter Margaret Helen was born on May 11, 1844.

Armistead Albert Aldrich

When the Mexican War erupted in 1846, James Hall joined Company H of the Second Regiment, First Brigade, Texas Mounted Volunteers, at Crockett on June 19. Colonel George T. Wood commanded the Second Regiment, with Captain John L. Hall (1809-1857) in charge of Company H.[5] Captain Hall, a Crockett hotel owner, was related to Joshua Hall. Enlisting as a private, James was promoted to first sergeant on July 29. Colonel Wood's regiment rode from Crockett to Point Isabel (Port Isabel today) on the lower Gulf Coast, crossed the Rio Grande into Mexico at Matamoros, traveled up the Rio Grande to the town of Camargo, and continued inland to Monterrey, where they fought alongside the volunteers of Colonel John Coffee Hays' First Regiment, Texas Mounted Riflemen. Company H mustered out on October 2, 1846, and James returned home to his family.[6]

Beginning with his election in 1847, and for the next ten years, James served as district clerk for Houston County. A Mason like his father, James belonged to Lothrop Lodge No. 21, achieving the honor of Worshipful Master in 1850. He received an appointment as postmaster for Crockett from February 17, 1852, until April 14, 1853, and he owned the building that housed a newspaper entitled *The Crockett Argus*. The 1850 census listed his real estate value as $3,000, which included his home in Crockett and any commercial property he owned at the time. A master of copperplate handwriting, as shown in his journal, Hall occasionally painted signs for local businesses.

An article in *The Crockett Printer* dated December 6, 1853, described the progress of Crockett since its early days: "The telegraph [has] entered our town, a substantial brick courthouse has just been completed, the Masonic Hall, Temple of Honor and Free Church are well attended; six stores, two taverns, a boot and shoe maker, four smith [blacksmith] shops, a wagon and three cabinet shops, a tannery and saddler's shop accommodate the public. Professional gentlemen offer their services to clients and patients, our bricklayers are busy, and all the usual means and appliances of civilized life may be found in our village."[7]

Frederick Law Olmsted of New York, who traveled through the area with his brother J. H. Olmsted and a guide a few weeks later, described a Saturday visit into Crockett to buy provisions and have a saddle repaired. The brothers "inquired at seven stores, and at the two inns, for butter, flour, or wheat-bread, and fresh meat. There was none in town. One inn-keeper offered us salt-beef, the only meat, except pork, in town. At the stores we found crackers, worth in New York 6 cents a pound, sold here at 20 cents; poor raisins, 30 cents; Manilla rope, half-inch, 30 cents a pound. When butter was to be had it came in firkins from New York, although an excellent grazing country is near the town." After the brothers inquired about the necessary saddle repair, the busy proprietor stated that he would try to finish the repair during the evening, but since he did not work on Sundays, he would leave the saddle at "the next store" to be picked up. Although most stores closed on Sundays throughout the country, the Olmsted brothers learned that the stores in Crockett and nearby towns customarily remained open, and in fact, made their "best sales" on those days. The saddler also explained that the only church in town welcomed anyone who wished to preach there.[8]

Five years later, according to the *Texas Almanac* of 1858, cotton and corn were the chief crops in the area with peaches in third place. Transportation to markets at Liberty, Houston, and Galveston could be achieved by steamboats on the river, and by ox and mule wagons when the river was not navigable, with the cost of transport ranging from $1.50 to $2.00 per hundred pounds. Five or six "different lines of coaches and hacks" provided mail service in Crockett. Schools, churches, saw and grist mills, and other businesses served a population of "five or six hundred; buildings, mostly of wood; distance from Galveston, about 170 miles; Alabama and Hall's Bluff are the principal shipping points. . . ."[9]

Where or when Joshua Hall met the widow Mahala Lee Roberts Sharp (1816-1885) was not revealed in James' journal, but because Joshua was a member of the Methodist church and locally famous for his love of dancing, it is likely that he met her at a church gathering or other social occasion. A daughter of Elisha Roberts, an early Texas settler and mayor of San Augustine, Mahala married Joshua in 1850.[10]

Mahala Roberts Hall

She brought two children from her marriage to John Marshall Sharp: Samuel Houston Sharp, Sr. (1839-1885) and Margaret Sharp (1840-1878). Mahala and Joshua had two children: Roberta, known as "Berta" or "Bert" (1852-1915) and Horace Oscar, nicknamed "Toby" (1854-1934). James referred to Mahala as "Mother," even though she was only three years his senior, and he gave Roberta and Toby the same love and attention he gave to his own children. He enjoyed a close relationship with Sam Sharp, and James was fond of Sam's wife Nellie and their infant son, named James Hall Sharp in his honor.

Although the changes in relationship dynamics due to Joshua's expanding family are unknown, James divorced Cornelia in 1858. On July 14, 1859, James married his step-sister Margaret Sharp, who was twenty-one years younger than James. They were blessed with four children: Florence (1860-died after 1880), James Wrigley (1862-1867), Josephine Martha (1863-1866), and Madison (1866-1874). Throughout the journal, James called his wife Margaret "the little woman" and occasionally "Maggie" or "Sis." Whether due to sadness or anger or remorse, he never mentioned his first wife Cornelia or daughter Margaret Helen in the journal. They were no longer a part of his life. But the transition had been deadly.

According to historian A. A. Aldrich, whose father O. C. Aldrich knew James, the "most unfortunate experience in [Hall's] whole career was when, in a fit of anger, he killed his friend, Isaac Peacock, who had assisted John McLemore in eloping with his daughter, Margaret."[11] *The Houston Weekly Telegraph* for Wednesday, March 23, 1859, stated that the events occurred on "Tuesday of last week," though the article must have been the reprint of a local piece, since the actual date of the incident was March 8, 1859. The application for Confederate pension submitted by Margaret Hall McLemore in 1916 affirms that she and John McLemore married on Tuesday, March 8, 1859, in Leon County, across the Trinity River.[12]

As reported in the same article, Hall had just finished his supper at Hall's Hotel, situated on the southwest corner of the square in downtown Crockett. While Hall was talking to someone who was not named, Peacock approached and engaged Hall in conversation. Angry that Peacock helped his young daughter get married in spite of his objections, Hall "bade him begone." Peacock refused to leave, and the two men first argued, then began to fight. During the altercation, Hall stabbed Peacock with a pocketknife. Peacock died the following Friday night (March 11). The newspaper article reported the knife blade as three inches long, and the fight as not premeditated. Because of darkness on the porch, witnesses "could not speak positively" about when Hall drew the knife from his pocket, or whether it was already in his hand when the fight began. Described as "a gentleman of education, liberal fortune, enlarged views, and essentially philanthropic purposes, such as characterize Maj. [Major] Hall in a high degree," he was nevertheless "at present a fugitive, wandering, we know not where." Given Hall's close relationship with his friend James Wrigley, it is likely that he went to Liberty.[13]

Hall was still missing a few weeks later, when *The Houston Weekly Telegraph* for April 13, 1859, printed a reward notice for Hall, mentioning his wealth as "a palliating circumstance in the recent killing." Governor Hardin R. Runnels offered a $300 reward for his arrest, and several citizens of Crockett offered $700 more. The murder remained an item of interest to E. H. Cushing, editor of *The Houston Weekly Telegraph*, for several months. On June 15, the *Telegraph* printed an item from *The Crockett Argus* stating that a new building, "erected by Mr. Isaac Peacock, deceased," in the northern part of town, had been bought "by an association of gentlemen" to be used as an academy.

By midsummer, Hall returned home and married Margaret on July 14. On November 9, the *Telegraph* printed an item from *The Liberty Gazette* stating that "Jas. M. Hall was tried at Sumpter last week, for killing Peacock, and the result was a mistrial, the jury being unable to agree. It stood between murder in the second degree and acquittal." Sumpter was the county seat of adjacent Trinity County. James Hall faced a second trial for the same incident in 1860.

How Hall spent the next two and one-half months is unknown, but by January 16, 1860, when the journal begins, he had decided to exchange his busy public life in Crockett for more peaceful days as a farmer. Hall undertook his new career with eagerness, purchasing tools and slaves, building a house, planting crops, and operating his gristmill. In April, he returned to Sumpter for a new trial, and this time he was acquitted.

While Hall dealt with matters at the farm and the mill during the summer of 1860, paranoia haunted many Texans, inspired the creation of vigilance committees, and drove men to violence. As described by historian T. R. Fehrenbach:

> a series of mysterious fires blazed along the North Texas frontier. Barns and buildings went up in flames in Dallas, Denton, Waxahachie, and several other towns. Newspapers reported 'abolitionists' were trying to burn out the South; horrible atrocity tales of slave risings, poisonings, and political murder—for which there was no basis in truth—pervaded the western counties of the heartland. At Dallas a large mob hanged three unfortunate Negroes, for no known cause. Three white men were lynched in Fort Worth, on the suspicion they had "tampered" with slaves. . . . Similar violence and panic was occurring in some degree across the whole South; the wildest rumors seem to have begun in Texas, but they rapidly spread northward as far as the Potomac. In Virginia and Mississippi, many people believed Texas was in a state of chaos, induced by Northern conspiracies.[14]

Southerners referred to the notorious events during this summer of chaos as the "Texas Troubles." Hall neither succumbed to panic nor took up arms.

In December 1860, whether due to a sense of isolation on the farm, obligation for past support, or a need to earn money, Hall went to Liberty to work for merchant Charles C. Lund at the latter's office, store, and warehouse. After a winter visit home, in March 1861 Hall returned to Liberty with Margaret and baby Florence. A year later, they settled into a newly built home in Liberty.[15]

James Hall supported secession and the Confederacy, but at age forty-two in 1861, he was past conscription age, which ranged from eighteen to thirty-five, beginning in April 1862. In September of that year, the maximum age rose to forty-five, but Hall remained a civilian. Although willing to help in other ways, Hall did not join the Confederate Army, probably due to his age and his reluctance to leave behind a young and dependent family. The safety of his family and slaves, a topic often mentioned in his journal, remained of paramount concern to Hall throughout the war.

While working for Charles Lund, Hall became an alderman for the city of Liberty and was elected mayor on June 21, 1862. In that role, Hall presided occasionally at a special mayor's court, and as a prominent citizen he attended many social events. He received a commission and served as the provost marshal for conscription. Hall took his turn patrolling the city, conducted a survey of needs for county families whose menfolk were away fighting in the war, and drilled volunteers for military service. At the same time, he grew bored from lack of business at the warehouse (due to the blockade by Union vessels off Galveston), and with Margaret away visiting the family, he suffered from great loneliness. Hall travelled to his farm in Houston County for a visit in October and returned to Liberty determined to resign from his positions as mayor and provost marshal. In December 1862, Hall moved back to the farm.

Now a fulltime miller, he employed Sam Sharp as his assistant. Since millers were exempt from military service, Hall avoided conscription into the army. He tried to have Sam Sharp exempted as well, but the Crockett enrolling officer refused Hall's plea. After being arrested, Sam joined the Confederate Army in January 1864. During this traumatic period, Nellie suffered a miscarriage, which infuriated Hall and embittered him toward the military.

In his journal, Hall noted the inflated prices for some ordinary goods and the lack of others, even as he adapted to the reality of wartime by becoming almost entirely self-sustaining. When Margaret, accustomed to purchasing fabric to make clothes, learned to spin thread and weave cloth on a loom, James took his own turn at the loom and expressed pride in making jeans fabric for a pair of pants for himself. He built a "cotton house" for the storage of cotton bales, his own plus those he purchased from neighbors with money from a business partner. Approached by a buyer for the Confederate Treasury Department, he "declined" to sell the stored cotton. His refusal was probably due to several reasons: he and his business partner planned to speculate in cotton when the war ended; the worthless value of Confederate money being paid for cotton; his need to barter cotton for cloth at the penitentiary; his resentment of the military; and his disillusionment with the Confederate government.

After the war Hall, like many others, perceived that commerce was the best way to rebuild Texas and the South. He returned to Liberty in April 1865, working first for Charles Lund and then for merchant James Wrigley. Hall's family and servants joined him in June, and in August, he was re-elected mayor. Charles Lund moved to Galveston, and Hall entered into partnership with James Wrigley on January 1, 1866. Hall remained in business with Wrigley and continued as mayor of Liberty until his sudden death from cholera on November 17, 1866.[16] James Madison Hall was buried in Liberty beside his small daughter Josephine on a quiet, tree-shaded bluff overlooking the Trinity River.

The title of the book is taken from James Hall's journal entry dated December 25, 1860. Hall is referring to a line by Alexander Pope (*Satires, Epistles, and Odes of Horace*. Satire i. Book ii. Line 127).

> "There St. John mingles with my friendly bowl,
> The feast of reason and the flow of soul."

Chapter 1

1860

With a second trial for the murder of Isaac Peacock expected in the spring, and no longer the Houston County district clerk after ten years of service, in January 1860, James Madison Hall turned away from public life. Inexperienced as a farmer, he relied upon common practices and his business skills, energetically investing in his new lifestyle and, depending upon the outcome of the trial, in security for his young wife Margaret. He needed a home, laborers, and tools.[1]

Monday January 16th 1860. This day [I] *commenced to improve the farm with one hand and with the ulterior object of permanently locating a home stead, Thus launching my barque upon an agricultural life, with rather poor prospects for success, but meeting the smiles and approbation of my dear little woman, and with a stout heart and a determination to succeed. Mr. Sam Sharp, Geo Border and John Varnadore visited the house and took supper. Mr. Varnadore remained all night, and with whom I contracted to erect me a good and substantial residence at a cost of $2000. Mrs. J. J. Hall also left on a visit to Mrs. Matthews with a view of purchasing a negro man for me. Thus I close the principal incidents of today.*

Sam Sharp was Margaret Hall's brother, George Border has not been clearly identified, but John Varnadore was a respected carpenter from Crockett.[2] Mrs. Frances Matthews was the wife of wealthy farmer Reuben

Matthews.[3] Only three years older than James, Mrs. J. J. Hall (Mahala) was his stepmother as well as Margaret's mother.

Tuesday January 17th 1860. This day I sent negro boy Joe to Crockett for three axes purchased from Genl. Collins. I then went in company with Mr. Varnadore to the site selected for the erection of my home, and from there to Leaverton's gin for the purpose of examining some 10 or 11 bales of cotton that I agreed to take from Mrs Peacock in liquidation of a debt due by her to me, for the sum of 400$ but found the cotton so bad and trashy that I refused to take it. Joe returned from Crockett with the axes, and Mrs J. J. Hall returned from her visit to Mrs Matthews having failed with her intention of purchasing the negro boy. I burnt brush in my new clearing in the evening and thus close the incidents of this day.

James P. Collins

Hall may have smiled as he wrote about General Collins. In an open letter published in *The Crockett Printer* on April 17, 1858, merchant Thomas P. Collins asked that correspondence to him be addressed as "General Collins," although he admitted he held no military rank, to distinguish him from his brother, James P. Collins, who was receiving his mail by mistake.

The Leaverton family was related to Joshua and James Hall. James H. Leaverton and his wife Lavinia, both born in Maryland, came to Texas during the 1840s. The 1860 census claimed that J. H. Leaverton (age forty-three) was a farmer with real estate valued at $2,500 and personal property worth $16,670. His wife Lavinia (age forty) and five children lived in the household, along with an overseer. Leaverton's property lay between those of Gaines Pennington and James Hall, and near that of William W. Peacock.

Evidently Hall did not plan to build and operate a cotton gin of his own, but intended to take his cotton to Leaverton's for ginning and baling. "Leaverton's gin" refers to a horse- or mule-powered cotton gin. (Steam-powered gins did not become available until the 1880s.) The word "gin," shortened from "cotton engine," referred to the building as well as the machine that separated cotton seeds from fibers. A screw press outside the gin building packed the fibers into a flat (uncompressed) bale weighing between 450 and 500 pounds, and the seeds were returned to the planter for his next year's crop. (At this time, the many uses for cottonseed had not been discovered, and most of it was destroyed.) Flatboats, keelboats, or steamboats carried the cotton bales downstream to port cities such as Galveston, where they were compressed into smaller bales and placed on steamboats or ocean-going vessels for shipment to New England or European textile mills.[4]

The 1860 census identified Sarah A. Peacock as a farmer and head of the household.[5] (She and her husband William W. Peacock were born in Maryland. Twenty-nine years old in the 1850 census, he had passed away by 1860.) Sarah Peacock owned real estate valued at $1,280 and personal property worth $3,670. Five children lived at home with her. Hall planned to purchase her cotton to satisfy a $400 debt she owed him, but finding the cotton full of burrs, twigs, leaves, and dirt, he turned it down because it would have brought a low selling price, causing a loss that would not have canceled the debt.

Wednesday January 18th 1860. This day Sam Sharp returned home from Hall's bluff and reports the Trinity River in navigable condition. Having put handles in the axes, I went to chopping in the clearing. Considering that I have but one hand, we are getting along pretty well. No other incident today.

"Navigable condition" meant that the water was deep enough for steamboats to travel upriver from Liberty or Galveston to deliver goods to Crockett and Houston County merchants and planters, and likewise to carry cotton bales downstream to commission merchants and factors (agents) in those same cities. Transportation of merchandise, cotton, and passengers along rivers such as the Sabine, Trinity, and Brazos enabled commerce to thrive between the Gulf Coast ports and the interior of Texas prior to the expansion of the railroads in the 1870s.

Thursday January 19th 1860. Today Sam Sharp, went to Crockett. I am still at work in the clearing. Old man Keen & Mr Whitley visited the house remaining to supper, no other incident occurring.

Joseph C. Keen (1784-1881) was born in Providence, Rhode Island. He moved to Mississippi, and in 1851, he and his wife Permelia Dailey Dean, a widow born in South Carolina, sold their land and moved to Houston County, Texas. Permelia Keen's brothers, Thomas Rutherford Dailey and Henry H. Dailey, moved to Texas with them. In July 1852, Joseph Keen bought 369 acres in the Elkhart District, and Thomas R. Dailey bought land close by, forming a small community. Keen had four children from an earlier marriage and seven children with Permelia. None are listed with the couple in the 1860 census, although any surviving children would have been grown and presumably on their own. (Permelia was fifty-seven in 1860.) Hall mentions their son Silas several times throughout the journal. Although a successful blacksmith and farmer, the seventy-seven-year-old Joseph Keen was unable to read or write.[6]

Friday January 20th 1860. I this day contracted with Mr Whitley for 2 yoke of oxen, with the yokes, bows[,] *rings and steeples and 1 chain all for the sum of $100. Mr Whitley left for the oxen which are to be delivered in a week. Still clearing—done a pretty fair day's work.*

Saturday January 21st 1860. Today negro Dan, went to town, and by whom I received two first rate iron wedges for rail splitting. Still occupied in clearing with some hopes of getting through in time to pitch a crop, at least I am doing as well as I could expect under the circumstances that surround me.

While Hall and Dan concentrated on preparing the land, Bill Hicks and Darby, owned by the elder Hall, cut and split rails for a fence to surround the clearing. Hall wrote that he "employed" the additional men, indicating that he intended to pay them for their work.

On Monday, January 23, Frank Stewart of Crockett began work "for the year as a field hand." However, when the 1860 census was taken in August, Stewart was enumerated as an "overseer" living with the family of Joshua Hall.[7] After the Civil War, Stewart married into the Hall family.

Still setting up housekeeping, on Wednesday, January 25, Margaret went with her mother to Hall's Bluff, where she bought an "earthenware" jug and four jars, amounting to 20 gallons, and she brought Hall "a box of oysters which were very acceptable." Hall delighted in eating oysters whenever he could get them.

Thursday January 26th 1860. Today Mr Renfro visited the house for the purpose of renting the lower field, which he did upon the following terms 1/3 of the corn & 1/4 of the cotton raised thereon, and he to receive one dollar pr [per] *hundred for all new rails split and put into the fence. I had not been able to chop this day in consequence of a pain located in my right shoulder blade. Still however at work in the clearing—weather cold with the wind from the North, and very cloudy.*

Three men named Renfro lived in Houston County at this time. Henry Rentfro (age fifty-one, a farmer born in North Carolina) lived with his wife and six children in the Elkhart area. His son John, age twenty-five, with a wife and a baby, may also have been the renter. A Thomas Renfro (age forty, a farmer from Georgia with a wife and four children) also appeared in the 1860 census.[8] In exchange for providing the land, Hall received a portion of the crop, specified in the journal as "1/3 of the corn & 1/4 of the cotton." Mr. Renfro (or Rentfro) provided draft animals and fodder, plows, seed, supplies, and labor, but since he did not live on the land, he was not considered a tenant.

After the Civil War, the farming practice of "thirds and fourths" led to tenant farming and sharecropping throughout the South. Tenant farmers lived on rented land and owned the crop because they provided the seed. With good management and successful harvests, tenants could become independent farmers. Also living on another person's land, freedmen and poor whites often became sharecroppers, offering only their own and their families' labor in exchange for housing, draft animals, tools, seed, and supplies. Sharecroppers usually received fifty percent of the proceeds from the sale of the crop, which was legally owned by the landlord since he furnished the seed. For necessities during the year (before the crop was harvested and sold), the sharecropper depended upon the landlord, who paid him a small wage or arranged for credit with a local merchant or at the landlord's own store. Sharecroppers settled the store account when the crop sold in the fall. If the sharecropper did not make enough money to pay off the account, then the debt rolled over to the next year. Sharecroppers often spent their entire lives in debt. This crop-lien system kept farm laborers in financial bondage well into the twentieth century.

Mr. Whitley delivered the two yoke of oxen on Friday, January 27, and Hall paid him twenty dollars on the account, with a balance of eighty dollars. Work continued in the clearing "though but slowly." The weather remained cold, "with [a] strong wind from the North, at night a heavy black frost."

Bill split 200 rails, while Darby split sixty-three on Sunday, January 29. The weather cleared and turned warmer. Building the fence began with logs between ten and twelve feet long. Each log was cut lengthwise in half, then fourths and eighths. Hundreds of rails were needed to complete the fence around Hall's newly cleared ground.

In Crockett on Monday, January 30, Hall attended an estate sale, where he bought two wagons, one for an ox team and "the other a horse wagon," costing $182. Without the cash, he signed a note, payable on January first of the following year, with Daniel M. Coleman, a prosperous farmer, and attorney William A. Stewart, the older brother of Frank Stewart, as securities.

Tuesday January 31st 1860. Still in Crockett and on today had a settlement with Mrs. C. C. Hall in which she fell in my debt $1006.75 and for which she *executed her note, which may be discharged in land. I also paid to Mr. Whitley the balance due him for 2 yoke of oxen heretofore purchased being 80$. At home Albert did not work in consequence of the cold, for the weather today had greatly changed, The wind from the North with a heavy freeze and ice plenty. No other incident today.*

Brothers Charles C. and John L. Hall, born in Maryland, were kinsmen of Joshua and James. Mary A. Hall, noted above, was the widow of Charles C. Hall (1812-1853). In the 1850 census, Charles (age thirty-five) and Mary A. (age thirty-two) had two children, Charlie (age seven) and Margaret (age four). A teenager in 1860, Charlie visited James and his family from time to time. John Hall (1810-1857) owned the hotel which became the scene of the deadly confrontation between James and Isaac Peacock. After his death, his widow Lavinia operated the hotel. Her son Sylvester (age twelve in 1860 and one of five children) also visited the Hall family.[9]

On Wednesday, February 1, Hall "purchased a negro woman named Louisa for which I paid in cash $1250." She remained with the Halls throughout the war.

She was not Bill Hicks' wife, who was also named Louisa.

Thursday Feb. 2nd 1860. Today I loaned to L. E. Downes $195.17 in cash, he going to Galveston. I also wrote to Mr. Wrigley at Liberty to send negro woman Rachael home, and I returned home [from Crockett] *in the evening finding all well and Albert at work in the clearing. The weather has moderated considerably but still cold, & a frost at night.*

Born in Maryland, Lodowick Elbert Downes (1812-1875) first came to Texas in 1839. Related to Joshua and James Hall, he lived with the Hall family for a while, building fences and doing other chores. After a short visit to Maryland, he returned to Texas in 1841. He taught school for a term, then went to work for Joshua Hall and a partner named McKeaver in their store. Joshua Hall and several friends occasionally played cards and gambled in the store on Sundays, activities which Downes so disapproved of that he quit working for Hall. Colonel John Long (1792-1859) hired Downes because

Lodowick E. Downes

of his integrity and strong religious beliefs (Downes helped found the First Methodist Church), and he gave Downes half interest in his mercantile business. Elected district clerk of Houston County in 1841, Downes served from 1842 until 1846, when James Hall took his place. A prominent businessman and influential citizen, Lodowick Downes joined numerous others who signed the 1850 petition to the Texas Legislature to levy a local tax during 1851. The original log courthouse, built in 1837 on the town square, remained in use, and by 1850, county residents and government officials recognized the need for a much larger building with space for offices and a courtroom. The local tax, approved by the Texas Legislature on December 2, 1850, funded a new brick courthouse in 1851 that stood until 1865, when it was destroyed by arson. (After this fire, courts were held in a building owned by L. E. Downes until another courthouse was erected in 1869.) In 1860, the forty-seven-year-old Downes and his wife Harriet had six children, real estate valued at $9,700 and personal property worth $30,950. (The Downes/Aldrich home still stands in Crockett.)[10] Downes was probably going to Galveston to buy goods for the store.

James Wrigley, a Liberty merchant and a Mason, was a good friend of Hall, and the two eventually became business partners. As will be seen, he would play a significant role in the lives of Hall and his family. It is not clear why Rachael had been staying with the Wrigley family nor for how long.

Hall kept his journal entries between Friday, February 3 and Tuesday, February 7 very short. Most notably, he sent two slaves named Martin and

Albert to Crockett with oxen in order to "bring home the wagons and negro woman Louisa, heretofore purchased." When they returned the following day (Saturday, February 4), they also brought five gallons of whiskey. Hall planted peas, and Bill Hicks split rails, but due to the cold, rainy weather, little farm work could be done.

On Monday, February 6, Hall went to Crockett, where he "collected from R. Duglass [Douglass] 73$, and paid out 30$ to McLemore." This passage contains one of only two references to Hall's son-in-law in the entire journal.

Hall returned home the next day with Sam Sharp, "who remained until dinner and then left for Crockett." That evening, Hall burned brush "in the clearing with Louisa & Laura."

Thursday Feb. 9th 1860. Today the little woman [Margaret] *received from Crockett by negro boy Dick a deed of gift from her mother, for negro woman Rachael. Still at work in the clearing. Weather, pleasant & clear with the wind rather fresh from the North.*

While Darby and Bill Hicks cut and split fence rails, Albert cleared land, including his own "patch." Beginning on February 12, Hall paid Darby in cash and tobacco and Bill Hicks in cash for their work. As noted on January 26, Hall arranged with Mr. Renfro to pay one dollar per hundred new rails, and on Saturday, March 10, Hall paid Bill Hicks "in cash $1. on a/c of rails." Hall kept a record of how many rails each man produced. By paying $1.00 per 100 rails, Hall was paying the same amount to both white and black workers, indicating his sense of fairness in regard to the work being done, regardless of who performed the labor.

The pattern of internal evidence indicates that Hall paid the slaves directly. The amounts were not large, and he probably paid them with pocket money. Since several hundred fence rails were required in order to surround the clearing and protect newly planted cotton and corn from free-ranging hogs and cattle, Hall was using payment as a contract to motivate the fence builders to work faster. Although paying slaves directly may not have been a common practice, Hall remained consistent throughout the journal.

For three consecutive days in February, beginning on Monday, February 13, Hall attended an estate sale at Hall's Bluff, where he purchased numerous unspecified items. He also wrote that the river was "in good boatable order and rising." Two flatboats laden with cotton "passed down" on Tuesday (February 14), and on Wednesday (February 15), the river "fell about 3 inches, and 4 flat boats well loaded with cotton" floated downriver that day.

Cotton bales from the previous fall, ginned and stored through the winter, were being transported downstream to Liberty or Galveston, where they would be consigned to a merchant or factor who sold the cotton for the best price he could get, retained a commission, and sent the balance of the money to the planter. If the planter were in debt for previous loans or expenditures, the money would be applied to the planter's account. Hall possessed a keen interest in the passage of flatboats and steamboats on the Trinity because he planned to send bales from his own cotton crop downriver to Liberty.

That same week (Thursday, February 16), Dan drove the wagon to Crockett, where he collected one and a half gallons of whisky, three plows, three pairs of trace chains, one pair of hames (parts of a horse collar to which the traces are attached), one pot and one spider, and returned to the farm. (A "spider" was an iron skillet mounted on three iron "feet" and having a very long handle, for use in open hearth cooking.)

Hall worked at home on Friday, February 17, where he finished "chopping out" the new ground "designed to be opened for this year's crop."

Saturday Feb. 18th 1860. Today I went to Hall's bluff, and purchased a few articles at Hurndon's [Herndon's] *sale. The river* [was] *down & one flat boat from Parker's bluff* [was] *laying there with 307 bales of Cotton. Sent Albert to the mill for wheat bran but disappointed in getting it. Still at work in the clearing burning brush. Weather today warm but cloudy and cold with heavy frost at night.*

Two months before, *The Crockett Printer* reported the events that led to the Herndon estate sale. Robert E. Herndon, described as "a stirring business man" of Hall's Bluff, had been shot and killed there by Dr. A. M. Still, "who was intoxicated." A friend of Herndon "standing by" then shot and killed Dr. Still. "Both lay dead together within but a moment of each other."[11]

Parker's Bluff, a steamboat landing on the Trinity River in Anderson County, a few miles upriver from the larger landing at Magnolia, lay about eighty-seven river miles above Hall's Bluff.[12]

Hall "sent the Cart to the bluff" for the items bought at Herndon's estate sale (Sunday, February 19), but discovered "considerable error in the bill, and several articles missing." The next day (Monday, February 20), he went to Hall's Bluff to pick up the articles from the sale and then alleviated the monotony of farm chores by traveling to Crockett, where he "visited" Mabie's Circus and Menagerie that night.

Mabie's Circus played in towns from Dallas to Houston, where it became "a favorite," according to *The Houston Weekly Telegraph*.[13] The circus featured "equestrian events" from Europe and America, a juggler, a weightlifter, a clown, and animals such as lions, tigers, panthers, leopards, a cougar and an ocelot, "tiger cats," hyenas, grizzly and black bears, camels, llamas, a "Burmese cow," alpacas, gray and black wolves, a white raccoon, badgers, porcupines, and "a wilderness of birds, and monkeys."

While in town, Hall bought "a magic watch" for Margaret at a cost of $175. Hubbard Brothers of New York City claimed to be the sole importers of the "magic" self-winding watch, made with an outer case of 10 karat gold and a "ruby action lever movement." The watch could be engraved and came with a warranty for accuracy. It sold for thirty-five dollars wholesale. A description of the watch appeared in *The New York Illustrated News* in 1863.[14]

Due to rain and hail, Hall spent the night in Crockett.

He returned home the following day (Tuesday, February 21) to find Albert "laid up from the result of an accident in cutting his foot with an ax, thus stopping my field opperations." For the next week, Albert was given light duty, such as going to the mill for bran.

With split rails accumulating, Hall began to lay out the "worm" of the fence on Thursday, February 23. At this time, Texas law required farmers to fence their property (houses, yards, outbuildings, and fields) against free-ranging cattle and hogs, animals notorious for damaging crops. Rocks were placed at the fence corners for support and to keep the vertical posts from rotting. The panels consisted of about seven rails, laid horizontally. The "worm" of the fence was the bottom rail, which set the distance and zigzag pattern of each section of the fence. Where the sections met, the rails interlocked, and additional support rails or stakes further steadied the corners. Fence rails were usually made of hardwoods, but with pine plentiful in East Texas, Hall may have been using that instead. By the time of the Civil War, stake and rider fences were widely in use and caused numerous difficulties for the armies. Split rails were placed horizontally, but were laid across stakes crossing both sides of the fence in an X shape, with a rail termed a "rider" placed in the forks of the stakes to hold the horizontal rails in place. A stake and rider fence was strong enough to withstand high winds and to prevent an invasion of wild and hungry hogs or cattle.[15] Hall did not state what type of fence he was building, but it was very likely a stake and rider fence.

That same day (Thursday, February 23), Hall hired Isaac Tanner and his son at the rate of $1.25 per day for both of them.[16] He and Tanner agreed for the latter to work for one month, beginning on Tuesday, February 28. The same day, he "let Darby have 1 lb of Tobacco in payment for his rails, making us even & square up to date."

Wednesday Feb. 29th 1860. We this day had Albert, Tanner & myself at work on the fence and reached the far corner with the worm. I let I. Tanner have 1 lb of Tobacco on a/c [account] *& Frank Stewart 5 lbs on a/c @ 50 cts* [cents] *per lb. The little woman completed me the first flanel* [flannel] *shirt I ever wore, and by the way it is pretty & comfortable and she has my greatful thanks for it. Weather, cloudy cold & extremely disagreeable.*

When the weather abated (such as on Thursday, March 1), Margaret set up a garden "at the old place for the benefit of the negroes." As a respite from work, she and Hall went fishing, probably at the mill pond (Sunday, March 4), where they caught five dozen "fine" sun perch. Married less than a year, they must have cherished this private time together.

With the worm of the fence around the "new ground" completed on Friday, March 2, the next day "all hands," including Hall, began "putting up the fence and came within 20 panels of enclosing the field."

While Tanner took the wagon to get a load of corn (Monday, March 5), Hall finished the fence "around the new ground field, and started one plow in the old ground field." With the land cleared, Hall needed more equipment, and on Tuesday, March 6, he accompanied Mahala to Crockett, where he bought two plows and three "singletree irons."

Everything seemed to be going well, but on the evening of Thursday, March 8, the fence "caught fire and consumed 10 or 12 panels which took all hands to put it out when nothing else was done." The next morning, Hall "made a singletree & ironed it and started 2 plows." But that evening, everyone "including the little woman had to fight the fire from the woods to prevent the fence from being destroyed, consequently no other work was done." Hall did not mention the origin of the fire or from which direction it came, but a north wind on Friday night brought frost that apparently put an end to the fire. More rails had to be split and placed in panels of the burned fence.

With plowing begun in the "old ground" (Monday, March 5), and Hall repaired and re-roofed an old smokehouse so that he could use it for a corn crib (Wednesday, March 7). They began to plant corn in the "old

Attorney Steward Alexander Miller (age fifty-five) and his wife Rebecca (age twenty-five) were both from Virginia. Their two small children had been born in Texas. Miller owned real estate valued at $17,740 and personal property worth $5,660. Miller served as mayor of Crockett in 1859.[17]

Isaac Adair followed Hall as Houston County district clerk beginning in 1857. Born in Alabama, he married Augusta Louise Smith, daughter of steamboat Captain John T. Smith of Houston County. In 1860, Adair (age thirty-three) and his wife (age twenty-four) had three small children. He owned real estate valued at $5,000 and personal property worth $3,000. A veteran of the Mexican War, Adair joined the Confederate Army as a private and rose to the rank of captain in Company H, Seventh Regiment, Texas Mounted Volunteers, which mustered at Crockett on October 28, 1861. Company H joined Sibley's Brigade in its expedition to New Mexico. Wounded at the Battle of Glorieta Pass on March 28, 1862, Adair died in Santa Fe, New Mexico, on April 9, 1862.[18]

ground, with two plows running" on Saturday, March 10. In Crockett on Monday, March 12, Hall bought a rake and two hoes, and he purchased a bay horse called Mustapha at an auction. Attorney Steward A. Miller, who lived next door to builder John C. Varnadore, sold the horse. Hall paid $124.75 for the horse and signed a note "on a 12 months credit" with William A. Stewart as his security. "I also gave my note to Isaac Adair for the sum of $120, for costs in sundry [court] cases."

Hall's trial for the murder of Isaac Peacock was scheduled for April, but less critical legal matters occupied much of his time and energy in March. For example, on Tuesday, March 13, on a motion made by Hall, "the Court quashed the bill of indictment in the celebrated Whitwell suit." Miss Whitwell, a school teacher, had sued merchant Thomas P. Collins for slander and won a settlement of $6,000.[19]

The journal entry for that day also noted that Hall paid S. A. Miller $105.75 "in cash for my note executed to him the day previous for the horse Mustapha . . ." but did not say how he acquired enough money to pay off the horse so quickly.

Still in Crockett on Wednesday, March 14, he lost a "500$ suit against Cooper, thus paying pretty dearly to accommodate a friend." Leroy W. Cooper (1822-1900) was a wealthy attorney with a wife and four children.

Judge Leroy W. Cooper

They arrived in Crockett from Georgia in 1856. After the Civil War, Cooper served in both the Texas Senate and Legislature, and he became a judge of the district court in Houston County.[20] The circumstances of the lawsuit against Cooper were not explained in the journal, but Hall may have joined the "friend" in the lawsuit against Cooper, or he may have signed a note as security on behalf of the "friend." Individuals often borrowed money on the basis of personal notes, which were co-signed by one or two close friends or relatives as "securities." If the borrower could not repay a loan or a debt of some kind, the securities then paid the amount out of their own pockets. This practice applied to the purchase of goods, livestock, and services. Hall often signed personal notes for debts, which he paid as soon as he could. He also served as security for others, including his father. The instance described on March 14, however, constituted an unusually large amount. He did not identify the "friend" or explain the nature of the lawsuit.

After attending another estate sale, Hall returned home on Friday, March 16, arriving in the evening. The next day, he "received a notice and a quietus, (but I say no more on this Subject)[.]" He also "paid Darby all I am due him for splitting rails save 59 for which I still owe." He never explained the "notice" and "quietus." Hall's obligation to pay Darby for the remaining rails is typical of him.

Bill Hicks continued to split rails, and the other hands planted corn until they finished on Monday, March 19. The next day, Hall repaired a wagon and noted that the "hands are busily engaged breaking out the middle or box between the corn rows."

Hall paid a visit (Wednesday, March 21) to neighbor John A. Williams, a thirty-three-year-old farmer from Alabama, "and took the upper Mills back at the price of $4000. He paying $1600 for the time he occupied them." Hall intended to become his own miller and completed the necessary legal documents on Tuesday, March 27, in Crockett. On Wednesday, April 11, however, Hall "let John Williams have the use of the mill for the balance of the month, he being at all expense for running it; for one half of what [corn meal or flour] is made, . . ." As Hall's trial approached, his uncertainty regarding the length of the proceedings as well as the outcome dominated his business decisions, and he made this short-term agreement with that in mind.

Thursday March 22nd 1860. Today my wagon got within 2 miles of home, when Isaac Tanner turned loose the steers & came home. It then took me until 12 o'clock in the night to return & get the wagon home. The hands finished breaking out the middles, weather clear & pleasant.

Hall continued to note the everyday details of his life. He went to Crockett to "fix the papers in the mill trade[,]" but accomplished nothing during the day and returned home at night (Friday, March 23). On the following day, the hands cleared land and planted a "potato patch." He also signed a note to the administrator of the Herndon estate sale for $137.73, payable in twelve months, with W. A. Stewart and James Collins, Jr., as his securities (Saturday, March 24). Because of errors in the bill and items he had purchased that were missing, it may have taken this long to create an accurate invoice. Without sufficient cash on hand, he signed a note for the items he had bought. Hall did not keep large amounts of cash immediately available, and he used the journal as a record of debts and payments.

James Collins, Jr., age twenty-six, had been born in Ireland and married eighteen-year-old "H. B." in 1860. According to the census, he owned no real estate but claimed personal property worth $8,600. His immediate neighbors in Crockett were W. E. Wingfield and W. A. Stewart, both friends of James Hall.[21]

Work on the "new ground" began with the "rolling" of logs to level it prior to plowing (Wednesday, March 28). Even that task did not go smoothly. Hall wrote on Thursday, March 29, "In consequence of a runaway scrape with the oxen, we lost all the afternoon. We succeeded however in catching Spot[,] when I sawed his horns off."

The term "runaway scrape" usually refers to the flight of Texas settlers toward Louisiana as General Santa Anna's Army marched eastward after the defeat of Texians at the Battle of the Alamo in 1836. By 1860, the term had come into common usage.

Three deaths occurred among the blacks in succession. Fifty-five-year-old Dan, born in Louisiana, died on Friday, March 30, of typhoid fever. On Saturday, April 7, two-year-old Green, son of Bill and Louisa Hicks, also died of typhoid fever. Although not much is known about Bill Hicks, the journal shows that he was loyal to the Hall family, and James, in particular, greatly depended upon him. The loss of little Green, occurring only a week after the death of Dan, was followed by the death of a woman named Angelina on Thursday, April 19, also of typhoid fever.[22]

Busy with chores, Hall continued to prepare for the outcome of his trial. After installing another fence, making "a road around the new ground field[,]" and "bedding the cotton ground," the hands began to plant cotton. Sam Sharp, who had frequently come from Crockett to visit, "moved up to the old house" on Monday, April 2, and on that same day, Hall "re-employed" Isaac Tanner for a month, paying him twelve dollars. Hall branded two of the oxen "on the right hip & turned them out."

Accompanied by Sam Sharp, Hall left home "to attend Court" in Sumpter on Thursday, April 12, his second trial for the stabbing of Isaac Peacock. (The first trial ended in a hung jury.) In Crockett, he "paid Cooper as Exr. [executor] of Peacock $1200 for his Peacock's interest in the Telegraph Mills and took a clear title for the same." Telegraph Mills had been the name of a post office until 1859. A new post office, called Elkhart, was established in another location in 1859. The Halls lived in the new Elkhart district.[23]

Pennsylvania-born Dan Dailey (age forty-nine) and his wife Mary (age thirty-five, born in Arkansas) had seven children, ranging in age from fifteen to one year old. All of the children had been born in Texas. Dailey's real estate carried a value of $91,000, and his personal property was worth $36,781. Hall and Dailey joined Captain John L. Hall's company during the Mexican War, serving from June 19, 1846, until October 2, 1846. Benjamin Bracken (Cornelia Hall's brother), John S. Harwell, and other neighbors also joined Captain Hall's company. Dan Dailey remained close to home during the Civil War, and Hall mentioned him numerous times in the journal.[24]

Hall and Sharp continued toward Sumpter, spending the night with wealthy planter Dan Dailey, Hall's longtime friend.

Hall and Sam Sharp arrived in Sumpter the next day (Friday, April 13), where they "found a great amount of sickness & many deaths." Both of Hall's trials were held at Sumpter, the Trinity County seat from 1850 until 1873. The trials were most likely moved to Sumpter on a change of venue since Hall was formerly an elected official of adjacent Houston County, where an impartial jury would have been difficult to seat.

An 1859 letter to E. H. Cushing, editor of *The Houston Weekly Telegraph,* described Sumpter as "laid off as most all county seats are in this State, in blocks at right angles. In the centre of the public square is the Court House, the most miserable I have seen in any part of Texas, the county being too poor and sparsely settled to afford a better one. There are several stores in the place and more than several doggeries [saloons], and they are well patronized. . . . There is a very good school, and divine service is held regularly." Although fights were common, the "grave yard is but thinly tenanted."[25]

After two postponements by the court, all of Hall's witnesses arrived on Sunday, April 22, and the trial began on Monday, April 23. The first day passed in jury selection and the testimony of two witnesses for the prosecution.

Tuesday April 24th 1860. Still in Sumpter. In my case the witnesses all testified and the arguments closed about 9 o'clock P.M. when the court proceeded to charge the jury and who retired to consider their verdict about 10 o'clock P.M. Today Madison Hall Bracken[,] *a young man whom I had raised and educated, departed this life, in the 19* [*sic*] *year of his age. at home still at work in the cotton, weather clear but cool.*

Madison Hall Bracken, who worked as a clerk in a Crockett store, began traveling to Sumpter on Saturday, April 14, but became sick at his (unnamed) brother's house. The following day (April 15), Hall went to visit him and "found him very sick with typhoid fever." The son of James R. Bracken, Madison was a younger brother of Cornelia Bracken Hall and had lived with James and Cornelia during their marriage.

Wednesday April 25th 1860. Still in Sumpter. Today the jury in my case came into Court with a verdict of "not guilty" thus setting me free again, on the occasion I treated the jury to all the champagne wine that the town of Sumpter did afford. And for the balance of the day and night myself & friends got into as comfortable a little "tight" as it ever befell man's lot to encounter with everything passing off to the entire satisfaction of all concerned. The remains of Madison Hall Bracken started for Crockett in the control of his father, to be interred in the grave yard at Crockett. At home hands still in the cotton, weather clear & rather cool.

On the following day, Hall "left Sumpter in company with Daniel Dailey and Guy Stokes and came as far as Dailey's residence where I was over taken by Sam Sharp and remained all night."

Hall noted that the remains of Madison Hall Bracken "were interred in their last resting place." Even though Hall did not mention his former wife in his journal, he had apparently been very fond of her younger brother.

According to the 1860 census, Guy Stokes was forty years old, a farmer owning real estate worth $1,000 and personal property valued at $12,400. (The 1850 census gave his age as thirty-two, meaning he had been born in 1818 rather than 1820.) Either way, he was born in Tennessee. He was not a member of the Stokes family of Crockett, but rather a member of the Howe family of Ellis County. Since he was traveling generally northward, he was probably on his way home to Ellis County.[26]

When Hall reached home (Friday, April 27), he found "my dear little woman well, but on a 'light tight' she having heard of my acquittal before I reached home." If Margaret's celebration was quieter than her husband's, it was no doubt as strongly felt, since she was now pregnant.

Relieved of anxiety about the trial, Hall checked on work at the mill (Saturday, April 28), went fishing (Sunday, April 29), and settled his account with John Williams (Tuesday, May 1).

Wednesday May 2nd 1860. Today Isaac Tanner's times [*sic*] *expired for which I had employed him. The wagon* [driven by Sam Sharp] *returned* [from Crockett], *with 12 bushels of corn and the things I purchased at Wall's* [estate] *sale* [Friday, March 16]. *I let Mrs Hall have 1 Bbl. of whiskey*[,] *40 Gals @ 80¼¢ per gal. making $32.00 Albert went to the mill, & got about 200 lbs flour, 3 bushels of meal, and I also let Mrs H. have 2 bushels of meal. The hands still at work in the cotton, weather clear & warm.*

Alert to conditions on the Trinity River, Hall noted the passage of steamboats. In May, the *J. H. Bell*, which acquired fame during the Civil War, brought his "groceries." The *Mary Hill* and the *Lucy Gwin* also traveled up and down the river.

Hall spent two days in Crockett (Thursday, May 10 and Friday, May 11) painting a sign for the store owned by merchants W. E. Haden and John Wortham.

On Saturday (May 12), John S. Harwell went home with Hall so that he could see the mill and machine shop. The thirty-three-year-old Harwell, born in Alabama, remained with Hall, working on the farm, until

W. E. Haden, born in Alabama, was twenty-five years old. He owned real estate worth $2,000 and personal property valued at $7,000. At the time of the census, he was living at Mrs. Hall's hotel. Haden enlisted with Captain W. R. Matlock's Company A, Eleventh Texas Brigade, on July 13, 1861. Others who signed up at the time included D. A. Nunn, W. A. Stewart, T. J. Stubblefield, and J. C. Varnadore. This company did not see active service. In September 1861, Haden joined Captain D. A. Nunn's company, which became Company I, Fourth Texas Mounted Volunteers of the Sibley Brigade and fought in New Mexico.[27]

Major John Wortham (1800-1867) had served as a land commissioner for Houston County (1837); major of rangers for Houston County (1839); trustee of Trinity College, then located on the Trinity River (1841); quartermaster of the Fourth Regiment, Third Brigade, Texas Militia (1842); and road commissioner (1844). He owned a plantation four miles to the northwest of Crockett, where he and his wife raised five children. He operated a steam-powered sawmill and gristmill about five and one-half miles from Crockett.[28]

he mustered into Captain R. S. Pridgen's company of cavalry at T. W. Dailey's store on June 29, 1861. Harwell later served with the First Texas Volunteer Infantry Regiment, Hood's Brigade. Wounded at Antietam on September 17, 1862, he had two fingers amputated, but he died on October 14, 1862.[29]

After helping Mr. H. Perry move out of the "mill house" (Tuesday, May 15), James and Margaret spent two days cleaning and another four moving in. Sam Sharp returned from a two-day trip to Crockett and "complained of being sick" (Friday, May 18), leaving Albert and Bill as well as Hall to drive several wagon loads of household goods from their house to the "mill place." Hall expressed dismay because of "an accident in letting the molasses barrel fall from the wagon." By Wednesday, May 23, the move was complete, and Margaret and James "commenced keeping house."

Hall settled accounts with the miller John Williams and discharged him, then hired Mr. Perry to operate the mill at $25 per month. According to the 1860 census, enumerated in August, Perry, a thirty-year-old farmer with a wife and two small children, lived on a farm adjacent to Sarah Peacock. Mary Neely and Joshua Hall were near neighbors of the Perry family.

To establish himself as a licensed miller, Hall next (Saturday, May 26) bought "a new ½ bushel Measure with the County seal thereon for the use of the Mill."

On Monday, May 28, Hall wrote, "we dressed the mill rocks," his first reference to an arduous task that would be ongoing. He did not state who "we" were, but presumably the work party consisted of Mr. Perry, Hall, and several of the hands. Hall mentioned neither John Harwell nor Sam Sharp, who remained ill until Wednesday, June 6, when Hall noted that he had begun to improve.

The "mill rocks," two large circular stones set on a wooden frame, were usually made of granite, but the best millstones, which contained quartz, came from France. Each stone weighed between one-half and two tons. The lower (bed) stone lay beneath the upper (runner) stone, with only a fraction of an inch between them. The distance could be adjusted, however, according to the desired degree of fineness of the grind. The stones had to be balanced precisely to avoid crushing the grain.[30] Dressing (or "pecking") a pair of millstones usually required two or three days, and at times of heavy use, the procedure had to be done every two weeks. Several men operated the hoist that raised and lowered the runner above the bed stone. The miller then used a pick to re-groove the pattern of furrows in both stones. The pattern of grooves, which was the same for each stone, could run either clockwise or counterclockwise, but the grooves did not lead to the center of the stone. Instead, the grooves were set off-center, and as the stones turned, the grooves crossed each other at an acute angle. The result was to shear, rather than crush, the grain. The grooves also allowed air passage to cool the meal as it flowed to the outer edge of the stone. A casing about six inches from the edges surrounded the stones, and a brush mounted on the runner guided the meal to a spout, where it dropped into a sack.[31]

The mill and adjacent pond demanded Hall's attention, and affected the health of his family, throughout the war years.

Although James Hall now lived in relative seclusion on the farm (he never referred to it as a plantation), he remained aware of the larger events encroaching upon his family, and the duel between newspapermen John C. Hepperla and Oscar H. Dalton brought those events to his doorstep.

In 1860, the Texas that Hall knew was about to race headlong into the Civil War. After almost ten years as an independent republic, Texans were accustomed to their own identity, government, and self-determination. Most Texans had migrated from Southern states, bringing with them deep cultural roots and a social hierarchy based upon Southern traditions. Texas, with its social and economic structures tied to agriculture, entered the Union in late 1845 as a state of slaveholders. The subsequent war with Mexico, in which Hall participated, ended Mexico's long-held claim to Texas. The Treaty of Guadalupe Hidalgo, signed in 1848, secured the boundary of Texas along the Rio Grande River and ceded to the United States an enormous amount of southwestern territory, which expanded the nation's southern border to the Pacific Ocean. With the discovery of gold in California in 1848, settlers streamed westward to California; the central area of the country began to fill up with American frontier families; and the moral issue of slavery followed them across prairie, river, mountain, and desert.

Throughout the 1850s, as each newly settled territory petitioned for statehood, the dilemma of slavery became hotly debated at all levels of society and government, and the citizens of the new states began to polarize into either pro-slavery or abolitionist sectionalism. (Abolitionists wanted an immediate end to the practice of slavery without compensation to the owners. They considered slavery to be immoral, viewed slaves as people rather than as property, and set up the Underground Railroad to help escaped slaves reach freedom in Canada.) Yeoman farmers who had moved westward and owned several slaves did not want their prospects of owning more to be denied. Southern planters, who had a great deal of money tied up in land and slaves, whose labor was critical to the production of cotton (the primary cash crop), feared the loss of their property and their political status in the U.S. Congress. The majority of Southerners, who did not own slaves but aspired to become powerful, socially elite planters, feared the loss of their distinct way of life. Thus threatened, Southerners talked of seceding from the Union to form their own separate nation. States that had entered the Union voluntarily, they argued, had the "right" to leave the Union voluntarily.

For years the arguments, debates, sermons, and soul-searching escalated until, on October 16, 1859, talk became action. Abolitionist John Brown and eighteen followers raided the federal arsenal at Harper's Ferry, Virginia. They intended to take the armory, distribute the weapons to Virginia slaves who would rise up in an insurrection, and emancipate all Southern slaves. Colonel Robert E. Lee and a force of U.S. Marines attacked the arsenal, capturing Brown and several of his men. A jury found Brown guilty of treason on October 31, and he was hanged on December 2, 1859. Moderate Northerners condemned Brown's raid, a point missed by many Southerners, as abolitionist approval of Brown and his actions increased Southern fears.

In April 1860, with a presidential election approaching amid deepening internal division, Texas sent pro-slavery delegates to attend the National Democratic Convention in Charleston, South Carolina. Democratic candidate Stephen A. Douglas of Illinois and his supporters refused to agree to a party platform that would ensure slavery in the Western territories. Southern delegates, including the Texans, withdrew from the convention. They gathered at Richmond, Virginia, and nominated John C. Breckinridge of Kentucky for president. Stephen A. Douglas received the National Democratic Party's nomination. The Republican Party, which rejected any expansion of slavery, met in Chicago and nominated Abraham Lincoln.

Throughout the presidential campaign, Governor Sam Houston urged Texans to remain loyal to the Union. Serving as first President of the Republic of Texas (1836 to 1838 and again from 1841 to 1844), and then as U.S. Senator (1846 until 1859), Houston adamantly opposed secession and engaged in a bitterly fought campaign against secessionist Governor Hardin R. Runnels in 1859. Texans were enjoying great prosperity after joining the Union, especially through the production of cotton, corn, and wheat, plus the sale of cattle, and a fast-growing population was busily creating a host of new towns. Planters and merchants needed to keep their commercial ties with Northern and New England banks, businesses, and textile mills. And the U.S. Army provided a degree of protection from Native Americans for settlers pushing westward. After working so hard for nearly ten years to enter the Union, Governor Houston could see no benefit in leaving it after only fifteen years of statehood. Many Texans agreed with him, whether or not they owned slaves, and they elected him governor in 1859.

By the middle of 1860, however, attitudes toward remaining in the Union began to change. Increasingly outspoken and volatile, Texas secessionists argued that raids by Mexican bandits on South Texas ranches and Indian attacks on frontier settlers proved the failure of the U.S. Army to protect the state's citizens. And unexpected events seemed to conspire in favor of the secessionists when, in July 1860, unexplained fires in several North Texas towns, including Dallas, fanned the atmosphere of anxiety into one of panic. After weeks of hot, dry weather, wooden buildings burst into flame. Loss of property amounted to hundreds of thousands of dollars. No one knew how the fires started, but ready to believe the worst, and aroused by newspaper editorials, Texans blamed abolitionists and slaves. Vigilance committees arrested and hanged blacks and whites suspected of starting the fires, poisoning wells, and attempting murder, events that became known to people across the South as the "Texas Troubles." Townsfolk soon realized that the fires had been caused by phosphorus matches that ignited spontaneously in the unusually hot summer, but fears of an abolitionist conspiracy and slave insurrection remained, and the "Texas Troubles" inspired fear throughout the Southern states.[32]

At home on his farm and safe from the dangers of the "Texas Troubles," James Hall first noted the presence of John C. Hepperla on Sunday, May 27. On that day, Margaret rode with Hepperla to visit her mother, and on her way home, she was thrown from Mustapha due to a loose saddle. Margaret was more irritated than hurt, and Hepperla, who must have helped her reach home safely, returned to Crockett. A few days later, Hepperla would be shot in the head during a gunfight over politics.

In the fall of 1859, John C. Hepperla succeeded attorney Preston Hay as publisher and editor of *The Crockett Argus*, a newspaper housed in a commercial building owned by Hall. *The Houston Weekly Telegraph* reported that "Col. Preston Hay has retired from the editorial chair of the Crockett Argus, where he has gained the name of one of the most forcible writers in the state. He has located himself in Austin. John C. Heppala [*sic*] takes full control of the paper. We greet him kindly."[33]

At the time of the 1860 census, Kentucky-born Preston Hay was fifty-three years old. He owned real estate worth $2,000, but no personal property value was listed on the census form. He stayed at the hotel operated by Lavinia Hall in Crockett. During the spring and summer of 1860, he visited James Hall, and they went fishing together. By 1866, Colonel Hay had moved to Huntsville, as indicated by an article in *The Galveston Weekly News* dated April 25, 1866. The article stated that "Col. Hay of Huntsville" had given a lecture in Houston two days earlier on the "Life, Character and Public Services" of Sam Houston.[34]

Born in Maryland, John Hepperla (age twenty-nine in 1860) remained the printer and editor of *The Crockett Argus* in 1860. Real estate worth $1,040 and personal property valued at $5,200 were reported in the census. Hepperla also lived at Mrs. Hall's hotel. He traveled to Houston, where he developed a positive relationship with E. H. Cushing, editor of *The Houston Weekly Telegraph.* Cushing regularly reprinted articles furnished by the *Argus.* In February 1860, the Houston paper noted that the *Texas Register*, "heretofore published in Galveston, has been absorbed in the Crockett Argus. . . . Mr. [B. F.] Davis, editor of the Register, is a finished writer. He takes position as junior editor of the Argus."[35]

In April 1860, Hepperla traveled first to Houston and then to Galveston to attend the Democratic State Convention. Hepperla and rival editor Oscar Harvey Dalton of *The Crockett Printer* became enemies over the 1857 election for the Governor of Texas, in which secessionist Hardin R. Runnels defeated unionist Sam Houston and served as governor from 1857 through 1859. In 1859, Runnels and Houston again opposed each other for governor, and this time Houston won. Hepperla backed Runnels, while Dalton favored Houston. In June 1860, their political feud ended in a gunfight. "An altercation took place on the streets between Oscar Dalton of the Crockett Printer and J. C. Hepperla of the Argus, in which pistols were used by both parties. The ball of Mr. Dalton is said to have glanced the forehead of Mr. Hepperla; while the ball from the pistol of the latter struck his opponent in the mouth, and the wound, it is said will doubtless prove fatal."[36]

News of the editors' gunfight was reported in the *Printer* and the *Argus*, as well as in Houston (*The Houston Weekly Telegraph*, June 12, 1860), Austin (*Austin State Gazette*, June 16, 1860), and Galveston (*The Galveston Civilian and Gazette*, June 19, 1860). Cushing revealed his disappointment in Hepperla in his articles about the shooting. On June 26, Cushing reported that Davis "has withdrawn from the editorial management" of the *Argus* to devote all of his time "to the practice of his profession." Immediately below that, he noted that Dalton "is getting well." The thirty-seven-year-old Dalton survived until March 25, 1861, when he died at home. Hepperla recovered from his head wound.[37]

Hall's journal entries for 1860 mention Hepperla several times. He "sent to Hall's bluff for a keg of printers ink and sent it to town [Crockett] to Hepperla" on Friday, June 8. Hepperla dined with the Halls on Sunday, June 17, and again on Tuesday, June 19, but, interestingly, Hall did not mention Hepperla's gunfight or head wound nor his thoughts about the incident. Perhaps due to his guilt over the death of Isaac Peacock, he did not wish to judge Hepperla, and at the time, Oscar Dalton seemed to be recovering.[38]

Hepperla remained in Crockett and visited with Hall early in 1861, but on Wednesday, February 27, Hall filed a lawsuit against Hepperla for unpaid rent and his "recovery" of the *Argus* office. As Hall stated, "after patiently waiting for 2 years he (Hepperla) refused to pay me one red cent." At the same time, Hall placed an advertisement for the sale of the "printing office" in *The Houston Weekly Telegraph* (Tuesday, February 26, 1861). Hall never received the rent money from John Hepperla, who enlisted with Captain John R. Woodward's Company G, Texas Volunteers, in Anderson County, on June 23, 1861. This company later became Company G, First Regiment, Texas Infantry. Hepperla died of typhoid fever in Virginia on November 13, 1861.[39]

Hall spent the late spring and early summer in routine chores such as repairing the stable; he visited with friends, with whom he went fishing; and he "loaned" his neighbor Mrs. Peacock beef and salt. Toby and Roberta, the children of Joshua and Mahala, came to visit, and Sam Sharp fully recovered from his illness. The slaves, whom Hall referred to as the "hands," worked continuously in the cotton fields.

In anticipation of a good yield, James Hall sought a ready market for his crop. He spent Wednesday, June 20, traveling from his home toward

Huntsville. He reached the Tuscaloosa landing on the Trinity River, ninety-three river miles south of Hall's Bluff, that evening and stayed at Wyser's Springs, which *The Houston Weekly Telegraph* (June 22, 1859) projected "to be a great attraction to the health seeking portion of the State. His [Wyser's] house is pleasantly situated on a high bluff, on the bank of the river. Good fishing and good hunting characterize the place, game of all kinds abounding all about." After the waters were "analyzed," it was expected that "these springs will become a leading place of resort for the whole surrounding country, during the summer months."[40] Hall spent the night there again during his journey home.

He arrived in Huntsville on June 21, "after a dry and warm ride[,]" and remained the following day. Although he did not state the purpose of his visit, later journal entries indicate that he made arrangements to sell his cotton to the penitentiary. The Texas Legislature had authorized the establishment of a state penitentiary in 1848, which was built the following year. Governor Peter H. Bell received $35,000 from the legislature to construct a textile mill inside the prison. By the late 1850s, the prison mill used 500 bales of cotton and 6,000 pounds of wool each year, and cloth production increased during the Civil War to make cotton jeans and woolen cloth for uniforms. In 1860, prisoners needed the cotton to make osnaburg, a coarse cloth used for sacks, work clothes, bedding, and other utilitarian items. Osnaburg cloth was originally made of linen, but "Texas osnaburg" substituted cotton for linen. *The Galveston Weekly News* reported on May 21, 1862, that "209 convicts in the State Penitentiary, [were] turning out near 6000 yards of osnaburg daily."

On September 10, 1862, the same newspaper stated that the penitentiary could not keep up with orders for cloth, and that current orders would not be filled for five to seven months. Texas soldiers received cloth first, then their families, and finally consumers. Retailers and speculators "need not apply, as they are the last to be supplied." Between December 1, 1861, and December 1, 1863, the prison sent more than 1.4 million yards of cotton and 292,000 yards of woolen cloth to the Confederate Army. The success of the prison textile mill led to wide distribution of cloth to prison inmates, Texas State Troops, the Confederate military, the families of soldiers, and the general public. During the war, however, Hall's family made their own cloth.[41]

Hall returned home without incident on June 24. Two days later he "settled with [Mr.] Perry for his last month's work" as miller. Hall did not hire anyone else to be miller during his upcoming absence.

On Monday, July 2, the hands began picking cotton. After "arranging [his] affairs," Hall left the farm again, this time on a much longer and more exhausting journey.

Hall and his father left for New York City on Tuesday, July 3, traveling by hot, crowded stagecoach to Liberty and by the steamship *Swan* to Galveston. There Hall bought "a through ticket"—a new type of travel arrangement—to New York for $82.50 (noted on Sunday, July 8). That day the Halls sailed from Galveston on the *Orizaba* "with a full list of passengers going to New York." After disembarking at Berwick Bay, Louisiana, they took the "Opelousas cars" (New Orleans, Opelousas and Great Western Railroad) to New Orleans (Monday, July 9). From New Orleans, they traveled by the Mississippi Central Railroad to Canton, Mississippi, then to Grand Junction, Tennessee, where they boarded the Memphis and Charleston Railroad (Tuesday, July 10). After traveling all night to Huntsville, Alabama, they crossed northern Georgia (Wednesday, July 11), and their route pressed on to Bristol, Lynchburg, and Alexandria, Virginia (Thursday, July 12). They continued to Washington City and Baltimore (Friday, July 13), and Philadelphia (Saturday, July 14), reaching New York City at six o'clock on Saturday evening, July 14. Passengers bought their own meals at stops along the way, and Hall suffered from lack of sleep throughout the trip. He and his father stayed at the National Hotel in New York while "purchasing goods." The weather in the city, he wrote, was "warm & pleasant, with 3 rains during my stay." His expenses amounted to $125 (noted on Saturday, July 14). They left New York on Thursday, August 2 and retraced their earlier route, taking the legendary steamer *Charles Morgan* from Berwick Bay to Galveston. They arrived home on Tuesday, August 14.

While they were away, Frank Stewart apparently worked as an overseer, as designated in the 1860 census.

Hall wrote no more entries in his journal until Thursday, September 6, when he and Sam Sharp began traveling south to Liberty. They passed through Crockett, where they were joined by George Frederick Numsen, who lived there, then continued to Sumpter, Livingston, and Grand Cane. They reached Liberty on Monday, September 10. While Hall took the buggy and mules to James Wrigley's home to be stabled, Sam Sharp visited Wrigley's warehouse. Hall, Sharp, and presumably George Numsen lodged at the City Hotel.

A native of Baltimore, George F. Numsen (1837-1888) was a tinsmith by trade. During the Civil War, he served in Hood's Brigade. In 1864, he married Jane Burkley Vaughan at Palestine in Anderson County, and they eventually had seven children. He returned often to Baltimore (three of his children were born there), and by 1880, he had relocated there permanently, becoming a "fruit preserver" according to the census.[42]

Hall examined land claims for the twenty-three-year-old Numsen, which required trips to Hardin and Beaumont; a side trip to Sour Lake was not explained. After returning to Liberty (Saturday, September 15), they next traveled to Galveston and from there to Houston, where they stayed at the Fannin House (Tuesday, September 18). Hall "examined the records of the County Clerk's office" and settled the land claim matter for Numsen (Wednesday, September 19). The same day, they returned to Galveston on the *Bayou City* and remained there at the Tremont Hotel until Saturday, September 22, when the two men boarded the *Swan* for the voyage upriver to Liberty. They arrived on Sunday, September 23. Due to the search for and retrieval of runaway mules and hard travel through driving rains, Hall reached home a week and a half later (Tuesday, October 2).

Sam Sharp stayed in Liberty, working as a salesman at James Wrigley's warehouse, until he came home for a brief visit (Friday, October 26). He left on Wednesday, October 31, for the return trip to Liberty by stagecoach.

With Margaret soon to give birth, James stayed close to home, building a "carriage house" and a "garden screen."

Friday Oct. 19th 1860. Today the little woman after much difficulty, tribulation and vexation was delivered of a female child at 7 o'clock A.M. weighing 10½ lbs. there being present Mother, Mrs Bird & myself, assisted by Rachael

& Louisa. hands still at work on the garden screen. Mr. McDaniel and Jo. Wright came to see me, and participated in a social glass, the toast being the new "responsibility", Mother remained all night and the rest left for home. weather clear, but rather cool with a frost at night.

Saturday Oct. 20 1860. Today Mrs. Bird, Mrs Leaverton, Father and the 2 children [Roberta and Toby] *came to see the little woman and the new responsibility, all remained to dinner, after which they all went home, & Rachael came up to nurse the little woman. Still at work on the garden screen. weather clear & warm in the day but cold at night with a hard frost.*

A week later (Sunday, October 28), Joshua Hall named the baby Florence Mahala Hall.

The "Mrs. Bird" mentioned on October 19 may be Mrs. L. A. Bird, enumerated in Angelina County in the 1860 census, since this is the only head of household with these initials in or near Houston County at that time. If this is the same couple, they moved to Houston County between July 7, when the census was taken, and October 19, when they were first mentioned by Hall. Born in North Carolina, Lundy A. Bird, age thirty-five, owned real estate valued at $1,000 and personal property worth $8,000. His wife Massaline, age twenty-five, had been born in Mississippi. Their four daughters ranged in age from eight to two years, and all were born in Kentucky. Hall's use of the formal "Mr." and "Mrs." suggests that the Birds were new neighbors.[43]

On Tuesday, November 6, Hall attended the national election at the "Elk Hart box, where 45 votes were cast, out of which Breckenridge [*sic*] & Lane rec'd [received] 41 and Bell & Everett 4." Southern Democrats John C. Breckinridge of Kentucky and Joseph Lane of Oregon vowed to protect states' rights and slavery, but did not favor secession. Conservative Democrats John Bell of Tennessee and Edward Everett of Massachusetts avoided the slavery issue and focused on the authority of the Constitution and the Union. (Everett represented the Constitutional Union Party.) Democrat Stephen A. Douglas of Illinois advocated the right of the citizens of each state to decide whether or not to permit slavery, rather than the federal government, but he was not in favor of secession. Although the Democratic candidates won the majority of the popular vote, they were too splintered into factions for a single candidate to carry either a majority popular vote or the Electoral College, and Republican Abraham Lincoln of Illinois won the majority of Electoral College votes. Hall did not state for whom he voted.

With the change of seasons, Hall frequently went hunting for ducks and geese. He also surveyed forty acres of Section 19 for "for J. A. Williams on a/c of W. H. Beazley."

William Henry Beazley (or Beasley) (1836-1863) owned property near that of John Williams, making him Hall's neighbor. Beazley was the son of Charles and Thursa Hyde Beazley. His wife Bertha (age twenty-one) had been born in Texas. No children were listed in the census. Beazley owned real estate worth $6,000 and personal property worth $3,280. He mustered into the Beauregard Cavalry, Twenty-Third Brigade, Texas State Troops at Brenham, Washington County, in May 1861. He died on June 20, 1863.[44]

Hall and John Harwell worked on the "garden screen" until Harwell "was taken sick in the evening with chills" on Tuesday, October 23. Harwell, who had been operating the mill, remained sick for several days. Hall took Harwell's place at the mill, where he ground "4 bushels of corn" into meal (Wednesday, October 24). The next day, Roberta was also "taken with the chill." They recovered, but the pattern of chills and fever would continue. Between Monday, November 12 and Wednesday, November 21, baby Florence suffered from a fever, and Mahala, along with neighbors Mrs. Peacock and Mrs. Bird, helped take care of her.

Hall "had the old place offered for sale" (Saturday, November 10), a reference to his home in Crockett. Busy with everyday affairs, Hall did not anticipate that a visit from Charles Lund in late November would turn his life in a new direction.

Merchant Charles C. Lund was born in Denmark around 1820. He and James Wrigley operated their business together as J. & J. Wrigley & Co. until they dissolved their partnership on January 1, 1855. Charles Lund opened his own mercantile business, and advertisements in *The Liberty Gazette* for November 17, 1856, indicate that he owned a store and a warehouse. He sold clothing, boots and shoes, "plantation goods" (fabric, hats, socks, and blankets), glassware and crockery, lamps, hardware, and groceries. About forty years old in 1860, he and his wife Mary and their daughters Caroline and Margaret lived in Liberty. Lund was a member of the Liberty Masonic lodge and held public offices as a city councilman, county treasurer, and mayor of Liberty.[45]

Charles Lund "came to see" Hall and remained for three days (Friday, November 23 through Sunday, November 25), during which time he and Hall hunted for ducks and visited with Mahala and Joshua. James did not state the nature or purpose of Lund's visit, but internal evidence indicates that Lund and James Wrigley had decided to go back into business together. Wrigley's brother John, with whom James formed a partnership after dissolving the one with Lund in 1855, was enumerated in 1860 as a farmer.[46] With John Wrigley no longer engaged in operating the store, James Wrigley re-established his business partnership with Lund, who asked Hall to come help them with the store and warehouse in Liberty. Hall agreed, although perhaps tentatively, but a crisis at the mill demanded all of his attention first.

A week of intermittent, heavy rain, together with "ice & a hard freeze" (Friday, November 23), stopped all of the outdoor work and filled the millpond with water.

Monday Novr. 26th 1860. Today John Williams came over, and in consequence of the rain & high water was compelled to remain all night. The levee of the mill gave way & a rend in [the] *dam was made about 26 feet wide, weather cool with hard rain all day, stopping any kind of business.*

Tuesday Novr. 27th 1860. Today I went to Fathers to procure some hands to assist in fixing the dam, John Harwell went to Wortham's Mill for lumber to repair the Mill, weather rainy & disagreeable.

Joshua sent Darby, Masaline, Albert, and Joe, plus three yoke of oxen, to help with mill repairs on Wednesday, November 28. John Harwell and Bill Hicks traveled to Wortham's Mill for lumber four times, for a total of 1,464 feet of boards. Hall also acquired twenty-nine pounds of nails from Joshua and a keg of nails from Joseph Keen. On Thursday, November 29, James received additional help from John Williams and Frank Stewart, and Mrs. Bird loaned the slaves Martin and Emory, as well as a Mr. Brown. Alex Baker and seventeen-year-old Charley Hall (son of Mrs. Mary A. Hall, the widow of C. C. Hall) came from Crockett to join them on Friday, and the Leavertons sent a man named George. Each evening, James went to see Margaret, who remained at her mother's. Rebuilding the levee continued until Friday, December 7, with some final details completed on December 9. However, this would not be the end of problems with the mill.

Hall now made preparations for his "visit" to Liberty. On Tuesday, December 11, Frank Stewart and Alex Baker, with the slaves Malinda, Laura, Conny, and Elisha "left in the wagon for Liberty." Hall "went as far as Crockett with them, and saw them safely off." After leaving Margaret and Florence with Mahala and Joshua, with whom they would remain during James' "visit" to Liberty, he rode away on his horse Hawk a week later (Monday, December 17). He stopped in Crockett to settle a debt with Lodowick E. Downes, then continued to Dan Dailey's, where he spent the night. He traveled twenty-eight miles that day. James reached Sumpter about eleven o'clock Tuesday morning, conducted business with "Messrs Ballinger & Robb[,]" and because of "a very hard rain" he remained in Sumpter overnight. He rode only seventeen miles that day. The following morning he left Sumpter "and after travelling 36 miles over a very bad & muddy road I arrived at Drew's cross road, where I haulted for the night, pretty well fatigued from the ride, expenses of the day $1.90. Weather clear & warm for the time of the year."

Drew's Landing was founded on the Trinity River in Polk County by Monroe Drew in 1838. He built a store and a hotel on the east side of the river to establish trade with the Alabama-Coushatta Indians, who lived on the west bank. During the Civil War, cotton, soldiers, and supplies brought overland from Polk and Liberty counties were collected at Drew's Landing and shipped downstream on flatboats built there. Drew's Landing, 226 river miles south of Hall's Bluff, was renamed Marianna in 1871.[47]

Thursday Decr. 20th 1860. Today I left Drew's in company with Dr. Hunsaker and Mr Halff, and after travelling 35 miles over the worst road in Texas, we arrived at Mr Hawkins' where we stoped for the night. At this place I found a marriage in perspective, with many interesting young ladies in attendance who wiled away the time discoursing sweet music upon the Piano Forte, in fact I almost thought myself a boy again so pleasantly did I pass the time, but as all things must have an end so I turned in for the night and had rosy dreams of the future, whether to be realized or not time only can develope, expenses for the day $1.10. Weather clear & rather warm.

After a twelve-mile ride, Hall reached Liberty on Friday, December 21, and went to see James Wrigley, with whom he stayed. Sam Sharp, who was still working for Wrigley, told Hall that "his magic watch had been stolen from him a few days before." On the same day he arrived in Liberty, Hall "went to work in the store, marking and arranging the goods, times dull."

Four years earlier, a colorful article in *The Liberty Gazette* declared that Liberty displayed:

> an animated appearance. On the arrival of the packet [steamboat] large numbers congregate at the landing, and on the following day, when the bulk of her freight is discharged quite a lively scene presents itself to the by stander. The peripatetic clerk is examining the marks on barrels and boxes, wagoners are loading up freight for up country, and the whole scene is truly refreshing

> to those who like to see progress. During the week wagons arrive with cotton and hides, and at night may be heard the tinkling of ox bells, belonging to teams in town. . . . We can inform all persons with certainty that any amount of Cotton will be purchased here at the ruling figures. They can send along the wagons.[48]

Although such activity must have continued, business at the store and warehouse had slowed quite a bit. Hall immediately missed his family. On Saturday, December 22, he wrote, "Today I am still in Liberty and still at work in the store, with very little business doing, I am however enjoying myself as well as I can, considering it is on the ides of Christmas, and I so far from the loved ones at home, . . ." The following day, he noted ". . . times are very tight and money scarce, but whiskey bears a premium, although there is plenty of the article in [the] market." He had intended to take the steamer *Swan* to Galveston on December 24, but the vessel left without him.

Tuesday Decr. 25th 1860. I am still in Liberty, and this being Christmas eve closed the doors, and set in for a regular bender. I took my Christmas dinner with my friend James Wrigley, which by the by was a splendid affair, and reflected credit on his amiable wife. There was a feast of reason and a flow of soul, together with a fine flow of champaigne etc. etc. Many times I toasted the loved ones at home, and thus passed the day very pleasantly, although it was cold, cloudy and drizzling rain during the entire day.

Hall returned to the store on Wednesday and Thursday, but business continued to be very slow. Friends from Houston County arrived on the steamer *John F. Carr* (Thursday, December 27), which brought 940 bales of cotton destined for the port at Galveston, and "we passed a pleasant time together."

Friday Decr. 28th 1860. Today I left Liberty on the steamer "Alice" in Company with James Wrigley, when we got to the mouth of the river, and fairly in the bay, the steamer Alice was compelled to drop her anchor in consequence of a severe norther blowing, the bay being too rough for her to proceed, it was very cold and no stove on board and thus I was compelled to pass a very disagreeable & unpleasant night. Today be it remembered that I have made a pledge not to drink any spiritous liquors for one year should life last so long, weather cloudy[,] *very cold, and a perfect hurricane blowing.*

Saturday Decr. 29th 1860. This morning I got out of my bunk nearly frozen after passing as I said in yesterday's notes a very disagreeable night, about 10. o'clk A.M. I saw a steamer coming out of the mouth of the river, it turned out to be the "Ruthven"[,] *she came alongside and the passengers were immediately transfered from the Alice to the Ruthven, my feelings can better be imagined than described*[,] *it was like passing from a dark and miserable prison to a luxuriant palace, after the transfer was complete the Ruthven weighed anchor and started for Galveston where we arrived about 5 P.M. The wind still blowing from the north like the devil which made it difficult to land, we succeeded however and I took up quarters at the Tremont* [Hotel]. *weather cloudy & very cold and at night it snowed to the depth of about 3 inches, so much for the sunny South.*

The *A. S. Ruthven* (144 tons) was a sidewheel packet built at Cincinnati, Ohio, in 1860. Named for Galveston merchant Archibald St. Clair Ruthven, the steamboat carried the Trinity River trade between Galveston and Liberty throughout the Civil War. During 1864, she transported guns, equipment, and personnel for the Confederate Quartermaster Department. The vessel remained in service on the Trinity until 1872 or 1873, when she wrecked at Parker's Bluff near Palestine. Her hull, protected by a one-inch thick covering of planks, contributed to her unusually long service.[49]

Sunday Decr. 30th 1860. Today I am still in Galveston and in consequence of the severe cold & sleet am compelled to keep housed and as close to the stove as possible.

Monday Decr. 31st 1860. Still in Galveston, and in consequence of the cold which still continues, was unable to transact but little business, I took a few oysters however and at night visited the Theatre, and after which I went to my old friend Archy Ruthven's where I partook of a fine supper, and saw a regular scotch gather [*sic*], *with many fine songs. The meeting was convoked to drink the old year out & the new one in, but in consequence of my temperence pledge I felt out of place and retired early. Thus I close my chronicles of daily events for the year 1860, now past and gone, and God only knows whether I will be permitted to live to keep one for the incoming year. weather very cold but clear.*

Archibald St. Clair Ruthven was born in Edinburgh, Scotland, on September 25, 1813, and he came to the United States in 1832, arriving in Texas in 1840. His wife Jane, a year younger, was born in New York. A Galveston cotton factor and commission merchant, Ruthven and a group of men planned the construction of a plank road from Houston to the Brazos River in 1850, but the road was not built due to a shift in interest to railroads. He offered life insurance, for whites and for slaves, as early as 1850, and he advertised insurance for "produce." He joined the Freemasons in 1841, organized a lodge at Houston in 1845, and served many important Masonic positions, including Grand Secretary and Grand Master during the 1850s.[50] Hall's reference to his "old friend Archy Ruthven" may have come from their association as Masons.

Ruthven organized a St. Andrew's Society for Scots in Galveston in January 1859 and served as the first president. At a celebration of the 100th anniversary of the birth of Robert Burns in 1859, the "sons of Scotia" delivered speeches, Ruthven sang "Ye Banks and Braes," and the organization's poet laureate George Gordon sang "The Bonnie Bairn." This is likely the same type of "Scotch gather[ing]" Hall wrote about.[51]

In his journal, Hall described his boredom and his need for his family, and he made no mention of the larger events about to consume the nation. He could not escape them, however, and before the next year ended, he would be drawn into the war in a way he never expected.

Chapter 2

1861

Tuesday January 1st 1861. Today I am still in Galveston, and adjusted my matters of dispute with Nelson Clements, I left Galveston at 3 P.M. on the steamer Ruthven bound for Liberty in company with James Wrigley and had a very pleasant passage, expenses while at Galveston $20. weather clear and cold.

According to an 1859 advertisement in *The Houston Weekly Telegraph*, Nelson Clements and Company was a New York City-based commission merchant and cotton factor with an office on The Strand in Galveston. In 1860, the Clements business "house" was "under the charge of A. S. Ruthven," who was "perhaps, more widely and more favorably known in Texas than any other citizen of Galveston." In the same glowing article published by *The Houston Weekly Telegraph*, Ruthven was described as a "man of strict integrity, and of fine business tact."[1] Hall did not detail his "matters of dispute[,]" but his friendship with Ruthven and the latter's integrity may have led to an amicable resolution.

Hall returned to Liberty on Wednesday, January 2, and packed his belongings. Riding his "celebrated horse Hawk," he left Liberty the next day in "extremely cold" weather. The roads were "very bad" and he suffered from "a severe pain" in his back throughout the journey. By the time he arrived home on Sunday, January 6, he felt "altogether used up from the severe pain still in my back, which rendered me almost helpless."

Nevertheless, he immediately attended to business matters relating to the farm. On Monday (January 7), he "rode up to the mill to see John Harwell and found him getting on pretty well." Margaret and baby Florence had been staying with Mahala and Joshua during James' absence, and he moved them to their home at the end of the week (Friday, January 11).

Tuesday January 8th 1861. Today I went in company with Father to Dailey's store, and from there to the election, there I met Richard Duglass the Assessor & Collector, give [*sic*] *in a list of property and paid him my taxes for the year 1860 and took his receipt for the same. I then went to the Mill* [house] *in company with W. B. Lacy and Mr. Cunningham where we all dined. John Harwell then went to the election & I returned to Mothers, where the little woman is still staying, waiting favorable weather to carry Florence home. weather clear & warm.*

The Thomas R. Dailey (1802-1876) family moved to Houston County from Mississippi during the early 1850s and purchased land on July 27, 1855. In 1859, Dailey deeded ten acres of his land for a cemetery and a church, which became known as Dailey's Baptist Church. Thomas' son Tandy W. Dailey (1828-1867) owned a store about one-quarter mile from the cemetery and the church. On June 29, 1861, Captain R. S. Pridgen swore in his company of cavalry at the store. Silas E. Keen, son of blacksmith Joseph Keen, signed up that day, along with Tandy Dailey, his three brothers, and his father. Thomas went to San Antonio to enlist in place of his son Milton, who had three small children, but he was turned down. Tandy, the only one of Thomas R. Dailey's four sons to return from the Civil War, died a bachelor in 1867 and was buried with Masonic honors at the Dailey family cemetery.[2]

William B. Lacy (age thirty-nine in 1860) was an "engineer" born in Alabama. He and his wife Elizabeth (age twenty-eight), also from Alabama, had five children. He owned real estate worth $250 and a personal estate valued at $2,000. J. Cunningham (age twenty-two in 1860) was a wagon maker. He did not give a value for real estate, and his personal estate was worth $700. He and his wife Eliza (age twenty), both from Alabama, had no children.[3]

After the election of Abraham Lincoln to the Presidency the previous November, South Carolina seceded from the Union in December, followed by the states of Mississippi, Florida, Alabama, Georgia, and Louisiana in January 1861. Early in December 1860, Texas secessionist leaders such as Oran M. Roberts and John S. Ford called for an election of delegates to a secession convention, which was held on January 8. Governor Sam Houston assembled the legislature in a special session and asked the members to declare illegal any actions of the proposed secession convention. Instead, the legislature authorized the convention, turned over the state government to it, and adjourned.

The secession convention met on January 28, and on February 1, the delegates voted for secession 166 to 8. After scheduling a statewide referendum on secession to be held on February 23, the convention elected seven men to represent Texas in the formation of the Confederate States of America at Montgomery, Alabama. The secession convention adjourned on February 4 with plans to reconvene on March 2 and directed its Committee on Public Safety to take control of federal property and to raise funds in the meantime.

Catastrophic events were now moving more swiftly than James Hall, secure on his East Texas farm, could imagine.

While the approach of war accelerated, Hall oversaw winter building projects.

Monday January 14th 1861. Today it rained in perfect torrants, swelling the Elk Hart to its utmost capacity, and putting us in fear that the mill levy [levee] *would again be washed away, towards evening however the wind hauled around to the North and the rain ceased. I concluded to tare* [tear] *down the old Machine shop, and commenced to remove the things out of it. Florence missed her fever, she has been for several days afflicted with the chills & fever which has greatly prostrated the dear little one, and I hope she may not have another attack of that horrible disease, weather of course cloudy, and very cool.*

As soon as the two-story machine shop was dismantled (Saturday, January 26), Hall directed John Harwell and Bill Hicks to begin framing "an upper story" for the house near the mill (Monday, January 28). The two men and Hall began "weatherboarding" the new part of the house on Saturday, February 9. Work on the house continued into March.

Bill Hicks had evidently been helping John Harwell at the mill. On Saturday, January 26, Hall wrote that Bill "ground 25½ bushels of corn."

Hall bought a 382-pound bale of cotton from Robert George of Crockett for 7 cents per pound (Saturday, February 2), and he "marked" seven bales of cotton for his father and sent them to the landing at Hall's Bluff to be picked up by a passing steamboat (Wednesday, February 6). Marking the bales meant writing the owner's name on the bale coverings in India ink.

Heavy rains threatened the levee at the gristmill (Thursday, January 31 and Saturday, February 9), but it continued to hold. Baby Florence, who suffered from chills and fever for several days, improved until she was well.

Several legal matters also occupied Hall's time. Joseph Wright, a grocer who was elected sheriff of Houston County in 1865 and 1866, served two citations "returnable to the District Court" of Houston County (Thursday, February 7). Hall filed a lawsuit against Mr. Bracken, his former father-in-law (Friday, February 8), and noted (Tuesday, February 19) the "celebrated case of Hall vs Hall was dismissed, and my other cases were continued." Although he did not elaborate upon the various lawsuits, and court records from that time have been lost to fires, he noted in his journal on Monday, February 25, that he "settled the cost in the case of Sharp vs McLemore for my old homestead." Two days later, he filed a suit against John Hepperla for "recovery" of the *Argus* office since Hepperla had not paid him rent for two years.

In mid-February, Charles C. Lund arrived on the steamer *Alamo* and visited with Hall and his family for several days (Saturday, February 16 through Tuesday, February 19). Earlier, Hall referred to his previous sojourn in Liberty as a "visit," and he made no statement in his journal that he intended to return to Liberty. His activities (such as adding a second story and weatherboarding the mill house) suggest that Hall planned to remain at the farm. It seems likely, however, that with war approaching, James Wrigley announced his intention to join the Confederate Army, leaving Lund with only young Sam Sharp as assistant. Lund needed Hall's experienced help to operate the business at the warehouse and store. Subsequent events show that Hall agreed to return to Liberty.

Hall loaned his horse Hawk to Lund for his return trip, and at this time he modified his references from "Mr. Lund" to "Charley Lund," suggesting a more comfortable relationship.

Hall did not reveal what arrangements he made with Lund; however, whatever they were, circumstances kept him at home.

At the same time, larger events began to escalate. The Texas Committee on Public Safety authorized Colonel of Cavalry John S. Ford to raise 600 men and to obtain the surrender of Ringgold Barracks and Forts Brown and McIntosh to prevent the U.S. Army from invading Texas through bays along the lower Gulf Coast or the mouth of the Rio Grande or, through arrangements with the Juárez government, from Mexico. Ford's orders included taking command of these forts as soon as the U.S. soldiers left. Colonel Henry McCulloch received orders to raise troops and bring about the surrender of U.S. forts on the northern frontier of Central Texas, while his brother Ben, commanding the Western Military District, sent state troops to outlying forts in order to secure the western part of the state from Indian attack.

The Committee also began to negotiate with Brigadier General David E. Twiggs, commanding U.S. troops in Texas, for the surrender of U.S. property at San Antonio. The aging Southerner had taken charge of the Department of Texas in December 1860, and while Twiggs sympathized with the philosophy of states' rights, he did not want a civil war to begin in Texas. Aware of the mounting secessionist fever and concerned about his soldiers, who were spread out across 1,200 miles, Twiggs sent four letters to his superiors in Washington asking for instructions. He received no answer. Pressured by the Committee, he agreed to surrender federal property, but demanded that his troops be allowed to leave peacefully, with their arms, and then only after a secession ordinance had been passed by the February 23 referendum.

After learning that Twiggs was about to be replaced by Colonel Carlos A. Waite, a staunch Unionist posted at Camp Verde northwest of San Antonio, the Committee ordered Ben McCulloch, leading about 400 Texans, to take over the U.S. arsenal. Early on the morning of February 16, McCulloch and his men left their camp on the Salado River, about five miles north of San Antonio, and marched into the city, where more than one hundred Knights of the Golden Circle joined them. Additional volunteers swelled McCulloch's force to about 1,000. Federal troops totaled only 160.

By six o'clock that Saturday morning, McCulloch and his men had taken control of the major streets in San Antonio. They placed guards over the federal ordnance, quartermaster, commissary, and clothing facilities. Commissioners authorized by the Committee on Public Safety halted General Twiggs, who was traveling by carriage to his headquarters at Alamo Plaza, and presented a letter requiring him to surrender all federal posts and property. To save his soldiers from attack by the Texans, Twiggs surrendered immediately, a decision that damaged his reputation and virtually ended his military career.[4]

On Monday, February 18, General Twiggs formally turned over the headquarters and arsenal in San Antonio along with all the other U.S. military posts and property to the commissioners. Through General Order Number 5, Twiggs commanded his troops to evacuate the camps and garrisons and to march to Indianola on the Gulf Coast. There the soldiers would be met by ships and transported to Union territory. They were allowed to keep their arms. When Colonel Waite arrived later the same day, he found the federal troops leaving for Indianola and the Texans in control. Although Waite assumed command on February 19, he realized it was too late to change the course of events.

The federal surrender gave Texas more than $23,000 in funds plus ordnance and weapons such as cannons, muskets, rifles, pistols, and ammunition, as well as wagons, horses, clothing, and commissary goods. The U.S. property at San Antonio, excluding buildings, amounted to more than $1.2 million, while the total value of property at all of the twenty U.S. military posts equaled $1.6 million. Most of the arms and equipment were used by the Sibley Brigade in its New Mexico campaign.[5]

Saturday February 23rd 1861. Today I went with John Harwell to the polls, and while there had to act as one of the clerks to the election. The vote at precinct No 7 stood for Secession 31, against Secession 5. I voted for it. weather cloudy & warm, until in the evening when the wind hauled around to the North & it became very cold with a heavy frost at night.

Like Hall, Texas voters approved the ordinance of secession on February 23. Many influential Unionists and everyday Texas citizens rejected the ordinance, but the final vote in favor of secession settled the matter. The secession convention met on March 2, and Governor Sam Houston announced that Texas had left the Union. Formal attachment to the Confederacy followed on March 5. The Texas Legislature was scheduled to meet on March 18, and the convention required all state officers to take an oath of loyalty to the Confederacy before that date; officials took the oath on Friday, March 15, but Governor Houston refused. His name was called again on Saturday, March 16, and again he refused. On Monday, March 18, the convention removed from office Governor Houston and Secretary of State E. W. Cave, who had also refused to take the loyalty oath, from office. The convention then appointed Lieutenant Governor Edward Clark, who was only too happy to swear the loyalty oath, to serve as governor. President Lincoln offered Sam Houston money and soldiers to help keep Texas in the Union, but Houston felt too old and tired to fight. He retired to his home in Huntsville, where he died on July 26, 1863.[6]

Tuesday March 12th 1861. Today at 12 o'clock I started for Liberty in the buggy with the little woman and Florence, and arrived in Crockett in good time, we remained there all night stopping at Lody Downes'. I employed Frank Stewart *for the balance of the year at the rate of $200 per annum. I left John S. Harwell in possession of my mill, and also left Charley Hall there. Harwell is in possession of the mill under a written contract for the current year. weather clear & pleasant.*

He did not specify the nature of Stewart's employment, but by contracting with Stewart and Harwell, it is evident that Hall intended to remain in Liberty for the rest of the year.

The following day, they continued southward toward the home of Dan Dailey, a distance of fifteen miles, "arriving there in the hardest rain perhaps that ever befel [befell] a poor devil to be caught in and also a severe north wind blowing that seemed as though it would cut one in to [two]. We were compelled to remain all night in consequence of the continued rain and cold." Two more days of travel brought them to Grand Cane, where they stopped "for the night." There, Frank Stewart caught up with them. He had left the farm after Hall and his family did, and traveling by stagecoach, he met them at Grand Cane on Saturday, March 16. After supper, "he started on the stage for Liberty."

Sunday March 17th 1861. Today we left Grand Cane and drove 23 miles and arrived safely in Liberty, where we were cordially received by James Wrigley's family he being absent at the time, but who returned shortly after. We are comfortably quartered at James Wrigley's where we receive every attention that friendship can bestow. weather cloudy & cold with drizzling rain.

Monday March 18th 1861. Today Frank Stewart started with the mules for the mill, to get my little wagon and to haul down a load. I let Frank have $20 in cash. Not much business doing. weather clear and cold.

James M. Wrigley, born at Johnstown, New York, in 1822, came to Texas in 1844 and settled at Liberty, where he was enumerated as a farmer in 1850. He married Ann Elizabeth Gayle (1829-1905), the daughter of Judge Billups and Ann Gayle (referred to as "Grandma Gayle"), on December 23, 1847. James and Ann Wrigley were the parents of three daughters and one son, all of whom lived to adulthood.

After dissolving his partnership with Charles Lund on January 1, 1855, Wrigley became a "commission and forwarding merchant," who received, stored, and shipped cotton, groceries, and other merchandise to Galveston. He also operated a stagecoach service to meet the steamer *Betty Powell* three times a week in its route between Galveston and Liberty. The stagecoach service carried the mail to Crockett.

In 1860, James (age thirty-seven) and Ann (age thirty-one) had three children: Lelia (age nine), John B. (age three), and Ida (age one). Wrigley owned real estate valued at $15,000 and personal property worth $2,000. During the Civil War, he served first with the Ninth (Nichols') Texas Infantry Regiment for six months. When the Ninth dissolved, he enlisted as a captain in Company B, Thomas N. Waul's Second Battalion of the Texas Legion, and rose to the rank of lieutenant colonel. After the war, Wrigley returned to his business as a merchant. At different times, Wrigley was elected city councilman and mayor of Liberty.[7] Hall and Wrigley remained close friends for the remainder of Hall's life.

James and Margaret quickly adapted to the lively pace of Liberty.

Tuesday March 19th 1861. Today I went up town in company with Jack Makimm and while there enjoyed the luxury of a nice shave by the barber. I am engaged in the store but not much doing. weather clear and cold.

Jack McKimm (age forty-two in 1860), a carpenter from Pennsylvania, was a former Liberty city councilman. His wife Sarah died suddenly in June 1860, leaving him with four children to raise.[8]

Two days later, Margaret and several ladies "went in hunt of blackberries. She & Mrs. John Wrigley walk[ed] over the railroad bridge, which is a considerable undertaking for a lady. I took a strole [*sic*] in their company on the other side of the river from Liberty, we met with poor success in getting berries however. weather changable & rather cool."

John (age forty in 1860) was the older brother of James Wrigley. John and his wife Sarah Hardin Wrigley had three children.

Friday March 22 1861. Today I went to the City to arbitrate a matter in controversy between Kellum & Stanwood. I also received a fine barrel of oysters from Galveston on the steamer, which I eat [*sic*] *(at least my share) with great gusto. weather cloudy & rather cool.*

S. K. Kellum owned Kellum's Springs in Grimes County, a "summer retreat" offering the services of a "resident physician" during the "watering season." The resort offered baths, single rooms, music, a "bowling saloon," a party every Tuesday, a full bar, and luxury foods such as "lobsters, oysters, and candied fruits." Lodging, board, and bathing cost $36 per month, $10 per week, and $2 per day and half price for children. In addition, Kellum's Springs provided "good stables and carriage houses[,]" mail service, and a school.[9]

Although the "controversy" between Kellum and Stanwood may have been resolved, Hall and James Wrigley next served as arbitrators in the case of Stanwood and Fatheree vs. Kellum (Monday, March 25). Since Dr. Thomas A. Stanwood and Dr. Ben B. Fatheree were both physicians, they may have worked for Kellum at his resort and had not been paid for their services. Hall "gave an award in favor of the plaintiffs for $543.50[.]"[10]

In between social, legal, and commercial obligations, Hall went fishing with Sam Sharp, who still worked at the store, and Ed (Edward Livingstone) Jones. A year younger than Sam, Ed Jones may have been introduced to Hall as a friend of Sam. Jones served in the Confederate Army throughout the Civil War. After the war ended, Jones worked at Wrigley's store, and he eventually married James Wrigley's daughter Lelia.[11]

Sunday March 24th 1861. Today I done nothing but loaf around the ware house & take an occasional <u>*smile*</u>*. weather changable & rather cool.*

To keep himself busy, on Monday, March 25, Hall "drew off 15 doz [bottles] of brandy [out of kegs] and bottled it up for sale." The next day he "sealed & labled" the brandy "ready for the market."

On Wednesday, March 27, Hall's cousin William P. Leaverton "and family with his negroes" arrived from Maryland. Hall did not state whether they had traveled by rail or by sea, but at Galveston, they boarded the *Ruthven* to cross Galveston Bay to Anahuac and steam up the Trinity to Liberty.

The Leaverton ladies checked into the hotel, and Hall arranged for the slaves to stay in "an old restaurant" (one no longer in use) that was owned by Jack McKimm. Hall does not say where Leaverton himself spent the next few days. The ladies left for Crockett by stagecoach on Thursday, March 28, while Hall waited for Frank Stewart who was "now hourly expected" to arrive with the wagon. Two days later, Stewart reached Liberty along with Bill and Louisa, "the little wagon and mules," and "sundry articles," probably clothing and household goods. "I am still engaged in drawing off wine. Mr. Leaverton [is] still here but very anxious to leave, he is floundering about like a fish out of water."

James and Margaret spent Sunday, March 31, with the Lunds. "Charley has a pretty place & very comfortably fixed, . . ." Hall wrote, and that evening they returned to the Wrigleys'.

Monday April 1st 1861. Today the little wagon in charge of Frank Stewart started up to the Mill, carrying William Leaverton and his negroes with a large quantity of the [their] *things. I am engaged in sealing the wine that I have been drawing off, for a few days, which is not entirely so pleasant a job as I anticipated. weather cloudy and warm.*

Hall seems to have enjoyed the visit with his cousin. He does not say whether the Leaverton family's relocation to Texas had been long-planned, or whether secession sympathies in Maryland plus the raising and drilling of troops in Maryland and Virginia for an attack on Washington City, according to *The Liberty Gazette* (January 11 and January 25, 1861), could have been reasons for them to leave. (In April, federal troops entered Maryland, took command of the state capital at Annapolis, and thereby gained control of the railroad lines to Washington, D.C.; Maryland remained in the Union.)

The Leaverton family bought land in Houston County near the Halls and continued to be residents in the area after the war.

Early in January, the citizens of Liberty raised the Texas flag on a pole 100 feet high in the "public square," accompanied by speeches in favor of the:

> repeal of the articles annexing Texas to the United States. During the delivery of the speeches[,] frequent bursts of applause greeted the speakers, and volleys of Musketry made the welkin ring in token of the intense approval of the step Texas is about to take in going out of the Union. The meeting then adjourned to the Court House, for the purpose of organizing a company of Minute Men, to hold themselves in readiness in case of any emergency.[12]

On Saturday, April 6, Hall along with Charles Lund, Sam Sharp, and Ed Jones "hoisted the confederate flag on the top of a 30 feet pole and it [is] placed on the top of the Ware house, where it now floats to the breeze, the emblem of the free." Hall and his friends had caught the excitement of secession fever and perhaps envisioned the return of Texas to an independent republic.

Although federal troops in Texas surrendered in February, Union soldiers in other Southern areas did not. Confederates fired on the federal garrison at Fort Sumter, near Charleston, South Carolina, on April 12, and the Union troops surrendered the next day.

On April 15, President Abraham Lincoln announced a call for 75,000 militia to enroll in the Union Army, and four days later, he ordered a naval blockade from South Carolina to the Rio Grande, later extending the blockade to include North Carolina and Virginia. Confederate President Jefferson Davis called for 100,000 volunteers for the army and authorized state militia units to serve for six months.[13] Although numerous Texans immediately joined the state militia (Texas State Troops) or the Confederate Army, as the war continued, the six-month militia companies were transferred to the Confederate Army. Texas needed the state militia for frontier service to contend with Indian attacks and for coastal defense to prevent a Union invasion. The conscription issue placed Texas governors in conflict with Confederate officers, who required more and more men to serve in the army. The matter would not be resolved until 1864.

Now a part of the Confederate States of America, Texas joined the larger swirl of events. Governor Edward Clark asked for 8,000 infantry troops and authorized John S. Ford and brothers Ben and Henry McCulloch to raise cavalry units, the service preferred by Texans, who generally disdained walking. Clark then created military districts to organize the recruiting effort and to establish camps of instruction.

By the time Colonel Earl Van Dorn, just appointed commander of the (Confederate) Department of Texas, arrived in Galveston from New Orleans on April 16, approximately 2,000 federal troops had left the state. Ignoring the agreement with Twiggs, Van Dorn and E. B. Nichols (a Galveston merchant) aboard the *General Rusk* captured Union troops on the *Star of the West* off Indianola on April 17. The U.S. soldiers at Indianola still awaiting ships also surrendered, but were soon paroled.[14]

Meanwhile, six companies of the Eighth Infantry, about 350 men from Forts Bliss, Quitman, and Davis, marched 700 miles across Texas toward San Antonio. These U.S. soldiers met Van Dorn and about 1,400 troops at San Lucas Spring on May 9. Faced with an overwhelming Confederate force, the federal soldiers surrendered. Officers were paroled, while enlisted men remained prisoners, spread out in forts and camps around the state. They were paroled at Baton Rouge, Louisiana, on February 25, 1863.[15]

On Tuesday, April 2, Hall noted, "Today I am engaged in filing and arranging the papers & vouchers belonging to the Trinity River Navigation Company." He continued working on the documents the next day, and that evening he suffered from "a pretty hard fever and the little woman says a chill preceeded it but I think not as I never have before had one of the articles, be that as it may. I do know that I had a fever which lasted nearly all night."

Thursday April 4th 1861. Today I am up, after spending a very sick night and went to work on the papers & accounts of the steamers belonging to the Trinity River Navigation Company. The little woman became very much alarmed for fear I was going to have a severe and protracted spell of sickness, but as I am up this morning she appears to be very much relieved, weather cloudy and rather warm for the season of the year with every prospect for a hard rain.

It is possible that the Trinity River Navigation Company Hall mentioned in this passage was the forerunner of the Trinity River Slack Water Navigation Company chartered in 1866. The purpose of the latter company was to establish year-round steamboat navigation on the Trinity River between Galveston and Dallas by building a series of dams and locks. The first dam, to be built above Liberty, had a proposed completion date of January 1, 1869, and the entire project was to be finished within three years, or the company would lose its charter. Among the directors of the Trinity River Slack Water Navigation Company were John F. Carr and Frank Hardin. The project failed, and the next company to propose continuous navigation of the Trinity River, also called the Trinity River Navigation Company, was established in 1892. Some clearing work began near Dallas, but did not continue downstream. Not until 1968, almost one hundred years after the initial projected completion date, did the Trinity River Authority build a dam (begun in 1966) and create a lake on the lower Trinity River near Livingston. The locks planned for the dam, however, were deleted due to the cost. Navigation of the Trinity River between Galveston and Dallas is no longer considered viable.[16]

On Sunday, April 7, Hall wrote that he sold Melinda, Laura, and Elisha, slaves belonging to Margaret, for $1,700, adding "I am indebted to her for the amt. [amount] of purchase money, I having used it." Hall did not state to whom they were sold, only that he and Margaret "made titles" for them (Monday, April 8).

With the store and warehouse located directly on the riverbank, Hall recorded the passage of steamboats up and down the Trinity, the type and amount of cotton or freight they carried, and conditions on the river. He noted the river's rise and the passing of the *Colonel Stell* upriver with "a large freight" (Sunday, April 7) and the *Alamo* downriver with "900 bales of Cotton" (Monday, April 8). The river continued to rise for several days, and he feared an overflow (Wednesday, April 10). On the following day, the *Lone Star* "came down the river, but in consequence of the drift having formed a raft above the rail road bridge, she could not get through. The Capt. chartered the steamer Swan to go to Galveston, in lieu of the Lone Star." On Friday, April 12, the *A. S. Ruthven*, with its reinforced hull, "went over the river to take the freight off of the steamer Lone Star." Hall dined on board the *Ruthven* with George Gordon.

Born in Scotland, Gordon was a clerk aboard the *A. S. Ruthven* and later became her captain. At different times, he worked as "captain, owner, master and clerk of steamers that worked the Trinity and called at Moore's Bluff. Gordon purchased 1,107 acres of land adjacent to Moore's Bluff, and eight of his ten children were born there. His wife was buried there in 1869." There were two homes, several outbuildings, and "an extensive garden where imported and native fruit trees were planted. Gordon died in 1888 and is buried at Moore's Bluff." Moore's Bluff stood only a short distance downstream from Liberty. In 1880, Gordon (age fifty-two) was enumerated at Liberty, with a listed occupation of farmer. He was a widower with five sons ranging in age from ten to twenty-three, all of whom were born in Texas.[17] George Gordon was a member of the St. Andrew's Society for Scots organized by A. S. Ruthven.

At the store, Hall spent two days (Tuesday, April 9 and Wednesday, April 10) "canvassing and carpeting the room intended for a counting room." When it was ready (Saturday, April 13), he and others ("we") moved furniture into "the new office in [the] rear of the store. . . ." The Lund warehouse and store had been built at the Trinity River landing where Gayle Street ended. Named for Judge Billups Gayle in 1856, the street passed south of the Catholic church and "in front of the South side of the Court House Square."[18]

On Monday, April 15, Dr. William George Washington Jowers (1812-1894) paid Hall a visit at the warehouse. Jowers, who appeared to be in "fine health[,]" was "doing business for several houses in New Orleans."

A physician born in North Carolina, William George Washington Jowers graduated from Transylvania University at Lexington, Kentucky, in 1835. After serving a term in the Mississippi legislature, he came to Texas in 1839 and practiced medicine in Crockett from 1841 until 1846. After his wife's death in 1846, he moved to Palestine in Anderson County. Elected to the Texas House in 1848, he represented Houston and Anderson counties. Jowers served two terms in the Texas House, three terms in the Texas Senate, and later became county judge for Anderson County. During the Civil War, he raised a company in Anderson County. Jowers lost most of his wealth during the war, but later regained it. He married four times and fathered eight children.[19]

During the spring of 1861, Jowers represented various factorage firms ("houses") in New Orleans. Once a planter's cotton reached a port such as Galveston or New Orleans, his factor, or agent, collected and sold the cotton to textile mills back East or in Europe, often Liverpool, England. Factors had long-standing relationships with planters. They loaned planters cash, kept their accounts, purchased clothing and household goods for them, married into their families, and at times managed their estates. Factors earned between two and five percent of the sale price of the cotton as their commission. Because so much of the South's economy depended upon uncertain harvests, borrowed money, changes in the worldwide cotton market, and wartime losses of stored cotton, many factorage firms went out of business during or soon after the Civil War.[20] Jowers most likely visited Hall to arrange for sales of Texas cotton to factors in New Orleans.

Although Governor Clark created military districts to organize the Confederate recruiting effort, the government needed money to buy uniforms, arms, and supplies for the troops, who expected to be equipped by the state. Texas had no system of taxation, however, and very few bonds left from the Compromise of 1850. In April 1861, Texas issued one million dollars in state bonds at eight percent interest. Clark authorized Galveston merchant E. B. Nichols to sell the Texas bonds in New Orleans, but Nichols found no buyers.

Neither could Nichols exchange the Texas bonds for arms because other Confederate states were paying cash for arms and sending purchasing agents to Mexico, Cuba, and Europe to buy more. At the camps of instruction held during the summer in each of the military districts, the recruits lacked supplies, weapons, and uniforms. Deluged with complaints, Clark sent three new agents (Hamilton P. Bee, Samuel Maverick, and Lemuel Evans) to Matamoros, Mexico, to purchase guns with the bonds, but they were no more successful than Nichols had been.

While James Wrigley traveled back and forth to Galveston on business, Hall worked at the store, where sales continued to be slow. He took an inventory of McKimm's "stock" (Monday, April 22) and conducted "some business in the railroad trade" (Thursday, April 25), but sales remained negligible. Frank Stewart arrived from Hall's farm on Wednesday, April 24, bringing "the little wagon," and Hall mentioned that the mules looked "very bad and much jaded." Hall mentioned Charles Lund's return from Galveston on Monday, May 13, after an absence of two weeks. On some days Hall admitted to "loafing" in the store, and he was not a man to enjoy inactivity.

As the spring passed, war with the Union came closer to the home front.

Wednesday May 1st 1861. Today the Liberty Guards turned out to receive the Polk County Guards under Capt D. D. Moore who are now on their way to the seat of war in Virginia. The Liberty Guards escorted them down to the ware house where they quartered[,] *but little business doing. I attended the store solus* [alone] *during the parade of the Guards*[.] *weather cloudy and warm.*

Thursday May 2nd 1861. Today the steamer Ruthven arrived from Galveston. The Polk County Guards were compelled to camp immediately in the ware house in consequence of a very hard rain, [in] *fact it continued to rain throughout the entire day making it exceedingly muddy & disagreeable out of doors. The weather was very cold for the season.*

On Friday, May 3, the Polk County Guards left Liberty on the *Ruthven*, bound for Galveston and transfer to another vessel headed to Virginia.

A six-month unit, the Liberty Guards were incorporated into Thomas Neville Waul's Texas Legion when the latter formed at Brenham during the spring of 1862. The Legion included infantry, cavalry, and artillery, totaling about 2,000 men. Lieutenant Colonel James M. Wrigley commanded the Second Infantry Battalion. After active duty in Arkansas and Louisiana, the Second Infantry Battalion was transferred to Mississippi and attached to General John C. Pemberton's troops at Vicksburg. All but one company of the Second Infantry Battalion were captured at Vicksburg on July 4, 1863, and Wrigley was wounded there. After the troops were paroled, Waul's Legion reorganized in Houston and spent the remainder of the war on guard duty at Galveston, finally disbanding in May 1865.[21]

The Polk County Guards, named by Hall on May 1 and 2, were in fact the Livingston Guards. Polk County Commissioners appropriated $1,600 "for uniforms and clothing . . ." for this unit, which became Company B of the First Texas Infantry. The First Texas, part of the Texas Brigade commanded by General John Bell Hood, took part in major battles and campaigns at Chickamauga, the siege of Petersburg, Gettysburg, Sharpsburg, Yorktown, Malvern Hill, Manassas, Spotsylvania, The Wilderness, and others.[22]

A few days later (Saturday, May 11), Hall noted that after working all day at the office, in the evening he "went up to town, and remained there for some time, drilling the K.G.C.'s." The Knights of the Golden Circle was a secret society, subdivided into groups known as Castles, with the primary goal of creating an independent empire that would include the South, the West Indies, Mexico, and Central America—territory approximating a circle. In spite of its secessionist philosophy, the movement never achieved much status in the South, except in Texas, where it was most popular in 1859 and 1860.[23] A major of Texas State Troops, Hall continued to drill the Knights and on Tuesday, June 11, he was elected company captain. Days later (Saturday, June 22), Hall wrote, "Today the Liberty Guards had a dress parade and went out on the cars [railroad] to Beaumont. I did not drill the K.G.C's in consequence of the absence of so many of the members with the Guards." As more and more of the Knights enlisted in the military, the organization faded away.

Hall noted the ebb and flow of business in the store, with "the rail road trade" providing the most "active" sales (Wednesday, May 15). The passage of steamboats and river conditions on the Trinity remained important topics.

Saturday May 18th 1861. Today the ladies from home in company with Ed Jones went out in hunt of black berries, they had not been gone long before the winds came and the rain descended in torrents, when they all returned, looking more like drownded rats than human beings. The Steamer Mary Lenard came down the river and in attempting to land carried away part of the lower landing and lost overboard a part of her cargo, but effected a landing finally against the Steamer Swan.

Hall spent Sunday, May 19, at home reading, and in the evening he and Margaret, James and Ann Wrigley, and a Miss Emma Johnson "took a strole" down to the landing to see the *Ruthven* arrive; "we all got a magnificent ice punch and returned home."

The following day, the *Mary Lenard* "went down the river in search of her lost cargo and returned in the evening." Hall did not mention the nature of the cargo.

Wednesday May 22nd 1861. Today I left Liberty on the Steamer Ruthven in company with James Wrigley and Geo Gordon, we had quite a pleasant run down the river and across the bay arriving at Galveston at 1 o'clock P.M. weather clear & pleasant.

The next day, Wrigley returned to Liberty, but Hall remained at Galveston, planning to continue to New Orleans by steamer.

Friday May 24th 1861. Today I am still in Galveston, with but little prospect of obtaining a passage to New Orleans. There was quite a large turn out of the Military in Galveston. The steamship "Rusk" weighed anchor and went over the bar after a prize ship, but returned with the pilot boat "Royal Yacht." weather clear & rather warm.

Saturday May 25th 1861. Today I am still in Galveston, and in consequence of the steamships all having suspended their trips between New Orleans and this point there is no prospect for my obtaining a passage to the former city. The mouth of the Mississippi river is not [now] *in a state of blockade by the Northern Government. weather clear & pleasant.*

Sunday May 26th 1861. This morning there was quite a large fire in Galveston, which consumed Briggs & Gard's store with several other houses. I left Galveston on the Steamer Ruthven at 9 O'clk A.M. for Liberty at which place I arrived at 10 P.M. and found the little woman well weather clear & pleasant.

Hall wrote the contract for the *Ruthven* "to carry the mails of the Confederate States" (Saturday, June 8). He worked at the store and continued to drill the Knights of the Golden Circle until most of them, who were also members of the Liberty Guards, left on June 22. When George Gordon returned from a trip to New Orleans on the *Ruthven* (Sunday, June 23), Hall reported that "every thing there [is] at a perfect stand still." At the time, Texas seemed to be at a safe distance from the Union blockade.

In late June, Hall took Margaret and Florence, Frank Stewart and a young black woman named Conny for a visit to the family in Houston County. They

Destruction of C.S. Privateer Royal Yacht, *8 November 1861.*

In Galveston Harbor, Texas by a cutting out party from USS *SANTEE*, commanded by Lieutenant James E. Jouett. Copied from: "Deeds of Valor," Vol. II, p.1, published by the Perrien-Keydel Co., Detroit, 1907. Courtesy of the Naval History and Heritage Command.

left Liberty on Wednesday, June 26, and arrived "at the mill" about four o'clock in the afternoon on Sunday, June 30, where they found John Harwell ill. Hall did not appear to be very concerned about Harwell's sickness. The next day, he "borrowed Harwell's horse" and went to visit his cousin William Leaverton. The two of them conducted unexplained business at Hall's Bluff (Tuesday, July 2).

In the same entry for July 2, Hall described "a large Comit visible at night situated in the N.W." The "Great Comet of 1861" was first seen by John Tebbutt (1834-1916) of New South Wales, Australia, on May 13 and observed in the northern hemisphere on June 30. Comet "Tebbutt" had a tail about 100 degrees long, stretching halfway across the night sky.[24] Many considered the comet a harbinger of the war.

By the time Hall and Frank Stewart returned to Liberty (Monday, July 8), leaving Margaret, Florence, and Conny at the farm, the war had come to Texas. Union blockade of the Texas coast began on July 2 with the arrival of the U.S.S. *South Carolina* off Galveston. Captain James Alden and his crew captured twelve ships between July 4 and July 12.

The blockade made it almost impossible to export cotton, the state's primary cash crop, to textile mills in Europe. However, the crop was a large one, and mills in Great Britain, France, Germany, and other countries were paying high prices. Long wagon trains hauled thousands of bales southward to Brownsville, where they were ferried across the Rio Grande to Matamoros, Mexico, beyond the reach of the blockade. The cotton was then sold to agents from Europe, placed on shallow draft vessels called "lighters," and transported to European ships waiting off shore. Cotton became such a crucial medium of exchange that Governor Francis R. Lubbock, who took office in November 1861, issued a proclamation prohibiting the storage of cotton near the coast to keep it from being captured by U.S. troops.[25]

On Monday, July 8, Hall noted that Captain Wrigley and the Liberty Guards had "started out on a Camp drill." Although Ed Jones joined Wrigley and the Liberty Guards, Sam Sharp had a very good reason to remain in Liberty.

Thursday July 11th 1861. Today I am engaged as salesman in the store with pretty active trade. Be it remembered & known that Samuel H. Sharp and Miss Mary Alexandrien Lamier [Lemaire], *were united together in the bonds of wedlock, and I rather expect at night there was some very sharp shooting took place, this however is only a surmise. Capt. Wrigley & Ed. Jones came in from their camp to attend said wedding, where all passed off pleasantly & agreeably to all in attendance, weather clear & warm.*

Friday July 12th 1861. Today I am busy as salesman in the Store, in consequence of Sam H. Sharp who on yesterday took unto himself a wife and is now sticking as close to her as a plaster. He being the regular Salesman, has now thrown that duty on me, doubtless for a few days, but I rather anticipate it will not last long. Capt. Wrigley and his company are still in camp. weather changeable & warm.

On the following day, he noted that Sam Sharp "did by a tight squeeze make out to come to the store but only for a few minutes." Captain Wrigley and his company "returned to town from their camp of instruction, whether benefited or not by the weeks work I cannot say but all however in good humor & a fine spirits [*sic*]."

Sunday July 14th 1861. Today I am busily employed in writing letters, and this being the anniversary of my marriage with the little woman I did not forget to write her and to drink her health & long life, weather changeable & warm.

By Monday, July 15, everything returned to normal, with Sam Sharp again working in the store as salesman, Captain Wrigley leaving on the *Ruthven* for Galveston, and Frank Stewart heading back to the mill with the mules and the little wagon.

While Hall handled sales, Charles Lund and Sam Sharp made "military belts" for the Liberty Guards (Thursday, July 18). The Guards also drilled at the warehouse (Friday, July 19). On Saturday, July 20, the Liberty Guards led by Wrigley "had a dress parade & company drill and to whom was awarded a stand of colors [flag] made by Mrs Lund of Liberty. It was presented by [attorney] Capt Trowell in a happy speech and received by Capt Wrigley on behalf of the Guards who responded in his usual happy off handed style, all passing off to the entire satisfaction of all concerned; but little business doing. . . "

Hall seemed to enjoy the military activities around him, even though he disdained fighting as a way to solve difficulties, and never expressed any desire to join the men going off to war. The youth's eagerness for adventure had mellowed into the adult's responsibility for the safety and well-being of his family and those who depended upon him.

The Confederate victory at Bull Run (First Manassas) on July 21, which routed the Union Army but failed to take advantage of the chaos to capture Washington, D.C., inspired Texans to join the military. Many enrolled in the militia units of the Texas State Troops, while others enlisted directly into the Confederate Army. A few Texas regiments organized during the spring of 1861, but most of the first infantry and cavalry units were created after the troops received some formal training in the camps of instruction that summer. A total of about 25,000 Texans, both infantry and cavalry, enrolled for service in 1861. The majority joined the cavalry. At this time early in the war, Texans had the choice of serving in either the Texas State Troops or the Confederate Army. Later, most of the militia units would be transferred to Confederate service. Altogether, an estimated 84,000 Texans participated in the war.[26]

Trusted by General John B. Magruder, whom he had met in California during the 1840s, Captain Leon Smith supervised the conversion of the merchant steamers *Bayou City* and *Neptune* to cottonclads. (A cottonclad steamboat bore cotton bales stacked around the deck as armor to protect sharpshooters during battles with Union gunboats.) Captain Smith led Confederate "cottonclad" steamships during the Battle for Galveston in January 1863 and at Sabine Pass in September 1863. After the Civil War, Smith headed to San Francisco to be reunited with his family. He opened a trading post in Alaska, where he was killed in 1869.[27]

Hall spent Sunday evening July 21 in drink and conversation with Wrigley, Dr. Fatheree, and steamboat Captain Leon Smith, who had worked for Charles Morgan's Southern Mail Steamship Company.

Since business continued to be slow, Hall noted details of life around him, such as sickness among the Wrigley family as well as Charles Lund, but Hall remained well and continued to work at the warehouse. "Mrs Lund gave us a call at the store and spent some time in the office which to us made the time pass very agreeably" (Thursday, July 25). The next evening, "George Gordon passed through town on a hand car [along the rail line] just from New Orleans." And on Saturday, July 27, the Liberty Guards "had a dress parade & drill on the public square."

Sunday July 28th 1861. Today I went up town in company with Charley Lund and after playing 2 games of billiards returned with him to his residence where I partook of a nice dinner served up in Mrs Lund's elegant style. After spending a couple of hours very pleasantly we returned to the river. The Str. Ruthven arrived and departed for Galveston, weather cloudy with occasional showers of rain. Ther: standing at 88°.

Thomas P. Ochiltree (1839-1902) called on Hall (Wednesday, July 31) and "spent some time." Ochiltree, a newspaperman and an attorney, served as secretary to the Texas Democratic Convention in 1859 and as a delegate to the Democratic National Convention in 1860. Ochiltree joined Hood's Texas Brigade, and after the Civil War he returned to his earlier careers. Ochiltree later served a term in the U.S. Congress and traveled to Europe on behalf of Texas businessmen.[28] Hall did not reveal the subject of their conversation.

As the summer passed, the Confederates built forts at San Luis Pass, Bolivar Peninsula, and Pelican Spit (a small island near the tip of Galveston Island, opposite Point Bolivar), and they set up an observation post on the roof of a building on The Strand. In response to Confederate cannon fire aimed at a Union pilot boat off San Luis Pass, the U.S.S. *South Carolina* bombarded Galveston for about half an hour on August 3, then sailed into open water. After the bombardment, Confederate General Paul O. Hébert ordered the cannons pulled back from the beaches first, followed by an order to evacuate Galveston. Many citizens were already leaving and businesses were closing.[29]

Because the long Texas coastline made it difficult to maintain the blockade, Union vessels concentrated on Sabine Pass, Galveston, Corpus Christi, Matagorda Bay, and Brownsville. Adventuresome captains with an eye to high profits ran the blockade to pick up cotton bales and take them to Cuba to sell as well as to deliver goods such as cloth, medicine, liquor, weapons, and some luxury items.[30] Most Texans made do with what they had, bartered for things they needed, and returned to old ways (such as weaving cloth at home). As Confederate money plummeted in value, gold, silver, and cotton became the currency. Early in the war, however, no one could visualize the lean days ahead.

Friday August 2nd 1861. Today the Steamer Ruthven arrived from Galveston with Capt McKeen's company in route for Virginia[,] *they making a fine appearance and being determined to do the Yankees all the damage possible.*

Mr [James] *Bolling* [a merchant] *went out on the cars with said Company. Frank Stewart arrived from the Mill, with the little wagon & mules bringing several articles and he looking very well from the trip. But little doing in the way of business, weather clear & hot, Ther: at 91°.*

Hall and Charles Lund voted for "state officers" on Monday, August 5. After Governor Sam Houston refused to take the loyalty oath to the Confederacy in March, Lieutenant Governor Edward Clark became governor, with a statewide election scheduled to follow on August 5. A contentious election campaign followed, with three candidates on separate tickets competing for governor of Texas: incumbent Edward Clark, Francis R. Lubbock, and Thomas Jefferson Chambers. Instead of a result that confirmed Clark's appointment, Francis R. Lubbock won by a slim margin (124 votes). The position of lieutenant governor also appeared on each ballot. Clark did not contest the election, but returned home and recruited the Fourteenth Texas Infantry Regiment. Governor Lubbock took office on November 7.[31]

With business declining, on the following day Hall "borrowed James Wrigley's celebrated mule Kate" and began traveling "up the Country to the Mills." He stayed overnight at the home of John F. Carr, a merchant, cotton trader, plantation owner, and steamboat builder, who lived at Smithfield in Polk County. The next day (Wednesday, August 7), Hall continued northward, accompanied by Captain John W. Redman (also spelled Redmond). On their way to Sumpter, Captain Redman "became very sick and was confined on the road side with several fits, which detained me on my journey very much[,] being compelled to wait upon and attend him[.]" Hall loaned Redman ten dollars in cash on July 19 without any expectation of repayment, indicating that he knew of Redman's reputation or had already had some business dealings with him. A steamboat captain, John W. Redman (census spelling), age twenty-eight in the 1860 census, had been enumerated at Augusta in Houston County. He was born in Texas, and his occupation was listed as farmer; however, no real estate or personal property values were given. No wife was named, but he and Mary Redman, age four, lived at the home of Darcus Edwards, age fifty, perhaps a relative or a close friend, who took care of the child. The loss of his wife may have led to Redman's heavy drinking.[32]

Redman would reappear in 1865 and become a burden during the last year of Hall's life.

Thursday August 8th 1861. Today Redman & myself left Sumpter and arrived in Crockett about 4 o'clock, when I parted company with him, I then started for the mill & met Father on the road, after riding 43 miles I arrived at the mills & found John Harwell my miller sick with chills & fever. I then rode down to Mothers where I found the Little woman & my pet Baby well & glad to see me. Father [is] *remaining in Crockett for the night. The balance of Mother's family I found sick*[,] *weather changeable & very hot.*

Hall stayed with Joshua and Mahala, where he rejoined Margaret and Florence, nicknamed "Fawn." He spent most of his time with John Harwell at the mill, putting a gutta percha belt on the gristmill and a leather belt on the wheat mill (Monday, August 12). He and John Harwell pecked (or re-grooved) the mill stones, while William Leaverton and "his negro man" helped raise and lower the runner stone. He also visited friends, went fishing, and took care of business matters in Crockett.

Working at the mill on Monday, September 9, Hall "learned that Mr Bird had this morning shot Neely's negro man George [in] a very cowardly manner although he did not kill the negro." Hall did not elaborate. Farmer Tom Neely, age twenty-five in the 1860 census, was born in Mississippi. He lived with his mother Mary, listed as head of the household, and with a younger brother and sister. Mary Neely's property was adjacent to that of Joshua Hall.

Just before his return to Liberty, Hall moved up to the mill house (Tuesday, September 10), while Margaret and Florence remained with Joshua and Mahala. Margaret and Florence visited him each day, and Roberta and Toby also went to the mill to see him. These visits were especially important since he would be returning to Liberty alone.

On Monday, September 16, Hall mounted the mule Kate and began the long journey southward. In Crockett he sold a one-third league of land in Denton

County and 640 acres in Jack County to G. F. Moore, and he arranged with Moore to buy 640 acres in Coryell County. After his "settlement" with Moore, he rode to Dan Dailey's, where he spent the night. The following day, he joined his friends Dan Dailey and Dr. J. B. Stone, who traveled together for thirty miles and spent the night at Colleta Alderman's, where he lost his "breast pin, with the little woman's daguerreotype likeness in it." The three men left Alderman's on Wednesday, September 18, and rode together for twelve miles, reaching Livingston at midday. Dailey and Stone remained in Livingston, and Hall traveled another seventeen miles to John Carr's. That night "there was an exceeding hard rain which lasted about 3 hours. Here I suffered severely from the fleas & bed bugs. In fact I got no rest throughout the night." The next morning, he rode a further sixteen miles but had to stop at Grand Cane because of "hard rain which lasted throughout the day. I having become well soaked." On Friday, September 20, Hall "left Grand Cane and rode 23 miles through the hardest rain I think I ever rode in before, reaching Liberty about 3. o'clock. Here I found James Wrigley's family all sick, Sam & his wife on the sick list also." Charles Lund and Ed Jones were the only ones well enough to attend to the store.

Monday September 23rd 1861. Today the Steamer Ruthven arrived from & departed for Galveston, bringing but little freight. Business very dull. I whipped James Wrigley's negro man Sam in the Ware house for running away. weather changeable and hot but rather cool at night.

This is the only instance recorded in the entire journal where Hall physically reprimanded a slave.

On October 4, Commander William B. Renshaw aboard the U.S.S. *Westfield* ordered the surrender of Galveston, but permitted a four-day truce to allow residents to evacuate. Confederate Colonel Xavier B. Debray, in charge of the evacuation, ordered Colonel Joseph J. Cook to move the troops, cannons, and supplies to Virginia Point, on the mainland, where he set up a new military camp. Galveston remained in Union control until January 1, 1863, when combined naval, infantry, and artillery forces led by Commander Leon Smith and General John B. Magruder retook the island.

Between Monday, September 30, and Friday, October 4, Hall mentioned that he was very sick, although he did not describe his symptoms, and he kept working at the warehouse. On Tuesday, October 1, he wrote, "Capt. Stovall with his Company arrived from Jasper County in route for Galveston to join the army[.] They made their head quarters in the Ware house awaiting the arrival of the Steamer to proceed on their journey."

Wednesday October 2nd 1861. Today Sam sharp and his wife left in my buggy for the Mill and to remain some time with his Mother. James Wrigley and Capt. Stovall's company left on the Steamer Ruthven for Galveston. I am still quite sick. But little business doing. weather changeable & very warm.

Business became "pretty heavy" on Thursday, October 3 and Friday, October 4, but dropped off again on Saturday, October 5.

Captain Wrigley returned to Liberty from Galveston (Monday, October 7), where he received "marching orders" for the Liberty Guards "and in consequence of which he got into a comfortable little tight on champagne."

The next day, however, Wrigley and "the hands raised the foundation or ground work of my new house." Hall had not previously stated that he intended to remain in Liberty indefinitely, nor that he needed a house. But to provide a home there for Margaret and Florence, he bought land from James Wrigley and began to construct a residence.

Wednesday October 9th 1861. Today I went home with Dr. Stanwood and partook of a fine oyster dinner, after which we had some excellent Piano music, performed by Miss Stanwood. Hands are now working briskly on my new house. The Steamer Ruthven left for Galveston with the residue of Capt Stovall's company. weather clear and pleasant.

Sarah Eugenia (Eugenie) Stanwood Mouton (1841-1915), daughter of Dr. Stanwood, became a widow soon after her marriage during the Civil War. She was later briefly married to attorney William F. "Bee" Hardin. Her book *Josephine Joseph—Texas Sketches*, about Galveston and Liberty, was published in 1900. Known as "Mrs. Mouton," she became editor and owner of *The East Texas Bee*, a weekly newspaper, in 1902.[33]

Wrigley and the workers finished the foundation on Hall's new house on Thursday, October 10. Work continued for several days, ground to a halt, then resumed intermittently, with supplies such as "flooring" brought by steamer from Galveston. At the same time, war-related activity increased.

Monday October 14th 1861. Today the Steamer Ruthven left for Galveston [after having her paddle wheel repaired], *with the cannon carriages for the Confederate States army at Galveston. James Wrigley arrived home from Houston on the cars.* [Wrigley had gone to Houston on the previous Saturday.] *He & 67 other members of the Liberty Guards were sworn into the service of the Government for 6 months to be stationed at Galveston. Business very brisk in the way of selling goods. Nothing doing on my house, weather changeable, with prospect of rain.*

Tuesday October 15th 1861. Today the balance of the members of the Liberty Guards arrived from Hardin County and were sworn into the service. Business very brisk in fitting out each member of the Guards with clothing etc. Nothing doing on my house. weather cloudy with rain all day long making it disagreeable.

Fitting out the Liberty Guards for their tour of duty at Galveston continued the next day. During a reorganization of the Guards on Thursday, October 17, James Wrigley was elected captain. Additional officers were: Joseph N. Dark, first lieutenant; B. F. Sterling, second lieutenant; and "B." Hardin, second lieutenant. Dark fought with Waul's Texas Legion during the Civil War, rose to the rank of major, and in 1866, he was elected county surveyor for Hardin County. He drilled for oil at Saratoga, which proved unsuccessful, and then turned to ranching.

He courted Kaleta Hardin, but they did not marry. B. F. Sterling, a carpenter, specialized in building coffins. After the war, he opened a wagon and carriage shop in Liberty. His son Ross Shaw Sterling (1875-1949) became president of Humble Oil and Refining Company, president of *The Houston Post-Dispatch*, and governor of Texas. Hardin is most likely William Franklin Hardin (1841-1898), nicknamed "Bee." He served in Waul's Texas Legion and survived the war, but grew disillusioned by the loss of the Southern culture. An attorney and a judge, Hardin was briefly married to Eugenie Stanwood Mouton. Hardin was not a "junior," as designated by Hall. Possibly Hall confused him with Augustine B. "Blackie" Hardin, who was a "junior."[34] Shortly after the election of officers, the Liberty Guards boarded the *Ruthven* and sailed to Galveston.

In honor of Florence's first birthday on Saturday, October 19, Hall "took a fine egg nogg." The following day, Margaret and Florence, along with Sam Sharp and his wife, nicknamed Nellie, "came down to Liberty safe & sound in my buggy, from their long & protracted visit up the Country. Frank Stewart with my little wagon & mules also arrived from the mill. I was overjoyed at the little woman's return who had been absent about two months on a visit to her mother's." Although work on their new house had slowed, for the moment life returned to normal.

Business picked up, and Hall spent several days "shipping freight" on the *Ruthven* to Galveston. Hall sent provisions such as cornmeal and potatoes, as well as recruits, to Captain Wrigley and the Liberty Guards aboard the *Ruthven* on her return to Galveston.

Monday October 28th 1861. Today I sent Charley Lund to Galveston on the Steamer Ruthven, with the bridles & saddles we had made up for the Confederate States army. I also sent Capt Wrigley some supplies for the Guards. Business rather dull. The workmen raised a part of the frame of my house. The sick at home are all well again. weather cloudy & very warm. I was taken very sick in the evening and passed a very unpleasant night.

Hall did not state the nature of his illness.

Wednesday October 30th 1861. Today I am able to be out though not well, and had to superintend the removal of the cannon carriages for the army from the Rail road cars. But little business doing. Frank Stewart [is] *still hauling brick. My house* [is] *progressing very slow. weather cloudy with hard rain from the North & very cold.*

The next day, feeling much better, he supervised transfer of the cannon carriages "to the steam boat landing." The carriages would be shipped to Galveston by steamer.

Friday November 1st 1861. Today [I] *am quite well. The steamer Ruthven failed to make her regular trip. John Wrigley took the hands off and stoped all work on my house. Frank Stewart still hauling brick. Charley Lund returned home by the way of Houston, on the rail road cars, looking quite well after his visit to Galveston. Business very dull, weather changeable, with wind blowing hard from the North, it abated and at night a hard frost, which is the first of the season at least in or about my locality.*

On Saturday, the "hands" returned to work on the house. After a busy day "selling goods[,]" Hall described further activity at the warehouse.

Sunday November 3rd 1861. Today the Steamer Ruthven arrived from Galveston with a large freight. George Gordon presented me with a nice barrel of oysters and which I enjoyed with no little gusto. Lieut. Dark arrived with 22 new recruits for the "Liberty Guards." I had to quarter them in the ware house. weather clear & cold, at night a hard frost.

Monday November 4th 1861. Today the Steamer Ruthven left for Galveston, with Lieut. Dark and his recruits on board, who had to say the least of it, behaved while in the Warehouse in a very shameful manner. I was compelled to patrol nearly all night, which did not set very well. weather clear & pleasant.

On October 3, 1861, the Liberty board of trustees established patrol duty within the city limits and placed pharmacist William Meyer in charge. The ordinance applied to all white men between the ages of eighteen and sixty. The state legislature formally authorized county patrols in January 1862. Hall patrolled for the first time on November 4. Even so, in the election held on Wednesday, November 6, he "attended the polls and voted for Jeff Davis for the Presidency of the Confederate States." Although discomfited by the need for security, Hall's loyalty to the Confederacy had not yet begun to erode.

Perhaps to give Margaret some time to rest, Hall took Florence on a visit to Galveston (Monday, November 11 through Saturday, November 16). With him traveled Ann (Mrs. James) Wrigley and her two-year-old daughter, Ida; Mrs. William Skinner, wife of a merchant; and a black woman named Rose. Hall and the ladies stayed at the Washington Hotel while in Galveston. He rented two carriages, and they went sightseeing around the city, visited the beach, watched the soldiers, and shopped. Hall and Captain Wrigley had several drinks ("phases") together in Galveston (Wednesday, November 13).

Early in 1861, the secession convention's Committee on Public Safety authorized General Sidney Sherman to set up batteries for the protection of Galveston. He ordered them to be placed in a defensive triangle at Bolivar Point, Pelican Spit, and Fort Point on Galveston Bay, with a fourth battery at San Luis Pass on the opposite end of the island. Fort Green lay at Bolivar Point, on the tip of Bolivar Peninsula.[35]

Hall and his party returned to Liberty on Sunday, November 17, and he resumed work on Monday. "There is a general leaving of Galveston[,]" he wrote on Saturday, November 30, "for fear the blockading vessels will commence bombarding the City." The *Ruthven*, he noted on that day, had brought a "very large freight[,]" which he and Sam Sharp stored at the warehouse.

Deliveries continued well into December.

Work continued on the new house, with "the hands" busy placing shingles on the roof for several days (Thursday, November 21). Hall "had to turn out as a patrol" on the night of Friday, November 22, which was notable because of a norther and heavy rain. Frank Hitchcock, captain of the *Ruthven*, gave him a barrel of oysters, which he enjoyed "hugely" (Sunday, November 24). Frank Hitchcock later became a partner with Hall for post-war cotton sales. By Tuesday, November 26, activity picked up at the store, and the workmen completed the "shingling in" of the house.

Wednesday November 27th 1861. Today I am quite unwell. The steamer Ruthven arrived from and departed for Galveston. Frank Stewart in consequence of being on a "bender" got into a difficulty with James Pickett, which came near terminating seriously, weather cloudy & warm.

Thursday November 28th 1861. Today I am still quite unwell, indeed so much so as not to be able to attend to any kind of business. Frank Stewart by pleading guilty got out of his difficulty by paying five dollars fine & costs of suit. The hands commenced laying the floor in my new house. weather changeable & rather warm.

James J. Pickett was an attorney in practice with his brother Edward B. Pickett, both prominent citizens.[36]

Friday November 29th 1861. Today I am much better. Business very brisk in the way of selling goods. The Ruthven arrived from Galveston with considerable freight, which kept me actively employed in the ware house. The Ruthven left for Galveston in the evening. The hands [are] *still engaged on the floors. weather cloudy with a strong north wind blowing & rather cool.*

The "hands" finished laying the floors of the house and began to install the ceilings (Monday, December 2). Hall himself tacked up the "canvass" on the interior walls, a step that preceded wallpapering (Wednesday, December 4). Work on the house advanced, with a Mr. Holtsclaw as "the principal workman" (Monday, December 9). Frank Stewart hauled brick for chimneys. On Thursday, December 12, Hall "received a deed from Capt. Wrigley [who was home on "furlow"] for the four lots upon which I am now erecting my new building."

Business at the warehouse improved for several days, then dropped off again. Hall continued putting up canvas in the house until Saturday, December 21, when he finished.

Sunday December 22nd 1861. Today the steamer Ruthven arrived from Galveston, with sergeant E. L. Jones and several other members of the "Liberty Guards" to spend Christmas with us. weather changeable & cold with hard frost at night.

Monday December 23rd 1861. Today the steamer Ruthven left for Galveston, and Mrs Wrigley and her children also left on her [the *Ruthven*] *to spend Christmas with her relatives in Houston. Sam H. Sharp and Frank Stewart whom I paid off and discharged from my service, left for my mills up the Country, in my little wagon. I am busy in the ware house, weather changeable and cold, with a hard frost at night.*

Hall had hired Frank Stewart on March 12 only for the remainder of the year, so it is not known whether Stewart's altercation with James Pickett influenced Hall's decision to let Stewart go.

Tuesday December 24th 1861. Today I am engaged in the ware house. I made the boys kill and salt down 1060 lbs. pork, weather clear & cold. I patrolled at night.

Wednesday December 25th 1861. Today being Christmas, no kind of business was done. The Steamer Ruthven arrived & departed. We had a fine flow of egg nogg to ware [*sic*] *off the dullness of the times, weather changeable & very warm for the season of the year.*

Hall returned to work, but there was very little business to attend to.

Saturday December 28th 1861. Today Charlie Lund and Sergeant E. L. Jones left on the cars for Houston. The remains of Col Terry also passed in the cars. I am busy in the store. The cannon so long looked for and anxiously expected arrived in the cars, at least two of them arrived, one weighing 9027 lbs & the other 8500 lbs. weather clear & pleasant.

Born in Kentucky, Benjamin F. Terry (1821-1861) came to Texas from Mississippi around 1834. He owned a sugar plantation in Fort Bend County and, with a partner, financed the first railroad in Texas, which ran from Harrisburg (Houston) to Richmond. In 1861, Terry and Thomas S. Lubbock organized the Eighth Texas Cavalry (Terry's Texas Rangers). While serving under Albert Sidney Johnston, Terry was killed in combat at Woodsonville, Kentucky, on December 17. His body was carried by train to Nashville, New Orleans, and Houston. Terry was popular and well-respected by civilians and the military.[37]

The two cannons were intended for the defense of Galveston.

In August, "a citizens' committee from Galveston" reached Richmond, Virginia, with a "requisition from General Van Dorn for heavy ordnance. Spurred on by the presence of blockaders off their city and a personal knowledge of its short ranged, inadequate batteries, William Pitt Ballinger, John S. Sydnor, and M. M. Potter" met with the Secretary of War who sent them to see "Major Josiah Gorgas, Chief of the Ordnance Bureau. He offered them four ten-inch Columbiads, two eight-inch Columbiads, and two soon- to-be completed eight-inch rifled pieces, adding that carriages for the guns and some thirty-two-pounders could be had in New Orleans." The men left Richmond on August 15 but encountered "a series of repeated delays, caused by railroad tie ups and the slush of fall roads in western Louisiana under incessant rains." In October, "the cannon were still mired deep in mud east of the Sabine River."[38]

Sunday December 29th 1861. Today I am engaged with 20 hands in removing the two cannons that arrived on yesterday from the cars to the steam boat landing, this was a pretty hard undertaking as we had no wagon to haul them, but was compelled to roll them on skids, as difficult as the undertaking was, I however succeeded and placed [them] *safely on board the Steamer Ruthven to be carried to Galveston. weather clear with a slight frost at night.*

The *Ruthven* transported the cannons on Monday, December 30. The next day, more arrived by rail from Beaumont, "three of the seven being

Columbiads and weighing as follows: 13.224 – 13.226 & 13.228 lbs." Columbiads were large, smoothbore cannons with 8- or 10-inch muzzles.

General Paul O. Hébert (1818-1880), a West Point graduate, engineer, Mexican War veteran, and former governor of Louisiana, replaced Colonel Earl Van Dorn as military commander of the Confederate District of Texas, New Mexico, and Arizona on September 18, 1861. In early August 1862, General Hébert ordered the guns Hall helped deliver to Galveston to be taken to the mainland, where they were scattered among several communities, including Liberty. This left Galveston without artillery protection from the Union Navy blockading the port, but also prevented the Union forces from capturing the Columbiads and smaller cannons.[39]

As Hall closed his notes for the year, he did not speculate upon events to come, "but trusting in his [God's] mercy I shall enter upon the trials of another year, with hopes of future success & prosperity through his goodness & favor." Hall repeated a similar prayer each year.

Chapter 3

1862

Wednesday January 1st 1862. Today I am busy in the Ware house. I assisted however in placing five of the cannon, balls and carriages on the steamer Ruthven to be taken to Galveston, weather changeable & cool.

Although Governor Edward Clark's agents had been unable to acquire arms through the sale of bonds, General Paul O. Hébert successfully secured weapons with the help of Confederate Secretary of War Judah P. Benjamin. In a letter to Benjamin dated October 24, 1861, Hébert wrote: "The few heavy guns ordered from Richmond [Virginia] are now on the route between Alexandria and the Sabine River. Much difficulty has been experienced in the transportation of these guns across the country—so much so, that the time of their reaching this point is very indefinite."[1]

Hall's efforts in moving the long-awaited artillery from the railroad to the wharf and onto the steamer remained a primary concern on the following day, when the *A. S. Ruthven* left with them, and again on Saturday, January 4, when the same steamer transported three additional guns. Hall again moved cannons from the railroad to the *Ruthven* on Sunday, February 2.

Hall continued working as a salesman in the store. On Sunday, January 5, he stayed at home reading and "passed a very pleasant time in romping for exercise with the children." Work on the new house continued slowly.

He wrote of the death of Henry Boothe (Wednesday, January 8), "a member of the Liberty Guards" who died at half past nine in the morning at the home of Charles Lund, "in consequence of which he was prevented from attending to business." On the following day, Mrs. Stanwood, "the consort of Dr. T. A. Stanwood" died about noon. She was taken to West Liberty (now Dayton) on Friday, January 10, for burial.

Hall continued to worry about the construction of his new house. On Thursday, January 9, he wrote, "Nothing doing on my house, which is now progressing so slowly that I have almost dispaired of ever getting it completed."

The work on the house, however, continued.

Friday January 17th 1862. Last night the Ware house was broken open and things were scattered around in rich profusion. The Steamer Ruthven arrived in the morning with some considerable freight. I was engaged in mending and nailing up the boxes & trunks broken open by the burglars. But little business doing. weather cloudy and rainy throughout the entire day.

According to Hall, "the black scoundrel" was caught in West Liberty on Sunday, January 19, and "severely punished." Hall did not say to what degree or by whom the thief received punishment.

Hall "glazed" the windows at his new house and worked at the warehouse, including the evening of Tuesday, January 21, "Charley Lund having other fish to fry." Hall finished installing the windows and began painting the ceilings on Friday, January 24. At last, on Tuesday, January 28, Hall declared, "In the evening be it remembered! That I moved the little woman, Fawn, bag & baggage into the new house, in order that I could have a home of my own although it is yet in a half finished condition, but we can get along in it until I can have it completed . . ." Details such as painting and wallpapering the rooms, securing carpets, and placing furniture continued for several weeks. Hall sent his slaves to the nearby swamp to get posts for a fence to be built around his house. During this time he hired Simeon Pattillo to build a smokehouse, well house, and stable, plus a barn and carriage house; the earliest references to this work are on Tuesday, February 18 and Wednesday, February 19. Freight arrived intermittently at the store and warehouse.

Tuesday February 11th 1862. Today I am engaged in the store as salesman, with quite a retail business. In the evening I am employed in making out accounts, at night I was Compelled to turn out to perform patrol service. weather clear, cool & a frost at night.

Wednesday February 12th 1862. Today I am engaged at the store. In the evening I went up town for the purposes of signing the bond as security for Charley Lund who had been appointed Collector of the war tax for the year 1861. weather clear & very pleasant.

Charles Lund left for Hardin County on Wednesday, February 19, "thus leaving me all alone to attend to the store and the Ware house." Sam Sharp had not yet returned from his visit to the family.

Hall remained engaged in finishing his new home and working at the store or the warehouse, as business steadily fell off.

Saturday February 22nd 1861. This being my birthday anniversary I celebrated it in a proper manner, with a large bowl of Egg Nogg & the etc. etc. that go with it. The steamer Ruthven left for Galveston. Charley Lund came home from Hardin Co. Boys still in the swamp getting [fence] *posts. Business very dull, in fact almost dried up. weather changeable and warm for the season.*

So tedious did the days become that he noted a ride into town on Hawk to get "finely barberized" on Sunday, February 23. He wrote out accounts at the store, sent his slave Charley to a mill for seven bushels of meal to ship to the Liberty Guards, and assigned other workers to repair the fence around James Wrigley's corn field with posts from the swamp. Some of "the boys" began building a fence around Hall's residence.

Friday February 28th 1862. Today the steamer Ruthven went down the river on a pleasure excursion and returned in the evening. There were a great many ladies on board, had quite a pleasant party and time passed swiftly and pleasantly. I am engaged at the ware house. I received a very interesting letter from Sam Sharp, who has been confined up the Country for some months. The boys are at work on my fence. weather clear & pleasant.

Sam Sharp left on December 23, 1861, but it must have seemed longer than two months to Hall.

Hall continued to work all day and patrol at night, and his leadership must have been greatly respected.

Saturday March 1st 1862. Today I went up town and fully organized the militia for this the town beat, during the time the citizens held a large mass meeting and at said meeting I received the nomination for the colonelship of the 5th Regt. 2nd Brigade [Texas State Troops]. *Business very dull. Boys* [are] *at work on my fence. weather clear warm & very windy.*

Authorized by Governor Edward Clark and the Texas Legislature, home guard units were organized throughout Texas. With so many men leaving to fight in the Confederate Army, the federal blockade in place to remind Texans of the possibility of invasion, and Indian attacks on the Western frontier, Texans joined militia units for local protection.

Wednesday, March 5th 1862. Today I made the boys plant 3 acres in corn. Business dull. In the evening the little woman, Mrs. [James] *Wrigley, Mrs. Sharp* [Nellie] *& I went fishing in the river. We had no success. Did not catch even a nibble. Weather clear & cold.*

Thursday March 6th 1862. Today the steamer Ruthven arrived from Galveston bringing but little freight. Business very dull. The boys at work on the house fence. Lieut. W. D. Williams arrived home direct from the Army in Virginia on a recruiting tour. He also brought the sad intelligence of the death of John Wrigley. weather clear and cold with a frost and freeze at night.

Lieutenant Watson Dugat Williams (1838-1881), half-brother of Eugenie Stanwood Mouton, was a steamboat pilot and captain. An 1860 notice in *The Liberty Gazette* announced that the Trinity was "in fine boating order" and that Captain Williams, of the steamer *Swan*, had headed upriver to Magnolia. Williams joined a military company early in 1861 and became its drill sergeant. On February 28, 1861, he and seventy-five men joined the Galveston County Rifles, boarded the *General Rusk*, and, under the command of B. F. Terry, sailed to Brazos Santiago to defend Brownsville. In early 1862, he arrived in Liberty after a recruitment tour, noted by Hall. On June 9, Williams joined the Liberty Invincibles and served with Company F, which became part of the Fifth Texas, Hood's Brigade. Williams received a promotion to captain in 1863. Although wounded at Second Manassas and Gettysburg, he remained with his company and was present at General Lee's surrender. He married Laura Bryan on December 11, 1865, as noted by Hall.[2]

John Wrigley had traveled to Houston and returned to Liberty on January 15, 1862. It is not clear whether he accompanied Lieutenant Williams to Virginia on the "recruiting tour" or had decided to join the army, or had traveled to Virginia on some other business. Since there was no fighting in Virginia at the time, Wrigley may have contracted one of the many illnesses prevalent in the Texas military camps there. However, Hall never explained the cause of Wrigley's death.

In 1850, James Wrigley's brother John (age thirty) was a farmer, born in Johnstown, New York, with property valued at $3,000. His wife Sarah Anne Hardin Wrigley was nineteen, and their daughter Adela [Adelia] was one year old. Ten years later, census records list John Wrigley as a farmer with real estate valued at $5,000 and personal property worth $5,000. He and Sarah had three children: Adilia [Adelia] (age ten), Mary (age four), and Ben (one month old), all born in Liberty County. John Wrigley served as a city councilman in 1851 and 1854. He died in Virginia on February 28, 1862, and his body was returned to Liberty for burial.[3]

Friday March 7th 1862. Today Charley Lund left on the cars to attend to the bringing of the remains of John Wrigley home for burial. I am very busy in the store selling goods. The boys are in the swamp getting posts for the fence. weather clear & rather cool.

Saturday March 8th 1862. Today Capt James Wrigley arrived on the freight train from Houston, to attend the funeral of his deceased Brother. I am busy in the store. The boys are engaged [in] *digging the grave for the remains of John Wrigley*[.] *weather changeable & rather cool.*

Charles Lund arrived on Sunday, March 9, with the body of John Wrigley. That evening, he was buried by "the Masonic fraternity with a large concourse of citizens in attendance although the place of burial was some 6 miles off, myself & family attended, weather cloudy with drizzling rain and at night a very hard rain."

At the store, Hall wrote out accounts. Entries in his journal state that the "Negroes" spent several days working in a nearby swamp, where they cut fence posts, and they dug a well for the new home. All of the outbuildings were completed in late March.

For a while, Sam Sharp's wife, who had been living with the Halls, returned to her mother's house there in Liberty. Hall referred to her as "Alexandrine," then "Alex," and finally as "Nellie." Her mother Mrs. Elizabeth Beale, who was born in Maryland, had three daughters (Lucy, Kate, and Susan) living at home with her.[4] Nellie's father was French Consul Alexander Lemaire, who had died many years before. Delayed by illness, Sam did not return to Liberty until Friday, March 28. Nellie and Sam began living with the Halls "permanently" on Sunday, March 30.

Hall maintained his involvement in the war effort.

Saturday March 15th 1862. Today James Wrigley & myself went up town, to attend the election for field officers of the 5th Regt. and also to muster & drill Company "A." of said Regt. I being a candidate for the Coloncy [Colonelcy] *had to play the amiable finely, after the polls were closed and I was elected I got on a little tight, but very gently, weather clear & pleasant.*

Sunday March 16th 1862. Today I went up town to get barberized, and then spent the residue of the day home with the little woman & boy [baby]. *weather clear & pleasant.*

Perhaps Hall was hoping that Margaret, who was pregnant, would give birth to a son. (If he meant "boy," he did not identify the child in the journal.)

Monday March 17th 1862. Today the steamer Ruthven arrived bringing some considerable freight, and I am busy in the ware house with the boys storing the same away. In the evening the steamer left for Galveston, and Capt James Wrigley left on her in as big a drunk, as ever I have heretofore seen him. Business dull. weather clear & pleasant.

At a party given by friends in Hall's honor for "having been elected Col of the 5th Regt." (Wednesday, March 19), "wit & champagne flowed pretty freely, all things passing off in fine style . . ."

A few days later (Saturday, March 22), Hall "went up town to attend the election of a Brig. Genl. & there voted for T. J. Chambers." Born in Virginia, Thomas Jefferson Chambers (1802-1865) was a teacher, attorney, surveyor, and land speculator. His home near Anahuac stood on a bluff, and Chambers County, created in 1858, was named for him. He ran for governor twice (1861 and 1863), but lost both times. During the Civil War, Chambers permitted the Confederates to set up a battery on his property to defend the mouth of the Trinity River, as well as his own wharf, and he served in Hood's Texas Brigade as a volunteer aide. Chambers was killed at home by an assassin on March 15, 1865.[5] Chambers openly criticized President Jefferson Davis and his government, and presumably his views agreed with those of Hall.

Even as Hall's slaves worked steadily on the fence surrounding the new house, they were often called away to work for others. They dug graves, stored freight at the warehouse or riverboat landing, cut timbers in a local swamp for construction of a county jail, and helped private citizens. Hall does not explain the circumstances, but on Sunday, March 23, planter Jerome DeBlanc "took upon himself to whip some 16 or 18 negroes, and among whom was Bob, whom he knocked down with a pistol inflicting a severe wound. I went to see him about it and came very near getting into a serious difficulty . . ." Although unable to work for several days, Bob did recover.

The following Saturday (March 29), Hall "went up town and fully organized the Company of Malitia [*sic*] for Beat No. 2 in Liberty Co. and then put it through the school of the soldier[.]" Beginning on Wednesday, April 2, Hall made out "the war tax rolls" for Charles Lund, a task that continued until Monday, April 14. With that completed, Hall began to write correspondence relating to the taxes for Lund, who was away on tax collecting tours (Tuesday, April 15).

Sam Sharp, who had arrived from the farm on March 28, returned to work at the store as salesman and bookkeeper on Thursday, April 3.

Friday April 4th 1862. Today we are still at work on the war tax rolls[.] *Sam is busy making out a/c's* [accounts]. *I sent the wagons down to Swilley's after corn and got 45 bushels which was all put into Capt. J. Wrigley's crib. Bill at work on the fence. The steamer Ruthven left for Galveston. weather changeable and warm.*

Swilley's Landing, on the Trinity River below Liberty, was ninety-four miles from Galveston. Liberty was 113 miles from Galveston, placing the landing nineteen miles south of Liberty.[6]

Freight, usually delivered by the *Ruthven*, arrived from Galveston, but by Monday, April 14, business was "very dull, in fact nothing in that line doing." Unknown at the time, however, a visit from Frank Hitchcock that day would lead to a successful venture after the war. Frank Hitchcock (age forty in the 1860 census for Galveston County) was a merchant with real estate valued at $1,250. The value of his personal property was not given. His wife Nancy (age thirty-two), sons Frank (age ten) and John (age seven) were all born in Massachusetts.[7]

Thursday April 17th 1862. Today Capt James Wrigley arrived home on the Steamer Ruthven, looking quite well. Sam Sharp, the little woman, Nellie, Mrs Lund, Miss Lizzie Robinson, Charley Lund and myself went out to gum lake on a fishing excursion and caught quite a nice mess, which we enjoyed in the woods with considerable gusto. Indeed we passed a pleasant day and all appeared to enjoy themselves hugely. Boys at work on the fence. weather cloudy and rather warm.

Gum Lake (or Gum Slough on various maps) was less than five miles south of Liberty. A low area with sloughs and bayous, it is known today as the South Liberty Oilfield.[8]

The following day was not so enjoyable. Captain Wrigley returned to Galveston, business remained dull, and the slaves were still at work on the fence. That night, Hall was "compelled to turn out on patrol service. . . ." It was "pitch dark & very disagreeable with a very hard rain coming down in perfect torrents." After "writing" in the war tax collector's office on Saturday, April 19, Hall returned to the store.

Tuesday April 22nd 1862. Today the steamer Ruthven arrived from and departed for Galveston. The river is now very high and still rising. Business entirely suspended and busted. The boys are still at work on the fence, weather clear & warm.

Wednesday April 23rd 1862. Today I have nothing to do but loaf around generally. The boys are still at work on the fence. The river is still rising with some fears of an overflow. weather clear & rather warm.

Thursday April 24th 1862. Today I am engaged in the war tax collector's office, and in getting up all the correspondence of the same. Business about played out. The boys are still jogging along at the fence, but very slowly, being called off pretty much every day and only working on it at odd times, but they will finish it sometime I have not a doubt. weather changeable & warm.

Because Hall was a prominent citizen and a generous man, his slaves were often called upon to do work for others.

Friday April 25th 1862. Today the Steamer Ruthven arrived from Galveston, with most of the old Liberty Guards, who were on yesterday regularly mustered out of the service of the Confederate States. No business doing. Boys [are] *at work on the fence. Charley* [is] *working in the corn. Weather cloudy & warm with strong prospects of rain.*

Sergeant Ed Jones "and several other members of the old Guards" arrived on Monday, April 28. They were "all looking in fine health."

Thursday May 1st 1862. Today the Steamer Ruthven arrived from Galveston, Capt James Wrigley came home on her. He appears to be in fine health. Sam Sharp went after my mules that run off on yesterday. He over hauled them about 10 or 11 miles up the road, and drove them back by dusk. Bill [was] *taken sick, and nothing doing on my fence. at night I had to turn out on patrol service. weather clear and warm.*

Bill recovered by Saturday, May 3, and returned to work on the fence. Due to intermittent rain, the Trinity continued to rise for several days.

Tuesday May 6th 1862. Today I procured three recruits for Capt Wrigley's Co. Capt Pickett's company arrived at Liberty in route for the seat of war, but pitched their camp here and doubtless will remain here for several days. River still rising[.] The boys are at work on my fence. weather clear & warm.

Edward Bradford Pickett (1823-1882), born in Virginia, was an attorney. Pickett joined the Twenty-Fifth Texas Cavalry under Colonel Clayton C. Gillespie on May 3, 1862, and was commissioned a captain. After action in Louisiana, he was ordered to Arkansas Post. He and his company were captured there by Union troops and sent to the federal prison at Camp Douglas, Illinois. Pickett returned to the Confederate Army after a prisoner exchange and served in the Tennessee campaign led by General John Bell Hood. Pickett rose in rank from captain to lieutenant colonel. Both before and after the war, Pickett served as a city councilman in Liberty; after the war, he was elected to two terms in the state legislature, functioned as president of the Constitutional Convention of 1875, and was the first president of the board of directors of Texas A&M University (1876-1882). He died in Liberty and was buried there.[9]

Captain Joe Dark's cavalry company, which had been "camped" there for a while, became "fully organized" on Friday, May 9. That same day, Charles Lund "left on another collecting tour, gathering up the war tax" for Hardin County. Hall remained at the store, while "the boys" worked at the warehouse. The Trinity continued to rise.

Hall recorded on Sunday, May 11, that Ann Wrigley gave birth to a little girl, but the child died, and on the following day, Hall "assisted Capt Wrigley in burying his dead infant." Although mustered out of the Liberty Guards on April 24, Wrigley and Ed Jones traveled to Houston on Monday, May 5, by rail. They may have re-enlisted at the time. By Tuesday, May 6, Wrigley was in the process of forming a new company. After losing his brother and his baby daughter, perhaps he welcomed the distraction of wartime activity.

The Trinity kept rising, and on Tuesday, May 13, Hall noted that the river was "all over the wharf." Not until Saturday, May 17, did the Trinity begin "to fall gently." A few day later (Tuesday, May 20), Hall wrote, "The boys are at work clearing the wharf of the drift wood left on it by the falling of the river, which is now receding very fast." On Thursday, May 22, the river reached its "low water mark." As will be seen, a post-war overflow led to widespread flooding throughout the Trinity watershed.

Ed Jones borrowed the mule Kate and left for the "up country on a recruiting expedition for Capt Wrigley's Company" on Wednesday, May 14. Hall remained at the store and warehouse, worked in the "war tax collector's office[,]" and patrolled at night. By Friday, May 16, business had come to a complete standstill.

Friday May 16th 1862. Today I went up town. Nothing doing in the way of business. The steamer Ruthven left for Galveston. Capt James Wrigley won 3 sets of china at a little freeze out. One set he presented to the little woman and he also presented one set to Nellie. weather changeable with a hard rain at night and rather cool.

Saturday May 17th 1862. Today I contracted with & sold to Messrs Dreyfus & Levy the remainder of our stock of goods, after the entire terms & conditions of the sale had been settled, we proceeded to take stock. The boys are at work on the fence. The river commenced to fall gently, weather changeable & warm.

Hall, with James Wrigley and Sam Sharp, inventoried the goods in the store, and Hall supervised their delivery "with two wagons constantly going" (Wednesday, May 21). The final delivery occurred the next day, when Hall had "a final settlement with Dreyfus & Levy (Thursday, May 22). Although the store inventory was sold, steamers occasionally brought freight to the landing. On Saturday, May 31, the *Ruthven* "arrived from Galveston with a large cargo of freight & with a great many passengers. The boys are busy storing freight." Such deliveries continued intermittently.

The Civil War came closer to the Hall family on Friday, May 23, when Captain R. V. Cook and his company "came over from Houston on the cars and took possession of Liberty as a military post. The County having been put under martial law."

On April 29, 1862, Admiral David G. Farragut and the Union Navy captured New Orleans, and the city became occupied by General Benjamin Butler and Union troops on May 2. After a suggestion by Farragut, commanding the West Gulf Blockading Squadron, Captain Henry Eagle of the frigate U.S.S. *Santee* sailed to Galveston in order to achieve the surrender of the city and to strengthen the blockade. On May 17, Captain Eagle, located off the coast of Galveston Island, gave the citizens four days to leave and threatened to begin bombardment on May 23. Hall did not mention the bombardment nor did his notes reflect panic about the proposed attack on Galveston or possible invasion of the mainland.

Brigadier General Paul Octave Hébert (1818-1880) replaced Brigadier General Earl Van Dorn as military commander of the Confederate District of Texas, New Mexico, and Arizona on September 18, 1861. Hébert first declared martial law for the coastal counties because of the threat of invasion (May 23, 1862), then added all of Texas (May 30). (Confederate President Jefferson Davis annulled the proclamation on September 12, 1862, stating that Hébert had overstepped his authority.)[10]

On Saturday, May 24, Hall wrote, "Today Capt Cook and twelve men went down the river in bateaux [flat-bottomed boats] for the purpose of searching out the cotton on the banks of the river." Shortly after taking office in November 1861, Governor Francis R. Lubbock issued a proclamation against storing cotton near the coast so that Union blockading vessels would not be tempted to sail upriver, or send troops inland, to seize it. Now, with the threat of bombardment and invasion imminent, Captain Cook and his men were making sure no cotton had been left at the landings or on the riverbanks.[11]

Protecting the cotton was critical to the Confederate war effort: first, the Confederate government needed to be able to purchase (or, if necessary, to impress) the cotton for sale to Europe in exchange for arms and ammunition; and second, the cotton was needed for the manufacture of military clothing, bedding, and field supplies such as knapsacks and tents (made by women's organizations in Houston, San Antonio, Austin, Dallas, and Jefferson, for example, and by men confined to the penitentiary). Cotton remained a bargaining tool in the South's effort to convince England, the South's primary purchaser of cotton, to support the Confederacy until England began to procure cotton from other nations and declined to become involved in America's Civil War.[12]

Monday May 26th 1862. Today Capt Wrigley arrived in the cars from Houston, and brought me an appointment from Genl. Hebert as enrolling officer for Liberty Co. under which I proceeded to enroll several conscripts. I went up town and drilled the officers of the 5th Regt. 2nd Brig. T.S.T. of which I have the honor to be the Colonel.—weather clear & warm. The little woman is still confined to her bed.

Three days after the bombardment of Galveston was supposed to begin, the Union vessels with their feared invasion force remained at sea.

Shortly after his arrival at Galveston, General Hébert surveyed the city and the island and concluded that they could not be defended from bombardment by Union ships or invasion by Union troops. He deemed it better for the island to be evacuated than to allow Confederate troops and civilians to be trapped there by Union forces. With that situation in mind, he devised a plan of withdrawal across the railroad bridge. In December 1861, soon after Governor Francis R. Lubbock took office, Hébert and Lubbock exchanged letters regarding Galveston. Lubbock made it clear that the city should be defended and that he would rather see Galveston "one blackened ruin" than allow it to be taken by the Union. However, if defense proved to be impossible, Lubbock recommended the destruction of cisterns, the transfer of livestock away from the island, and the burning of all grass (to deny forage to Union horses).[13]

The proposed abandonment of Galveston became public knowledge, infuriating Texans who resented Hébert's aristocratic manner as well as Lubbock's acceptance of the possible need to sacrifice the city to the enemy.[14]

On Sunday, May 25, Hall noted that Margaret "is very sick with neuralgia in her face, so much so, as to confine her to her bed." Margaret Hall suffered from Trigeminal Neuralgia, or *Tic Douloureux*, a rare disorder of the trigeminal nerve on either side of the cranium. Each spasm, occurring on only one side of the face, feels like an electric shock. The attacks, which can be set off by touching certain sensitive places on the face, last several seconds and can continue, one after another, for minutes. Trigeminal Neuralgia may be in remission for weeks, months, or years, and its return is unpredictable.[15]

Four days later (Thursday, May 29), Margaret was well enough to "look after her household affairs."

Each day, Hall enrolled conscripts for the Confederate Army, noting on Friday, May 30, that he had "[put] many into the army who would not otherwise have joined." He "received the appointment of Provost Marshal for Liberty County" on Sunday, June 1, and granted travel or exemption permits. Hall rented a small house from William Meyer to serve as his office and moved in "desks & papers" on Monday, June 9.

A pharmacist, William Meyer (age forty-four in 1860) had been born in Strasburg, Germany. An 1855 advertisement in *The Liberty Gazette* stated that he sold "a general assortment of Plain and Fancy Groceries," including lobster, as well as wine, brandy, and schnapps "for medicinal purposes." Meyer served on the city council (1859-1864) and organized the patrol within the city limits beginning on October 3, 1861. He died on March 9, 1867.[16]

The summer brought even more changes for the Hall family. Margaret and Nellie began packing trunks for a trip to the farm on Tuesday, June 10. Hall often referred to such trips as going "up the Country" (Tuesday, June 10). He delayed their departure to have his wagon and buggy repaired (Friday, June 13), and he bought two horses: "Rat" and "the fine sorrel gelding known as Jack McKim's Rob . . ." Rat cost $150 while Rob cost $300. Repairs to the wagon were finished late in the day on Tuesday, June 17. The next day, Margaret, Florence, and Nellie, traveling by buggy, with Sam riding Hawk, "and the little wagon & mules with the negroes & baggage left Liberty for the Mill, there to spend the summer, leaving me all alone in my glory to get along as best I may." Immediately (Thursday, June 19), Galveston merchant Frank Hitchcock, with his wife and two young sons, moved into Hall's house. Hall placed his own things in the "back room of the store and there took up [his] head quarters." Hall's slaves (including Bill Hicks), who remained in Liberty, helped the Hitchcocks by "hauling furniture" to the house. Like many others, the Hitchcock family left their home in Galveston to find safety on the mainland.

While Sam Sharp was en route to Houston County, on Friday, June 20, Hall recorded that Sam received "his commission as Assessor & Collector of Liberty County, I am busily engaged in arranging his tax books in order to facilitate him in his collections." Sam returned from Hall's Bluff on Saturday, June 28.

Saturday June 21st 1862. Today I am engaged in the office. In the evening I was compelled to attend the session of the board of Aldermen for the City of Liberty. I being a member of said board, and under the laws of the corporation an election was gone into and I had the extreme honor of being elected Mayor of the City, into which office I [was] *duly installed after taking the oath of office. (Sam Sharp & the ladies reached the mills as I am informed by letter. I make this note in order to date the time that my little woman commenced boarding with her mother.) Charley Lund* [is] *engaged in the office. Boys* [are] *at work at Capt Wrigley's. weather clear & hot. Ther: 94°.*

Hall recorded the temperature at three o'clock each afternoon during the summer.

June was not the usual time for elections. Records indicate that there was no incumbent mayor. Since Hall was a member of the city council (board of aldermen) and did not plan to join the military, he was a good choice for the position.[17]

Hall wrote out and completed the "war tax rolls of non rendered lands" (Monday, June 23 and Tuesday, June 24), advertisements for the "sale of land for which the tax had not been paid . . ." (Thursday, June 26), and continued his duties in the provost marshal's office. Although his work as a merchant had slowed, Hall spent his days serving as mayor of Liberty, provost marshal, conscript officer, colonel of Texas State Troops, and he helped both Sam Sharp and Charles Lund make out their "war tax rolls." Hall's slaves cut and hauled timber from the swamp and helped to build the county jail (Tuesday, July 1). On Wednesday, July 2, he finished the war tax rolls for Charles Lund, "thus completing all the work in the tax collector's office until after the 1st Monday in August next, at which time his sales of non rendered lands comes off."

On the following day, he kept to himself "in order to take a little more active exercise." That morning, he went hunting, killing two squirrels, and in the evening he and Frank Hitchcock "went up the river in a bateaux" to buy eggs from Jim Rodgers, then returned to town. Bill and Masaline "commenced with my little wagon to haul lumber from the cars, to the wharf, and in hauling the 4th load broke my wagon down. So it goes! And so passed my days amusement."

While Hall worked in the office the next day (Friday, July 4), Charles Lund "commenced to post up" their "commercial books." Bill Hicks made an axletree for the little wagon, and Jack McKim hauled "the lumber from the cars to the wharf under my contract." There was plenty of activity to keep Hall busy while his family was away.

On Sunday, July 6, the *Ruthven* brought forty-four bales of cotton from Galveston "and reported seven sail of vessels off the Island preparing to bombard the City."

Early in 1862, General Hébert received orders from Secretary of War Judah P. Benjamin to send all of his troops, except those at the artillery batteries on the coast, to serve with General Earl Van Dorn in Arkansas. Hébert complied, of course, but he then had even fewer troops to defend Galveston. To prepare for the May 23 bombardment and expecting a superior force of Union troops to overtake the city, Hébert ordered Colonel Joseph J. Cook in command of Galveston Island not to surrender, but to stall for time during the planned evacuation by spiking some of the artillery in the coastal batteries and moving others to the mainland. Unwilling to be left behind, Galvestonians fled the island. The May 23 deadline came and went, and nothing happened. Captain Eagle's promised bombardment of Galveston was a bluff designed to frighten the troops and citizens of Galveston into surrendering the city without a fight. Neither Hébert nor the citizens of Galveston knew that Captain Eagle lacked enough marines to capture the city and was waiting for Admiral Farragut to send reinforcements.[18]

After several weeks, the panic dissipated, and residents began returning to Galveston. The seven ships mentioned by Hall on July 6 were maintaining Captain Eagle's bluff.

In August, Hébert applied for, and received, a transfer to Arkansas.[19]

Of great interest to Hall (Saturday, July 5) was the novelty of watching John Brodhead "dive in his diving suit, in order to try and raise the Steamer Alice, which has been sunk in the river over one year." The work of a professional diver, with his round brass helmet, wetsuit, and oxygen apparatus, would have appealed to Hall's curiosity as well as his business sense. The salvage of engines, boilers, and other equipment from sunken steamboats had occurred often in the past, but during the war it became a vital necessity. Although the South contained plenty of timber for steamboat hulls, superstructure, and paddlewheels, machinery parts that were traditionally bought from Northern foundries were no longer available. Salvaged machinery could be used in a new or rebuilt steamboat, or incorporated into mills, cotton gins, and other commercial ventures. With Northern and foreign commerce cut off by the blockade, and the South's increased need for ships to conduct coastal trading and run the blockade, raising the *Alice* could have served a dual purpose.

The salvage operations described by Hall on July 5 were not successful. Hall's friend George Gordon and a partner named James Bannerman, owners of the *Alice*, sold the remains of the vessel "together with her tackle, apparel, furniture, rigging, boilers, engines & machinery and all the appurtenances . . ." to Watson Dugat Williams on April 21, 1866. Williams probably intended to salvage what he could from the steamer.[20]

Hall ordered the forty-four bales of cotton moved to the railroad for storage "on the cars," then had five bales ferried "over the river" (Monday, July 7). The following day, he supervised the storing of Frank Hitchcock's "freight," and "getting 29 bales of Cotton off the lower wharf, which the steam boat hands broke out and did not remove." Hall also "sampled some cotton" at the warehouse (Thursday, July 10). To sample cotton from each bale, he gently pulled the strands of cotton fibers, or staple, between his fingers as he examined them for length, color, cleanliness, strength, and flexibility. These qualities determined the grade of the cotton, which was, and remains, the basis for establishing the price per pound for a bale. Fluctuating supply and demand within the worldwide market, then and now, also affects the price.

Although Hall supported the Confederacy, he was unwilling to make certain sacrifices for the new government. On Friday, July 11, Lieutenant R. V. Cook and a group of soldiers "arrived from Houston and attempted to press my mules into the service as a military necessity, which put [him] on a high horse & uncomfortably tight." Hall felt "tolerably sick from my dissipation" the next day, but he was "able to be up and about the office."

Monday July 14th 1862. Today I am engaged in the office. Sam Sharp left on Hawk for Tarkingtons' prairie on an electioneering tour. Frank Hitchcock and family left on the Steamer Ruthven for Galveston, leaving me a batchelor's establishment to keep. The boys are engaged in hauling Mr Hitchcocks furniture down to the boat and in hauling my pughes [poles or stakes] *up home. Bob is at work for Charley Lund. This being the third anniversary of my marriage with the little woman, I celebrated it in a becoming style, and hoping that our future life together may be spent as pleasantly as the past three years, for I can truly say that the last three years has been an oasis in my life: weather clear & hot. Ther: 98°.*

Hall bought 280 poles "from Jim Rodger's negro man Charley" on Sunday, July 13.

Tarkington Prairie, founded in 1822 on the Nacogdoches to Lynchburg road in the northern part of Liberty County (near Cleveland), grew into a lively town by the Civil War, with stores and shops, a mill and cotton gin, a Masonic lodge, and a post office. Many veterans settled there after the war. The town became an important stop on the cattle trail to the Gulf Coast.[21]

Although Sam Sharp received a commission as tax collector/assessor, he still faced an election to the office. (The commission may have been a temporary appointment, to be followed by an election.) Then, as now, the tax assessor/collector was chosen by voters.

Tuesday July 15th 1862. Today I am busily engaged with the boys and little wagon in moving my furniture back home from the river. I have put them all back in the positions it [*sic*] *all occupied before my little woman left for the up Country. Charley & Sleepy are busy pulling fodder. In the evening I went to the office. weather changeable, with occasionally light showers of rain throughout the day: Ther: 82°.*

The next day, while Hall worked in the office, the "boys" worked "for the Corporation in getting out timber for the Convent bridge and in hauling the same."

Thursday July 17th 1862. Today I am busy in the Provost Marshal's office. The boys are at work for the Corporation, in mending the Convent bridge. I took dinner with Charley Lund & passed a very pleasant and agreeable time. weather clear & hot: Ther. 92°.

The "Corporation" referred to the city of Liberty.

The Ursuline Convent was founded in February 1859 by five nuns, four from France and one from Quebec, Canada. The nuns opened a girls' school for boarders as well as day students. Although the school was successful, it closed in June 1866 due to a loss of French-held trust funds. The property then became a day school for boys. Dr. T. A. Stanwood and his family lived next door to the convent and school.[22]

Friday July 18th 1862. Today the Steamer Ruthven arrived from & departed for Galveston. I am busy in the ware house with the boys in braking out and shipping freight, all the Galvestonians now in Liberty left on the Steamer for home, preferring to take the risk of a bombardment from the Lincoln fleet rather than sojourn any longer in Liberty. Bob is at work with Lieut Sterling making mess boxes. weather clear & hot. Ther: 94°.

Hall spent his days working at the warehouse and the provost marshal's office, and he fulfilled his obligations as mayor of Liberty by attending meetings to conduct the business of the city. His slaves were also busy helping others. Besides repairing the bridge at the Ursuline Convent, they dug a grave for "poor old Charley Bealing who died in Beaumont and whose remains was brought over on the cars for burial here" (Saturday, July 19). Bob and Bill Hicks worked on the home of William Meyer, although Hall did not state the nature of their work (Wednesday, July 23 through Saturday, July 26).

Sam Sharp returned from his "electioneering tour" on Sunday, July 20, "looking quite well & harty [hearty] and not much fatigued from his trip . . ."

Monday July 21st 1862. Today I am engaged in the Provost Marshal's office. Sam Sharp [is] *attending to his duties as Assessor & Collector. Bill finished the garden fence at last, and in the course of human events may get the entire fence completed. J. H. Smith, familiarly known as old deaf, was taken sick on yesterday and died today at 40 minutes after 3 O'clock P.M. Sam Sharp and I set up with his remains part of the night & Charley Lund the rest of the night. weather clear & very oppressive. Ther: 98°.*

John H. Smith was indeed deaf. In 1860, he was seventy years old, a sailor, who had been born in New York.[23] (John H. Smith is not to be confused with Texan scout Erasmus "Deaf" Smith.) Smith was buried "with Masonic honors" the next day. (Hall's men spent Tuesday, July 22, digging the grave and "in assisting at his burial.") At the request of Mrs. James Wrigley, (Thursday, July 24), Hall and Charles Lund "examined" his papers and noted that he had "bequeathed every thing he had" to her. According to the 1860 census, Smith owned more real estate than personal property. Thus Hall's experience as district clerk of Houston County remained invaluable to him as mayor of Liberty.

Late in July, Hall took the *Ruthven* to Galveston, where he stayed at the Washington Hotel (Tuesday, July 29). He visited with Frank Hitchcock and his family as well as other friends, noting that business in Galveston was "perfectly dead. The blockading vessels are still off the bar being five in number." The following day, Hall and his friends "chartered a hack and went down to Prince's establishment, where we had a regular jolification and spent a pleasant time. Upon our return we drove over to the gulf and had a regular sea bath which done me great good. I found however after I arrived in the City that I had forgotten my watch and had to employ a negro boy to go down the Island after [it], who returned in the night with my watch[.] [T]hus passed one of the most pleasant days that I have had this summer."

On Thursday July 31, Hall left Galveston with Frank Hitchcock on the *Ruthven* for Houston, "at which place we arrived at night[,] when a general meeting took place in the Cabin, & which passed off to the entire satisfaction of all concerned . . ." One can imagine the scene from the romantic age of paddlewheelers: a group of friends seated around a table, cards and drinks at hand, cigar and pipe smoke billowing above their heads, the music of laughter, and the gentle rocking of the vessel. Evenings like this were rare for James Hall, and he enjoyed them deeply when they occurred.

The next day, Hall said goodbye to Frank Hitchcock and left Houston on the railroad, arriving at Liberty around noon. That evening, he "remained at home feeling somewhat fatigued from my journey, or from some other cause . . ."

Saturday August 2nd 1862. Today I am busily engaged in the office. Charley Lund left for Hardin County to close up his war-tax collection & to make his sales of non rendered property. Sam Sharp is busy in his office. Boys are at work on the fence. weather clear & hot. Ther 94°.

Captain Peacock paid a visit to Hall at his new home on Sunday, and he spent the rest of the day "reading & writing" (Sunday, August 3).

Monday August 4th 1862. In the morning I am busy in the ware house braking out freight for the Steamer Ruthven, which left for Galveston. This being the day of election for State and County officers I attended the polls. I also held the sale of non rendered property for the war tax and sold about half the land in Liberty Co. Boys at work on the fence. weather clear & hot. Ther: 94°.

The following day, Hall worked in the "war tax collector's office making out certificates of sale" and that evening he "went home with Richard Cole and spent the night there." Sam Sharp remained in his office.

Hall returned to the war tax collector's office (Wednesday, August 6 and Thursday, August 7). Charles Lund returned from Hardin County, where he had been collecting taxes (Wednesday, August 6). Sam Sharp began making out his tax rolls for Liberty County (Thursday, August 7), and he and the slaves weighed cotton (Friday, August 8).

On Friday, August 8, Hall noted that he had "a sort of settlement" with Captain James Wrigley, "and took his general power of atty [attorney], to wind up the old business between us during his absence to the seat of war." Wrigley then "left on a hand car [by rail] for Houston to join his company [Waul's Legion] which is now ordered to Little Rock in Arkansas." Hall would not see James Wrigley again until after the war.

Hall remained at the war tax collector's office, and Sam Sharp made out the tax rolls for Liberty County. On Monday, August 11, Hall wrote, "E. H. Cushing arrived from Houston on the cars and came to see me." Cushing was the editor of *The Houston Weekly Telegraph*, who had closely followed Hall's legal troubles in 1859. Hall did not explain the reason for Cushing's visit.

Thursday August 14th 1862. Today I am very busy writing in the office of the war tax collector. I purchased from Nicholas D. Hamel of Chambers County a very likely negro girl about 19 years old, by the name of Mima [Jemima] *for which I paid him 1200$. Boys* [are] *in the swamp getting out pughes* [fence poles]. *Sam Sharp is still at work on his* [tax] *rolls. Bill* [is] *at work on the fence. weather changeable & hot: Ther: 95°.*

References to Jemima appear frequently in the journal.

Hall's days as mayor of Liberty were drawing to a close. Since each member's term had expired, the city council met on Saturday, August 16, and "ordered" an election for "seven trustees or aldermen" to be held on the first Monday in September. The next mayor would be elected from among them. Hall did not run for public office, and Charles Lund took his place as mayor, serving until the 1865 election.

In that same entry, Hall noted, "The boys worked on the fence in the forenoon and in the evening I gave them [a] holliday." This would not be the only such occurrence.

Hall and Sam Sharp worked on the Liberty County tax rolls for several days and noted on Wednesday, August 20, that the "County Court is busy examining them." The examination continued the next day. The County Court had to approve his tax rolls before Sam Sharp could conclude his work as tax assessor/collector. (Perhaps the records were incomplete, since Hall continued working on the tax rolls until Monday, August 25, when he finished.) That same day (August 25), he added, "In consequence of the negligence of T. W. Key I am disappointed in not having the will of old man Smith probated, he having failed to give the notices required by law." Thomas W. Key was a member of the city council, serving from 1862 through 1868.

Leaving Sam Sharp and Charles Lund to manage the remaining business and tax collection details, Hall rode away from Liberty on Wednesday, August 27, to visit Margaret and the family at Hall's Bluff. Bill and Jemima traveled with him. They crossed the Trinity River at Liberty and "went up on the west side of it. [W]e drove 23 miles and camped for the night." Their route passed through Cold Spring and Huntsville to Tuscaloosa, where they crossed the river to the east side, and continued northward toward home, arriving safely on Monday, September 1.

As soon as they reached the mill house, Hall left the wagon and mules "with the servants" and, in the evening, rode Hawk "down to Fathers where I found the little woman and my pet daughter Fawn, enjoying fine health, and who were much pleased to see me. I also found Father's family well."

Hall immediately set to work. He visited with J. H. Leaverton to buy fodder (Tuesday, September 2), and he visited with his cousin William Leaverton and friends Mr. Keen and Charles Beasley. On Friday, September 5, Hall learned that Captain and Mrs. James Wrigley had been in Crockett for a week. He did not see Captain Wrigley, but Ann Wrigley visited with the Halls from Saturday, September 6 until Wednesday, September 10. Hall and "the children" picked ninety-five pounds of cotton on Thursday, September 11. (He did not identify the children.) At the mill on Friday, September 12, Hall gathered his tools and "had a partial settlement with Mr. Pennington in relation to toll corn[,]" with a final settlement on Monday, September 15, then turned his toll corn over to William Leaverton that same day. He picked cotton "by way of amusement" (Friday, September 12) and on other days as well. On Friday, September 26, Hall's slaves were "busy driving up beeves to put into a drove[,]" and he sold seven of his wife's cattle to D. L. Burton for $140 (Saturday, September 27). That day he also "contracted to purchase some cotton" from Charles Beasley.

Tuesday September 30th 1862. Today I received from Charley Beasley 5 bales of Cotton, weighing 565.[,] *536.*[,] *538.*[,] *538.*[,] *& 501 lbs for which I paid him 10¢* [per pound] *cash.—Wm. Leaverton started for Navarro* [Crossing], *but had to return in consequence of the high stage of the Trinity River, weather changeable and warm with strong prospects of rain. Thus I close the jottings for the month of September.*

Throughout the war years, many Southern planters held onto their cotton.[24] It is not clear whether these were the first bales Hall was buying in partnership with Frank Hitchcock, or if he had decided as an individual to begin stockpiling cotton for sale after the war, when demand would be great and prices high. On the following day, Hall and William Leaverton rode "nearly all over the neighbourhood in search of cotton, but without any success . . ." and although Hall did not buy any cotton that day, his neighbors now knew he was prepared to do so.

In Texas, because of the blockade, the only outlet was at Brownsville, where the bales were ferried across the Rio Grande to Matamoros, Mexico. Agents from European textile mills waited there to purchase wagon trains of cotton from Texas, Louisiana, and Arkansas. Planters sending their cotton bales to Brownsville risked losses from damage en route, bad weather, government impressment, corrupt agents, and outright theft. They also had the extra costs of teamsters and wagons, livestock and forage, plus fluctuating fees levied by Mexican customs officers. The Texas and Confederate governments bought cotton cheaply or impressed it if a planter refused to accept either a low price or, later, depreciated currency. Hall was providing his neighbors cash during hard times without the risks of sending their cotton to Brownsville.

Saturday October 4th 1862. Today I had a settlement with Father and divided with him the lands that we held in common, I made the deed to Mother for the same. The little woman is still quite sick [from Trigeminal Neuralgia]. *I am busy taking a copy of the old field notes, taken in 1838.* [*sic*] *of my Trinity lands. weather changeable & hot.*

Margaret recovered quickly, according to the journal entry for Monday, October 6. On Tuesday, October 7, Hall wrote a new will "in consequence of my having divided and deeded away Father's interest in the lands that we held in common . . ." He disposed of his property "differently" from an earlier will, but did not describe the provisions. Nellie Sharp and William P. Leaverton served as witnesses. The timing for these two transactions may have been influenced by his upcoming return to Liberty (with its exposure to wartime events) as well as the impending birth of another child.

The next day (Wednesday, October 8), at seven o'clock in the morning, Margaret gave birth to a son weighing eleven pounds, one ounce. The family sent for Dr. Murchison, but he "arrived too late to be of any service."[25] Mahala, James, and several of the black women assisted with the delivery. Hall named the baby James Wrigley to honor his friend and celebrated the birth of his first son with "a big egg nogg, which was not bad, by the way."

With Margaret improving steadily, Hall and Bill Hicks left for Liberty on Monday, October 13, and arrived the following Friday, October 17. Hall found his friends well, but business was "perfectly dead. The Yankees [are] in possession of Galveston and Capt Black's Cavalry Company [is] stationed at Liberty to guard and protect the Rail Road bridge over the Trinity River," he wrote that day.

On the same day that Hall's son was born, Commodore William B. Renshaw (1816-1863) and a flotilla of eight U.S. ships captured Galveston. Captain Eagle and the *Santee* had left because the disease of scurvy, due to a lack of vitamin C, appeared among the men aboard his ship, and he sailed away to get medical help. (Untreated, scurvy can cause death.) Renshaw's ships included the *Westfield*, his flagship, and the *Clifton*, both ferry boats, the *Owasco*, a gunboat, and the renowned *Harriet Lane*, built in 1857 as an armed sidewheeler for the Revenue Cutter Service (now the Coast Guard). Besides its military role, the *Harriet Lane* had also served a ceremonial function for foreign guests of the United States. Renshaw arrived at Galveston on October 4 and gave the city four days to evacuate, contingent upon the Confederates not bringing more weapons onto the island. Sent by General Hébert then at military headquarters in San Antonio, Confederate Colonel Xavier B. Debray took charge of Galveston on October 5. He agreed with General Hébert's assessment about defenses and instructed Colonel Joseph J. Cook to leave the island. Cook removed troops, guns, and machinery to Virginia Point on the mainland across Galveston Bay, where he established a military camp. Cook left behind only a few troops to defend the railroad bridge and one gun. Once more, residents fled the island. On the morning of October 8, Captain Jonathan Wainright of the *Harriet Lane* along with a party of Union marines and sailors came ashore. To their surprise, uniformed firemen greeted the Federals at the wharves and guided them to the custom house, where the mayor gave Wainright the keys to the city. Remaining Galveston citizens watched the peaceful surrender. Wainright took over the custom house, and the occupation of Galveston began. Governor Lubbock hurried to Virginia Point. He learned from Colonel Debray that the Confederates had no vessels for scouting or for defense operations. Lubbock arranged for the purchase of the *Bayou City* and placed Commander William W. Hunter in charge of naval operations at Galveston. The Confederates next began to make plans to drive the Federals from Galveston Island.[26]

U.S.S. Harriet Lane

(1861-1863) Halftone reproduction of a wash drawing by Clary Ray, circa 1898.
Courtesy of the U.S. Naval History and Heritage Command Photograph.

Hall had little work to do at the store, and Sam Sharp ran the warehouse. Hall returned to the provost marshal's office, and Sam began "packing up things" to take to the house near the mill on the Elkhart (Tuesday, October 21).

On Wednesday, October 22, Hall "tried Mr. R. O. W. McManers [McManus] for treason against the Government, the evidence not being sufficient he was discharged." (Since Hall was no longer mayor, he conducted the trial as provost marshal.) Robert O. W. McManus (age forty-seven in 1860) had been born in New York. In 1860, he gave his occupation as farmer, with real estate valued at $30,000 and personal property worth $10,000. His wife Sarah (age thirty-eight) had been born in Louisiana. Two daughters and three sons, ranging in age from twenty to ten, all born in Texas, lived at home. In 1852, McManus captained the steamboat *Washington* on the Brazos River. According to an 1855 advertisement in *The Liberty Gazette*, McManus offered forwarding services between Liberty or Moore's Bluff and Galveston to Trinity River merchants and cotton planters in Polk, Tyler, Trinity, and Houston counties. Hall did not describe the nature of the "treason."[27]

Capture of U.S.S. Harriet Lane, *1 January 1863*

Engraving published in *Harper's History of the Great Rebellion*, page 421, depicting Confederates boarding the *Harriet Lane* from the C.S. gunboats *Neptune* and *Bayou City*.
Courtesy of the U.S. Naval History and Heritage Command Photograph.

Monday October 27th 1862. Today Sam Sharp riding my horse Hawk and Bill with the mules and little wagon pretty well loaded left Liberty (after bidding us all good bye) for the Mill up the Country. To which place I have now fully concluded to remove and settle down I hope permanently with my little woman and babies. Weather clear and cold, with a frost at night.

The following day, Frank Hitchcock gave him "a pair of fine blocks" (buhrstones), suggesting that he knew of Hall's plan to return to Houston County. On Friday, October 31, Hitchcock "deposited" $15,500 with Hall to buy cotton "up the Country." As early as August, Hall must have been thinking about whether or not to leave Liberty, since he did not run for mayor in the regular election. It is probable that, in August, Hall and Hitchcock discussed their intention to buy and store cotton as they waited for the blockade to end and trade to resume (see journal entry for September 30).

Although preparing to leave Liberty, Hall remained at the warehouse. He shipped freight from the warehouse to the rail cars and supervised the moving of items belonging to Hitchcock from the warehouse to the railroad for shipment to Houston. On Tuesday, November 4, he visited his friend Richard Cole and, with a group of friends, went "ducking . . ." Hall "bagged" fifteen. After a "splendid" dinner, all of the men returned to their homes.

During the same day, he sent a letter by Attorney Abraham B. Trowell "in route to Waul's legion in Mississippi & by whom I sent a letter to Captain Wrigley, notifying him of my intention to remove from Liberty up to my Mill, where my family has been for the past five months." That evening, he visited with Charles Lund "and spent a pleasant time with him & his family. I then returned to my solitary abode to cogitate upon the past." After "loafing around [his] office" (Wednesday, November 5) and putting freight from the warehouse on the rail cars (Thursday, November 6), Hall moved his office to the warehouse at the river (Friday, November 7), where he could be "more comfortable." Afterward, he went hunting, killing "two nice turkeys and one duck[,]" which were all he could "conveniently carry home."

Saturday November 8th 1862. Today I am busily engaged in the Conscript office reconscripting those heretofore discharged by reason of disability[.] *Sam H. Sharp, with the little wagon & mules*[,] *arrived from the mill having left there on Wednesday last, taking just 4 days to come down. He left my little woman and babies well. The boys* [are] *still at work housing the potatoes, weather clear and cool, with a hard frost at night.*

After a Sunday morning spent in the "Conscript office[,]" Hall spent the evening "writing up this journal and some letters to my little woman & dear ones at home[.] Sam Sharp kept Hall company at home (Sunday, November 9).

Monday November 10th 1862. Today I am again very busy in the conscript office enrolling soldier[s] *for the army of the Confederate States, & so continued until the army Surgeon Mr G. Forgason left. The boys finished digging & housing the potatoes, weather cloudy and warm with strong prospects of rain.*

Tuesday November 11th 1862. Today I am busily engaged in fixing up my papers in the Conscript office and in putting the office in good trim for my successor whomsoever he may be, weather cold, with a strong north wind blowing and a very hard rain at night.

Hall wrote out the muster roll for all of the conscripts "since I have held the office of enrolling officer for Liberty County, and also in arranging all the papers belonging to said office" prior to his resignation (Wednesday, November 12).

Thursday November 13th 1862. Today I am still busy in the office and finished making out my rolls as Enrolling officer, and sent the same to Head quarters together with my resignation of the same. At night I attended a dancing party given in the Empire Saloon given in honor of the returned soldiers from Virginia, weather cloudy & cold, & very unpleasant, with light showers of rain.

Military district headquarters were located in Houston. Hall sent the documents relating to his role as provost marshal to Brigadier General H. P. Bee at state headquarters in San Antonio (Saturday, November 15).

But Hall's sojourn in Liberty was not yet over.

In October, General John Bankhead Magruder (1807-1871) received orders to take command of the Department of Texas, New Mexico and Arizona, with headquarters at Houston. He arrived in October and officially replaced General Hébert on November 29, 1862. To drive the Federals out of Galveston, Magruder ordered the conversion of steamboats to cottonclad gunboats, recruited other steamers to become service vessels for the gunboats, and planned the details for the upcoming battle to retake the city and the island.

As early as December 2, 1861, Commander William W. Hunter of the Confederate Navy sent a letter to General Hébert suggesting a defense strategy for the Trinity River. Hunter stated that there were three "passes" in the river, two being shallow and suitable only for small boats. The passes were "much obstructed by logs and shoals." The third and "main pass" was through a canal, "the entrance to which would be under the guns of a battery" at Chambersia or Anahuac. The canal was about four and one-half feet deep "at mean tide." Hunter recommended placing a battery with 500 infantry at Anahuac, which would be "a sufficient force to command the entrance to the Trinity River." Anahuac, he wrote, "is on the mainland, on the east side of the bay, and there is a good road to Liberty and Beaumont."[28] T. J. Chambers offered the use of his property (Chambersia) for the battery, and Confederate soldiers occupied Fort Chambers during 1862.

Almost a year after Commander Hunter wrote his recommendations, and with Union forces in control of Galveston, the Confederates began to take action. On Wednesday, November 12, Hall noted, "The Government steamer Col Stell arrived here from Lynchburg in quest of negro men to assist in erecting fortifications at the mouth of the Trinity River and in sinking obstructions in said river to prevent the gun boats of our enemy from ascending the same."

Friday November 14th 1862. Today I went up town and remained there pretty much the whole day expecting to attend a mass meeting of the people called for the purpose of devising ways & means, to obstruct the mouth of the Trinity River in order to prevent the gun boats of our enemy ascending the same, but from the luke warmness of the people no meeting was holden, and everybody appeared to be resigned to their fate if the enemy should come and take the village which does not at all seem improbable. weather changeable & cool.

The *Colonel Stell* returned to Liberty "from the mouth of the river" on Sunday, November 16, but no defensive works had begun due to the lack of a labor force. The following day, while Sam Sharp and Masaline left for Hall's Bluff, Hall "attended a mass meeting at the Court house for the purpose of furnishing labor to obstruct the navigation of the river as against the advance of the enemy's gun boats, but I regret to say that no definite action was taken and the Government steamer Col Stell was compelled to leave without the hands for which she came, thus making two grand failures, to arrouse the people to a sense of their dangers."

No doubt, Hall was glad he had decided to move back to Houston County permanently (Monday, November 17). Although Hall's Bluff was accessible by the Trinity River, the distance from the coast made it an unlikely target for an invasion force.

With very little to do, Hall interceded on behalf of two ladies with Colonel Clayton Crawford Gillespie (1822-1876) for the release of a soldier, with unknown results (Thursday, November 20). On the same day, Hall paid Simeon Pattillo for his work on the house. He concluded Sam Sharp's paperwork as tax assessor and collector for Liberty County, submitting the records to the County Court on Friday, November 21. The next day, the court approved the accounts and "discharged [Sam] from further liability upon his official bond as such."

That day (Saturday, November 22), Hall "went up town and assisted the ladies in erecting a stage upon which to represent some tableaux which exhibition is for the benefit of the suffering soldiers in our army in the way of purchasing clothing, shoes, etc."

Liberty resident Camilla Hardin wrote to her brother Lieutenant William F. "Bee" Hardin on November 22 about the program to be held on the following Monday night. Funds raised by the program were intended for E. B. Pickett's Company, which had been captured by the Union Army, and many of the sick and starving men were imprisoned in boats. Ms. Hardin wrote, "They [Pickett's Company] are at Post Arkansas, Ark. And I assure you that we are in excitement about costumes, 'attitudes' and scenery. Oh, yes! A peck of trouble! We will have simple pictures as [we] cannot prepare now for any other kind: such as 'Ruth and Naomi,' 'Dressing Moses for the Fair!' . . . School scene and the closing scene will be Dr. Robert [White] persuading Old Abe [Lincoln]."[29]

Monday November 24th 1862. Today I am busy writing, Mr. & Mrs. Perkins came over on the cars from Houston. [Henry E. Perkins was an attorney and a land agent living in Houston.] *At night the ladies of Liberty gave a grand tableau representation at the Court house, the proceeds of which are to be disbursed for the benefit of the soldiers in the Southern Army. At the exhibition I had to act as scene manager, Master of Ceremonies, take my part in the various tableaux and in fact was a perfect Major Domo of the affair. The house although very large was crowded, there not being less than three hundred persons present, the receipts being about one hundred and sixty-five dollars. The Tableaux were received with great éclat and every thing passing off to the entire satisfaction of the audience as well as all the parties concerned. weather clear & rather cool.*

Hall clearly enjoyed his multiple roles, and the success of the evening uplifted his spirits.

While Hall waited for Sam Sharp to return to Liberty with wagons, mules, and extra hands to move his household goods, he conducted an auction of the "stock of goods" belonging to merchant Joseph E. DeBlanc beginning on Tuesday, November 25. "I only charged him 2½ per cent for my trouble in crying off the goods, but having nothing to do, prefered to do that, rather than loaf around town." However, on Wednesday (November 26), during the auction, "a general spree among the soldier[s] stationed here in Liberty, they being all drunk and refusing to obey the orders of their officers, put the whole town into commotion and broke up the sale[.]" Hall resumed his work for DeBlanc the next day and again on Saturday, November 29. Hall finished making out bills for auctioned items on Sunday, November 30, and "thus closed [his] labors in that particular."

Increasingly impatient to leave, Hall noted that a Mr. Allen, an "old gentleman" from Houston County, arrived in Liberty with "his wagon & team and by whom I expect to send forward some of my furniture to the Mills . . ." (Friday, November 28). Allen stayed overnight with Hall and on Saturday (November 29), he left for Crockett with a portion of Hall's furniture. Although Allen's arrival might have been a coincidence, because of the rapid turnaround, it is possible that the gentleman had been sent by the family.

Monday December 1st 1862. Today I went up town and settled in full with Mr. DeBlanc for the things purchased at his auction sale, at night I visited a ball given in the Court house by the members of Capt. Black's Company now stationed in Liberty, weather cloudy and cold with occasional showers of rain.

The following day, with Bob's help, Hall began packing furniture and household goods in earnest. Unfortunately the weather was "cloudy, cold and rainy, making it exceedingly disagreeable and preventing us from doing much towards packing up." A railroad "train of cars" from Houston ran off the track, injuring several passengers, and Bob became ill on Wednesday, December 3. Hall stayed at home sitting near the fire "inconsequence of the rain & cold" (Thursday, December 4) and then went "up town and loafed around the stoves" (Friday December 5).

Hall learned of the death of Frank Barziza on Saturday, December 6, from one of the Barziza brothers. Barziza "departed this life on last Thursday after a lingering illness of some time with consumption." He was buried at Liberty with Masonic honors. Hall did not state that he attended "the ceremonies[,]" but details indicate that he probably did. Francis Louis Barziza (1822-1862) was an attorney, born in Virginia, who set up a law practice at Wheelock in Robertson County with his younger brothers William Lee and Phillip Ignatius, Jr., during the 1840s. They relocated to Chambers County and became planters. Their youngest brother, Decimus et Ultimus, became a noted Houston attorney and legislator.[30]

Without work to keep him busy, Hall searched for things to do. He traded his interest in a tract of land plus twenty-five dollars in cash for a four-year-old roan horse (Tuesday, December 9) which he named Ratler. The horse was stolen from the stable the next night. Hall thought Ratler had been taken by Joseph Wright, the previous owner, but the following day (Thursday, December 11), he learned that the horse "was left at the residence of James Rodgers on the Trinity River." He sent Bob, who was now well, to get the horse.

Charles Lund returned from a trip to Houston by rail (Friday, December 12) bringing two pair of cotton cards worth $25 per pair. In normal times, cotton cards sold for 25 cents per pair. Cotton and wool cards were hand-held wooden paddles with tiny metal teeth covering the inner side of each paddle. Holding the paddles by their handles, a worker stroked the top paddle across its mate to comb the cotton on the bottom paddle. Combing cleaned, straightened, and smoothed the fibers until they formed a roll, which was twisted into thread on the spinning wheel.[31]

On Monday, December 15, Hall attended a dinner at Dr. Stanwood's residence to celebrate the twenty-first birthday of his daughter Sarah Eugenia, and afterward the guests moved to the courthouse, "where we had a first rate dancing party, and as usual I had to act as master of ceremonies on the occasion, towards the small hours of morn the party closed, everything passing off quite pleasantly."

Unable to wait any longer for his wagons, Hall packed up "the most valuable part" of the furniture and decided to go to Crockett, leaving other articles behind for the moment (Wednesday, December 17). He bought "the celebrated horse Gladiator" and a buggy from Dr. J. O. Shelby for $600 in Confederate money (Thursday, December 18). He next purchased "a beautiful upright Piano Forte" for Margaret from Dr. Stanwood for $300, placed as much as he could in the buggy, said goodbye to friends, and headed north to Houston County and his family (Friday, December 19).

Dr. John Orville Shelby was a physician practicing in Liberty from 1850 until the mid-1870s. After serving in the Civil War, he became a representative for the Freedmen's Bureau (1866-1868). Shelby twice received a special military appointment to serve as county judge. In 1868, Shelby and Dr. Felix Smotridge shared offices in the latter's home. Shelby became county treasurer (1869) and postmaster, and he served on the city council from 1870 until 1872. Dr. Stanwood later lived in Dr. Shelby's home in Liberty.[32]

Hall spent his last night on the road at the home of his friend Dan Dailey, and the next morning (Tuesday, December 23) he met Bill Hicks with the wagon and mules en route for Liberty. He gave Bill $5.50 for expenses on the road. Hall then drove from Dailey's to Crockett, a distance of fifteen miles, where he unloaded the buggy to have "the balance iron" repaired.

Hall was probably referring to the fifth wheel, a piece of curved iron on each side of the running gear that kept the front of a wagon or buggy from "swaying excessively or toppling on turns."[33]

Hall then reloaded the buggy and continued the additional ten miles to his house at the mill, "where I found all my loved and dear ones enjoying good health, and who were overjoyed to see me."

Thursday December 25th 1862. Today I remained at home with the little woman and babies and enjoyed a fine Christmas dinner with several nice egg noggs gotten up in a style as only the little woman knows how to fix them. I contracted with Mr Thomas Dailey for 1000 lbs of pork at 14¢ [per pound]. *The drafting of the Militia came off in Crockett and Sam Sharp was drawn to serve under the three months call for the protection of our coast. weather cloudy and warm, with occasional showers of rain.*

Hall bought a little more than 2,000 pounds of fodder from Mr. Renfro, and he hired three blacks plus Chester and Ann, who belonged to Joshua, to salt 1,100 pounds of pork, bought from L. A. Bird. He also bought 937 pounds of pork from Thomas Dailey and hired Chester to cut it up. After Chester and Ann salted down the pork purchased from Dailey, "we killed ten other hogs which weighed 1480 pounds" in terms of pork (Tuesday, December 30). He paid Chester and Ann a total of $9.50 for their work. From Dr. William F. Corley, a farmer and physician, Hall bought twenty-five bales of cotton at 17 cents per pound (Monday, December 29). With Mr. Pennington's contract as miller at an end, Hall took possession of the keys to the mill (Wednesday, December 31).

Of greatest concern during this time was the illness of Nellie Sharp, who was pregnant, requiring repeated visits from Dr. Murchison, Mrs. Bird, and Mahala Hall.

On Wednesday, December 31, Hall concluded his journal for 1862 "now past & gone, and whether God will permit me to live to keep [a record of] the events around me of the incoming year is more than I can know, but trusting in his mercy I shall enter upon the duty, which is pleasing to me and may be profitable to my family and myself hereafter."

During the year to come, the Hall family remained safe, but not necessarily at peace, on its East Texas farm.

Chapter 4

1863

On Christmas Day, 1862, three companies (about 260 men) of the Forty-Second Massachusetts Infantry Regiment under Colonel Isaac Burrell arrived from New Orleans to reinforce Commander William B. Renshaw's 150 men holding Galveston. Just before daybreak on January 1, 1863, Confederate General John Bankhead Magruder ordered an attack on the Federals by land and by sea. Confederate Commodore Leon Smith commanded the cottonclad steamboats *Bayou City* and *Neptune*, while Brigadier General William R. Scurry directed the land force. Within hours, the Confederates forced the Union troops to give up the city. Commander Renshaw destroyed his flagship, the U.S.S. *Westfield*, to keep it from Confederate hands, but unfortunately he and fourteen of his sailors perished in the resulting explosion.

Union ships reappeared in January in another attempt to capture Galveston, but the carefully contrived appearance of heavy fortifications and artillery discouraged the Federals, who lacked the necessary troop strength to take and occupy the city. (Union ships returned in November and retook all of the Texas ports.)

The fate of the Columbiads and other artillery pieces transported by Hall is unknown. They may have been used in the defense of Galveston, moved to artillery emplacements on the mainland, or distributed to coastal towns. But Hall's efforts helped prevent a Union invasion force from landing on coastal Texas soil in 1862.

Back home in Houston County, Hall immediately took control of the mill. On Thursday, January 1, he wrote, "As I have now got the entire control and possession of my mill I contemplate jotting down her earnings and out lay for the current year, it is agreed however between Sam Sharp & I, that he shall act as the miller, I attending only during his absence." After some maintenance work, they began grinding corn. A week later (Wednesday, January 7), Sam ground fourteen bushels of corn before riding to the "Shilo Camp ground" to report for militia duty. Shiloh was a small community about ten miles southwest of Crockett, which grew up around a church and a revival campground established by Stephen F. Box in 1834. The campground served as a mustering area for Confederate soldiers.[1] Hall noted on Friday, January 9, however, that Sam returned that day from "the Camp at Shilo[,] he having been discharged from his enrollment in the Militia in consequence of a severe gun shot wound he received when quite young." A journal entry written by Joshua Hall on November 27, 1851, stated, "Sam got shot." Born in 1839, Sam would have been about twelve years old at the time. There is no description of the nature or location of the wound.[2]

Hall settled quickly into the rhythm of farming. He purchased two field hands: a mulatto man named John "or Squire" (age nineteen) from a Mr. McCord for $1,600 (Wednesday, January 7), and a black man named Bill (age thirty-four) from Thomas W. Reed for $1,800 (Thursday, January 8). On Saturday, January 10, Hall "sent" Bill, with the mule and cart, to get his clothing from the Reed place, which lay across the Trinity River in Leon County. Bill returned the next day, without his belongings, but "all safe." Bill made the trip across the river and back unescorted. Bill initially belonged to Elisha Tubbs, who had just died, or his son Jesse, before being bought by Thomas Reed. Hall referred to his new man as "Bill" and to Bill Hicks as "Hicks" in order to distinguish the two. Bill adopted the Tubbs name after emancipation. (For clarity, these names will continue to be used.)

Hall directed the men to haul wood and set out garden posts, and from Mr. Renfro he bought 300 pounds of fodder and eight bushels of peas. He bought lint cotton from Jesse Tubbs, totaling 5,244 pounds, and he paid Tubbs' son, "young Jesse," $700 "on a/c [account] of said Cotton." On the following day (Wednesday, January 14), Bill Hicks and Louisa arrived from Liberty with

Hall's wagon after nine days of travel "and in consequence of the horrid state of the road they hauled almost nothing, the mules being badly cut up and very much jaded."

Hall planned to build a new farmhouse, and on Sunday, January 11, he and Sam Sharp "rode down in the bottom to select a good ford, and to select a site upon which to erect a house and make some permanent improvements . . ." He did not elaborate.

Captain Peacock and Solomon Levy stopped in with Hall for the night of Monday, January 12. They traveled from Crockett "in a buggy" and were on their way to Magnolia. They left the next morning, and Hall went to the mill, where he ground twenty-two and one-half bushels of corn.

Winter weather impacted activities for several days in mid-January. Two storms caused Elkhart Creek almost to overflow (Tuesday, January 13 and Sunday, January 18); another storm brought several inches of sleet and snow (Wednesday, January 14); and a hard freeze left between one-quarter of an inch and an inch of ice in all the containers holding water (Thursday, January 15). Icicles hanging from tree limbs and the eaves of the houses measured about six inches long (Thursday, January 15). During this unusually cold weather, Hall and Sam Sharp, along with "the boys," killed six hogs, which were then cut up and salted for preservation (Thursday, January 15 and Friday, January 16). Pork was an important element of their diet.

The men then returned to building a fence around the garden.

At 8:00 on the morning of Sunday, January 25, Nellie Sharp gave birth to a son, who weighed 7¾ pounds and was named James Hall Sharp. Present at the delivery were Margaret and her mother Mahala Hall, Massaline (Mrs. L. A.) Bird, Sam Sharp, James Hall, and two slave women, both named Louisa. "Nellie sustained herself very well under the circumstances and had rather an easy time than otherwise." They nicknamed the baby "Major" to "distinguish him from the little woman's child James, alias Jim." Hall's pride in being so honored by Sam and Nellie rings from the journal entry.

After the excitement of the baby's birth, the days grew quiet. Staying close to home, Sam built a loom for Mahala. Margaret bought a spinning wheel from Mrs. Beasley for seven dollars in cash (Friday, January 30). Because of the Union blockade, very little cloth reached Galveston or other

Texas ports except by blockade runner. Women who previously could afford to buy cloth now had to make their own.

Once cotton had been cleaned of any trash such as leaves or sticks and stripped of its seed, the fibers were carded ("combed") into rolls, then spun on the wheel to make thread. The thread was reeled, to keep it from knotting, and then dyed with bark, leaves, moss, berries, or earth. After the thread had been dyed, it was placed on spools and taken to the weaver to be made into cloth on a loom[3] As the war progressed and the blockade continued, the Halls became more and more self-sufficient.

Hall sold the *Argus* office to D. Richardson (Friday, January 30) for $1,023.05 "and gave him 12 months time on it, dating from the 4th of October last, & drawing 10% interest after maturity." The next day, Sam Sharp drove the buggy to Crockett, where he sold Hall's "old homestead" to William F. Johnston for $2,000 cash. By selling his properties in Crockett, Hall permanently divested himself of his former life in the town and acquired money for future needs.

Construction of house and garden fences and gates, repairs to the mill, planting a garden, finishing the loom, and unusually cold weather marked the days of early February. Another hard freeze formed ice one-half inch thick in "all the vessels that had water in them" (Wednesday, February 4). Sam set up the loom for Mahala and "put it up in running order for her" (Thursday, February 5). That night, Florence "was taken very sick which kept me up nearly all night." The weather that day was "cloudy and cold as the devil with a hard freeze and plenty of ice."

In his journal entry for Saturday, February 7, Hall noted that several of the slaves worked "on the road leading to Palestine." That same day, he described the wedding of John and Jemima "after the style of negro marriages, they had a general blow out with a congregation of all the negroes in the neighborhood and seemed to enjoy themselves hugely." A few days later (Friday, February 13), during a hail storm, Masaline ran away, and on Monday, Hall learned that he was "in jail at Crockett." Rather than force him to return to the farm, Hall sent Sam Sharp to Crockett (Thursday, February 19), where Sharp sold Masaline to Mr. R. B. Arrington, a Massachusetts-born clerk and bookkeeper in 1860, for $1,500.

Hall wrote to Frank Hitchcock "in relation to cotton" and Sam built a "first rate wagon gate for the house yard" (Tuesday, February 10). Hall obtained garden seed and shrubbery from Mahala on February 10, and the next day Margaret planted "english peas, eschalots, lettuce, horse raddish and other vegetables." Florence's fever abated, and Hall declared her to be well (Wednesday, February 11). The slaves "finished the house fence" and began building a fence around "the little field in front of the house" (Wednesday, February 11) and "in making a large wagon gate" (Thursday, February 12). While Sam Sharp ground corn at the mill, Hall and Margaret planted "apple trees, grape & fig cuttings," and vegetables (Thursday, February 12).

During this time, heavy rains almost destroyed the mill. During the night of Friday, February 13, "it rained very hard with severe thunder & lightning and a perfect hail storm." The next day, "the mill dam gave way & required the labor of all hands nearly the entire evening to repair the break." More showers followed, flooding the area, and by Monday, February 16, the slaves worked to repair "a rent [rend] in the levee. Sam Sharp ground 11½ bushels of corn by way of assisting to run off the water which is very high and I am fearful that the levee will be swept away. Weather cloudy and rainy. In fact it rained incessantly throughout the entire day raising the Elk Hart about as high as I ever saw it before." The next day, after more rain during the night, the men began "carrying sand" to fill another break in the mill dam. "The water is fearfully high in the Elk Hart and the mill dam is just on the wiggle, the water however is falling a little and probably the mill dam may stand the presure [*sic*]." By Thursday, February 19, the worst of the flooding receded. "The water is drying up a little from the face of the earth. The Elk Hart is falling a little and I now think the mill levee is safe against this last freshet." This was only a temporary respite from difficulties with the mill.

One evening "the boys went after a load of wood and bogged down and in their effort to get the wagon out of the bog broke an axle tree, thus giving more trouble. . . . The whole face of the low lands is still covered with water"

(Tuesday, February 17). While the slave hands split and hauled rails to build a cow pen, Bill Hicks made an axle tree for the wagon (Thursday, February 19). Hall spent several days making a reel to help Margaret wind thread from the spinning wheel, and when it was finished, he "reeled cotton thread" for her (Monday, February 23). As the water drained away, Hall retrieved nails and building materials from the "Brown house" on the property (Tuesday, February 24), and tore down a smokehouse from "the old place" for additional building materials (Thursday, February 26).

Hall celebrated his birthday on Sunday, February 22, with "a fine dinner" prepared by Margaret and attended by Mahala and Mr. and Mrs. Bird. A few days later (Wednesday, February 25), he made a "brooch holder" for Margaret.

Heavy rains swelled the Trinity River, and Hall noted the passage of the *Lone Star*, southward bound for Liberty, on Tuesday, March 3. That night, the steamer *Alamo* arrived at Hall's Bluff with "most" of Hall's "house hold furniture" from Liberty "on board." The next evening, after working all day, he and Bill took "the little wagon & mules & drove down to Hall's bluff, after some of my articles, which I found on the bank of the river where they had been landed by the Alamo. I was compelled to camp out at night & sleep[,] what little I got on the bank of the river, which was exceedingly disagreeable[.]" The weather was "very cold."

Thursday March 5th 1863. Today I am engaged at the bluff in watching my things, and which I found in a damaged condition. The Steamer Alamo passed down the River from Magnolia, she lay at the bluff about 2 hours & then proceeded on her way to Liberty. The boys are busy hauling my things home, they made 2 loads with the mule team & one with the ox team, in the last load by the mule team I returned home from the bluff. My horse Gladiator run off & Hicks has been out all day hunting him but without success. Sam is engaged in pecking the mill rocks and putting them in good running order. Weather cloudy & cold with very high wind blowing and occasional showers of rain & very disagreeable.

Two wagon loads followed the next day, and on Sunday, March 8, while Bill Hicks continued to search for Gladiator, several of the other men went to get Hall's gin stand and dining room table. With his furniture now at home, he began "fitting up the rooms for bed chambers and in putting matting down on the floors" (Saturday, March 7) and "arranging [his] desk and papers" (Sunday, March 8). While working at the house, he "lost one of [his] gold sleeve buttons." This is one of his few references to wealth. Steamboat Captain G. W. "Wash" Rose visited Hall on Sunday, and the next day, Rose accompanied Bill Hicks, who was still searching for Gladiator, as far as Dan Dailey's place about 25 miles away. At an estate sale (Tuesday, March 10), where Hall had gone to purchase seed cotton, he learned that Gladiator was at a neighbor's. He retrieved the horse, paid the man five dollars for taking care of Gladiator, and led him home. That night Bill Hicks returned safely from Dan Dailey's.

Hall's gin stand, a small, wooden machine with metal interior parts, was designed to separate cotton seeds from fibers. In 1793, Eli Whitney invented the "cotton engine" (later shorted to "gin") to speed up the labor intensive process of separating seeds from fibers by hand. Whitney's ginning machine, or "gin stand," used two wooden cylinders placed inside a frame box. Powered by two leather belts, a cylinder with rows of spikes inserted into the wood rotated in one direction, while a brush cylinder mounted behind it rotated in the opposite direction. The spikes passed through a stationary metal bar with metal teeth, or "ribs," that allowed the cotton fibers, but not the seeds, to pass through. The brush cylinder removed the fibers, or "lint," and air currents carried the lint to an opening for discharge. The seeds fell to the bottom of the box to be periodically removed. However, the spikes often loosened from the cylinder, and circular saws came to be preferred. Whitney's original concept is still in use, although cotton gins today are far more complex.

By the 1860s, farms and plantations operated small cotton gins, here referring to the building, which usually contained one gin stand. An area beneath the elevated ginning floor remained open on three sides. Tied to wooden gears by long sweeps, horses or mules walked in circles beneath the ginning floor. As the animals walked, the sweeps turned the gears and transmitted power to the two leather belts attached to the gin stand. The belts activated the cylinders inside the machine.

After the cotton was cleaned, or "ginned," it was stored in a small room on the ginning floor or dropped into the lint room, an enclosed area on the fourth side of the building, beneath the ginning floor. Workers, who had earlier brought seed cotton from the field to the gin building in baskets, now gathered the lint into baskets and carried them outside to a mule- or horse-powered screw press. After the lint had been squeezed into bales, wrapped with bagging, and tied with ropes or metal bands, each bale was weighed, the average being 450 pounds, although 500-pound bales were not unusual. Slaves drove wagon loads of the bales to a cotton house, where they remained stored until time for transport by wagon or shipment by flatboat or steamboat to a market town or to a port.

East Texas and coastal planters sent their cotton to factors at Liberty or Galveston. Factors then shipped the cotton to New Orleans, New York, or England (very often to Liverpool). Galveston served as Houston's port until the Port of Houston was established early in the twentieth century.[4]

In addition to growing his own, Hall bought seed cotton (cotton bolls picked from the plant but still containing the seeds within the fibers) to be ginned, and lint (cotton without the seeds) to be baled. On Tuesday, March 10, 1863, for example, he purchased 14,859 pounds of seed cotton from a deceased neighbor's estate. Although Hall owned a gin stand, he did not set up a cotton gin or screw press. Instead, two days later, he "made arrangements with Mr John A Williams for the use of McElroy's gin & had the cotton hauled there." (Williams was a near neighbor. The young black man named John spent several days transferring the cotton by wagon.) He stored the bales for later sale, according to his agreement with Frank Hitchcock. Hall bought 80 bales from T. R. Dailey and his son Milton Dailey (Saturday, March 14), and he continued to buy and store cotton throughout the remainder of the war.

For Hall, setting out a garden, making the house more comfortable (such as installing window panes), grinding corn at the mill, buying cotton, fishing, and visiting friends and relatives filled the spring days.

On Friday, March 20, Hall sold his "office in town" to L. E. Downes for $1,200. A few weeks later (Saturday, May 16) he gave Downes a title for lots 31 and 32 in Crockett.

Friday April 3rd 1863. Today the boys are still engaged in planting corn. I drove my horse (Gladiator) and buggy to Crockett in order to carry Margaret Hall home after her visit out on the Elk Hart for the past two weeks[,] *while in Crockett I paid Messrs Sorley, Smith & Co the sum of $134.54 upon which they had sued me. I also paid Wall's estate $232. To John Miller $65. To Kenneth Murchison as J. P. the judgment that Miller & Collins obtained against me and Daniel Dailey amounting to 58$. To S. A. Miller as atty for C. G. Forshey a Judgment that he obtained against me for $70.53 principal & interest up to this date. I also collected from W. A. Stewart on a/c of a claim I hold against Commins' Estate the sum of $197. I returned home in the evening in company with W. A. Stewart, Wm. Wingfield and Joseph A. Wright. Sam ground 21 bushels of corn. weather clear & pleasant.*

Hall had purchased items at an estate sale he identified as Wall's on May 2, 1860. This was most likely the estate of William F. Wall, who had served as postmaster for Crockett in 1851, 1853, and 1857 or 1858. Hall was the Crockett postmaster in 1852.[5]

Margaret Hall (1846-1931) was the daughter of Charles C. Hall, who died in 1853, and Mary Ann Hall. Margaret married John Shepard Shivers in 1869. In 1860 her mother was the head of household with real estate valued at $3,500 and personal property worth $250. Mary Ann's children were Charles (age seventeen in 1860), Margaret (age fourteen), and Amanda (age eight).[6]

In 1860, Virginia-born Steward A. Miller was a fifty-five-year-old attorney with a twenty-five year-old wife (Rebecca), also born in Virginia. The couple had a four-year-old son and a two-year-old daughter, both born in Texas. Miller owned real estate valued at $17,740 and personal property worth $5,660. Miller and his family lived next door to carpenter and builder John C. Varnadore. Miller had been elected mayor of Crockett in 1859.[7]

William A. Stewart (age thirty-one in 1860) was the older brother of Frank Stewart. A lawyer born in Georgia, he owned real estate valued at $6,000 and

Thomas P. Collins

personal property worth $5,000 in 1860. He and his wife "S. L." (age twenty-six) had three daughters. In 1880, Stewart was a widower with his three daughters living at home. Stewart represented Houston County in the Sixteenth Texas Legislature (1879).[8]

William E. Wingfield (age thirty-two in 1860) was a merchant. Born in Virginia, he owned real estate valued at $1,700 and personal property worth $3,450. His wife Helen (age twenty) was also born in Virginia. Their son Charles (age four) was born in Texas. They resided in the same neighborhood in Crockett with W. A. Stewart, James Collins, Thomas P. Collins, attorney William B. Stokes, and newspaper publisher Oscar Dalton.[9]

Work on the farm remained constant. Hard rains and hail in early May caused newly planted corn to be hoed and replanted. Hall made Florence, whom he called "Fawn" or "Pet," a pair of shoes. He also ground corn, went hunting and fishing, and bought food staples when he could. For example, Sam Sharp rode to Magnolia, a round trip of forty-four miles, to purchase fifty pounds of sugar at 33⅓ cents per pound (Monday, April 20). Frank Stewart bought fifty pounds of sugar in Magnolia, at 6 cents per pound (Monday, May 18). Hall sent Rachael to Crockett on Hawk to buy ten pounds of coffee, costing $3.18 per pound (Thursday, April 30). He noted these prices for his wartime record-keeping. Prices and availability of these everyday items were important to Hall in his roles as farmer and provider.

Hall depended on young Frank Stewart for numerous tasks (he was twenty-one in 1860; see Chapter 1). For example, on Sunday, April 26, Hall, Joshua, Sam Sharp, Frank Stewart, along with Bill Hicks and Joe, "went down to

Hall's bluff in order to run the division line between Mother's lands and my own. We succeeded in making the survey, after which we all returned home." Stewart also accompanied Joshua Hall on a trip to Huntsville, presumably to the penitentiary, but returned without accomplishing their unnamed business (Wednesday, May 6 through Sunday, May 10). On Friday, May 22, Stewart "left for the army to join Capt Smith's company of Burnett's Regiment in Genl. Walker's division." With the campaigns at Vicksburg and Gettysburg about to begin, the Confederate Army needed every available man.

Saturday May 23rd 1863. Today Bill is still at work plowing the corn in the lower field. Mr Keen came over & I settled in full with him for the work he done on my wagons & buggy. Hicks with the little wagon & mules, and John with the large road wagon & four yoke of oxen, left in route for Liberty. The little woman and children in the buggy, and Nellie riding Rat all went down to Mothers and then out after blackberries. I am at work setting out potato slips. Sam ground 16 bushels of corn. weather cloudy with occasional showers of rain in the morning, but clear and warm in the evening.

The following Monday (May 25), James Hall told everyone goodbye and, driving the buggy, left with Nellie for Liberty. They stopped in Crockett for dinner, where Hall "collected" $1,200 from L. E. Downes, who gave him an additional $1,500 "to be invested for him in goods at Houston." After dinner, they continued to Daniel Dailey's, where they spent the night, a total distance of twenty-five miles that day. The next day, they traveled twenty-nine miles, passing through Sumpter, and stopped for the night at Mr. Alderman's. Hall and Nellie "found the roads very heavy & considerably washed up, making the travel exceedingly fatiguing . . ." (Tuesday, May 26). They caught up with the wagons the following day, and Hall "met George Gordon [see Chapter 2] in the stage on his way to Woodville to purchase cotton for the Government." After a distance of forty miles, they "stopped for the night at Mr. Smith's, where we had wretched fare." On Thursday, May 28, after traveling another thirty miles, they reached Liberty.

There they found Nellie's mother, Elizabeth Beale, and one of Nellie's sisters "quite sick and confined to their beds." Born in Maryland between 1824 and 1827, Elizabeth (Waring) Lemaire Beale owned a home in Liberty valued at $500 in the 1860 census. She first married Alexander Lemaire, French Consul to Liberty, who was lost at sea around 1843 (the same year Nellie was born). About 1852, she married John S. Beale, and they had three daughters, Lucy, Kate, and Susan, who were still living at home. Mrs. Beale lived until 1871.[10]

Captain Wrigley's family members were also ill, although they were "generally up." Hall's friend and former Liberty City Councilman Jack McKim was "nearly dead with the dyptheria [*sic*]." And Charles Lund had gone to Houston. "In fact I found nothing as I expected to find it[,]" he wrote on Thursday, May 28.

Although Hall stayed with James Wrigley's family the first night, he moved to Captain Tom Peacock's home the next day. Jack McKim passed away about eight o'clock on the morning of Friday, May 29, and was buried on Saturday with Masonic honors. While attending McKim's burial service, Hall lost a meerschaum pipe given to him by Captain Peacock.

Bill Hicks and John arrived with the wagons on Friday night, and they "camped" at the warehouse. Charles Lund returned by train from Houston on Saturday (May 30). After giving Nellie $101 on Sam Sharp's account, Hall "went over on the return trip of the same train to Houston . . ." He accompanied Mrs. Carrie Bolling, wife of merchant James Bolling, and Dr. Stanwood's daughter Eugenia. Nellie remained in Liberty. Hall and the ladies stayed at the Capitol Hotel while in Houston. Contemporary visitors to Houston may be surprised at Hall's comments about the city dated Sunday, May 31: "Today I am still in the City of Houston, which I found the most dull and unpleasant place that I ever passed a Sunday in before. I have no notes to make upon the passage of the day, weather clear & very hot." Hall would be equally surprised at today's bustling city—even on Sunday.

Hall spent Monday, June 1, shopping for items requested by "the various person[s]" who had asked him to purchase them. His friend and business partner Frank Hitchcock traveled to Houston from Washington County purposely to visit with him, and that night they attended the theater together. Hall began noting the temperature, which he did each summer, and recorded 90° Fahrenheit "in the shade" at three o'clock in the afternoon. After shopping for goods and packing them for travel on Tuesday, that night he went to the theater again with Frank Hitchcock. His business concluded on Wednesday (June 3), Hall returned to Liberty with Eugenia Stanwood on the Texas and New Orleans Railroad, arriving about one o'clock that afternoon. Hall moved from Captain Peacock's to Mrs. Beale's, where he planned to stay until ready to return home. He noted personal expenses of seventy-five dollars while in Houston.

Hall continued to "settle up" his "old business" in Liberty (Thursday, June 4). He had the wagons loaded with goods and "started them up home. I collected from Mr Levy the sum of 20$ for hauling some freight for him from Crockett." He also wrote that he was "very unwell" from diarrhea. "Today I am still in Liberty [Friday, June 5] and succeeded in settling up the business of the firm of James Wrigley & Co. after a fashion. I took a bond from said Wrigley with Charles C. Lund and Edward P. White as securities in the sum of $20.000 for the payment of the out standing liabilities. I then retired from said firm." This retirement, however, would not mark the end of his association with Lund and Wrigley.

Edward P. White was the Sheriff of Liberty County from 1862 through 1865. A native Texan, he was born around 1825.[11]

Hall and Nellie began the return trip on Saturday, June 6, again in the buggy drawn by Rob. The horse was "in rather poor condition" compared to his state when they left home, but Hall does not explain why. They caught up with the wagons on Sunday, June 7, some eight miles below Livingston. Hall "was exceedingly sick nearly all day and was compelled to lay by the road side for some hours." However, they reached Livingston later that day and put up at Bishop's Hotel.

Monday June 8th 1863. Today we left Livingston and drove 24 miles to Sumpter where we stopped for the night at Mr Teagarden's hotel, this distance I drove suffering very severe pain and cramp in my bowels, we met 26 wagons in one train all loaded with cotton, they were from Louisiana and bound for Brownsville for army supplies. Expenses of the day 2$. weather clear & hot: Ther: 88°.

Wagon trains took bales of cotton to Brownsville, where they were ferried across the Rio Grande River to Matamoros, Mexico. European agents in Matamoros bought the cotton from individuals, civil and state governments, and the Trans-Mississippi War Department. Small vessels called "lighters" carried the cotton downstream to the Gulf of Mexico and across the bar to ships with European registry lying off the coast. U.S. naval ships could not stop foreign vessels from transporting the cotton. The Confederacy used the money from cotton sales to buy arms and ammunition, as well as other goods intended for the war effort. Blockade runners also took cotton bales to markets, such as Havana, Cuba, and returned with various goods. Fast, lightweight schooners could sail within the shallow waters close to the Texas coast and enter bays that larger, heavier ships could not reach, but being Southern vessels, they were subject to search and seizure if captured by the U.S. Navy, and transport by the blockade runners was dangerous due to the possible loss of ship and cargo. For successful blockade running captains, however, their profits were well worth the risk.

Tuesday June 9th 1863. Today we left Sumpter and drove 42 miles home. My horse [is] *very much fatigued and nearly given out. I was sick throughout the entire day and only kept up by the excitement of finding my family all well. I found the little woman and children all up as well as Sam. Pet had been sick during my absence. Expenses while in Crockett 5$. I learned from Sam that the mill had ground 176½ bushels of corn during my absence from home. weather changeable & very hot: Ther: 98°.*

Hall continued to be sick until Thursday, June 11, but that day Nellie became ill "from her recent trip to Liberty & back." He did not record the nature of her illness, but she apparently recovered rather quickly because he did not mention it again.

Hall spent Friday, June 12, "lying flat on my back from the effects of a spider bite received last night." That evening, the wagons arrived home from Liberty after nine days on the road with Bill Hicks and John, livestock, and goods "all safe and sound." He gave the other men a holiday on Saturday.

The next two weeks passed quietly. The slave hands chopped out the bottom cotton field and then split rails "to finish enclosing the mill field" on Monday, June 22. Sam weighed 20,000 pounds of seed cotton that Hall had bought from Mrs. Beasley on Wednesday, June 17 and Thursday, June 18. John took the wagon to get cotton from Corley's gin three days in a row (Tuesday, June 23 through Thursday, June 25, plus Sunday, June 28). John continued bringing wagonloads of cotton well into July. Hall and Sam Sharp "put the wheat mill in good running order" and began to grind wheat on Thursday, June 25.

Then, on Friday, June 26, after daily rain showers on Wednesday, June 24 and Thursday, June 25, the "mill dam broke and washed away about fifty feet of the levee." Mr. Keen, who had come to the mill, had to remain overnight with the Halls because of the "high water in the creek occasioned by the braking of the levee." A new cycle of crises began.

After waiting a day for the water to run off, Hall sent Bill Hicks "around the neighborhood in order to procure some hands to repair the mill levee." With the addition of four men ("one from Mr. Beasley, 2 from Mr. Dailey and one from Dr. Murchison"), Hall and his hands spent Monday, June 29, repairing the levee, only to have "high water from the upper mill" destroy their work late in the afternoon. They began again the next day, and by day's end they "got the levee of sufficient strength to resist the high water let down from the upper mill." Between rain showers and numerous tasks, Hall's men continued to work on the mill levee until Wednesday, July 15, when they finished all he planned to do at that time.

Hall and Sam Sharp also made repairs to the mill forebay. Hall's mill was most likely built according to frontier standards of the day. The wooden building was probably one story high, standing on a bank of the Elkhart, with a large mill wheel on one side. Above the mill building, on Elkhart Creek, stood a dam, Hall's "levee," built to stop enough water to create a millpond. The dam had to be strong enough not to collapse due to flooding from the river, smooth enough not to trap debris, and far enough from the mill to allow flood waters to pass around the building without destroying it.

Water from the millpond was then diverted into a millrace by means of a gate. Water pressure from the pond plus the fall, or drop, of the millrace turned the paddles of the mill wheel. At Hall's mill, a wooden trough, or flume, carried water from the millrace to the wheel, where a gate was raised or lowered to control the flow of water into the pit beneath the wheel. The forebay was the area beneath the flume, just in front of the control gate.

Hall's attention to the forebay suggests that this was an undershot wheel; that is, the water struck the paddles near the bottom of the wheel. (With an overshot wheel, a flume carries water to the paddles at the top of the wheel.) Gravity carried the water past the wheel and down the millrace to re-enter the Elkhart below the mill. Shafts and gears transmitted power from the water wheel to the millstones, which ground the corn and wheat.[12]

During this time, the children Florence and James became ill with fever and chills. Sam Sharp, Roberta, Nellie, and the slave couple John and Jemima sickened also. By Thursday, July 23, Hall himself was suffering from chills and fever and wrote "in fact my house is now a perfect hospital." Although Florence may have been stricken with typhoid fever, according to Hall (Wednesday, July 15), the others showed symptoms of malaria, transmitted by mosquitoes breeding in the millpond. The first symptoms occur ten days to four weeks after infection and repeat in cycles of forty-eight to seventy-two hours. Chills, fever and sweating, headache, nausea and vomiting, muscle pain, and anemia are a few of the symptoms. Quinine was used to treat malaria, but the blockade had cut off supplies of medications.[13]

By the time everyone except Jemima had recovered (Monday, July 27), water in the millpond had fallen to such a low level that the mill could not operate. Two days later "some person went to the upper mill and pulled up the gates, thereby giving me the benefit of their whole head of water." Although the water immediately filled the millpond, by the next day (Thursday, July 30), the water had drained away, and the millpond returned to the previous low level. On Sunday, August 2, Hall noted that Florence and both Conny and Jemima were again sick with fever, and he wrote, "I am satisfied that it is the influence of the millpond, that produces so much sickness in my family."

While battles raged in Vicksburg and Gettysburg, Hall and his family remained isolationist in philosophy and practice. Sam Sharp rode to Crockett on Friday, July 3, "to have his name stricken from the Militia roll." The next day, Hall himself was "drafted in Crockett to serve with the Militia." On Monday, July 6, Hall drove the buggy to Crockett, where he "procured a Surgeon's certificate and was discharged from the Militia, so far as the Surgeon could do so."

One month later (Monday, August 3), Hall and Sam attended the election for state officers. "Be it remembered that I voted for T. J. Chambers for Governor because I am opposed to all those who advocate Military necessity as paramount to the Constitution and laws of the land." Hall was probably referring to the Constitution of the Confederate States of America, which was based upon the U.S. Constitution. Chambers lost the election to Pendleton Murrah, Texas' last Confederate Governor (1863-1865).[14]

It appears contradictory that Hall, who had served as provost marshal in Liberty, now avoided being drafted into the militia. It may be that, like many others at the beginning of the Civil War, he thought the fighting would be concluded in one or two battles and a new Southern nation would be established within a few months. Southerners generally believed that states which had voluntarily joined the Union could voluntarily leave it, and underestimated the North's determination to hold the country together. As the war continued, soldiering lost its romantic, adventuresome appeal. It may be, too, that Hall learned of the devastating Confederate losses at Vicksburg and Gettysburg in July, knew that the Confederacy was now divided at the

Mississippi River (which was controlled by the Union Army), and hoped for a diplomatically accomplished peace. Whether or not his philosophy had changed, Hall had no intention of leaving home.

The balance of the summer and early fall passed quickly. For example, on Sunday, July 19, Hall wrote, "I let all the negroes attend a protracted meeting of the Methodist Church, held at the Elk Hart meeting house. I should not suppose that they were benefited much by their visit, although as I learn, there was plenty of hollo-ing and whooping on the occasion."

On Wednesday, July 22, Martin "with the wagon & 5 yoke of oxen, loaded with five bales of cotton, started for Huntsville." Martin belonged to Joshua because, Hall added, "John went down to Father's to work." (That is, John went to Joshua's to work while Martin was away.) The penitentiary was buying cotton from planters to make cloth. Two days later, Sam Sharp, riding Gladiator, started for Huntsville "to attend to the procuring of some domestic [cloth] from the Penitentiary." He returned on Tuesday, July 28, with 150 yards of "Cotton cloth" for Hall's family and the same amount for Mahala and Joshua's family. "The wagon got down to Huntsville after much trouble and the loss of two yoke of oxen, which escaped and returned home."

Wednesday July 29th 1863. Today the boys quit splitting boards and commenced pulling fodder, which required their immediate attention. I ground 19 bushels of corn and 5½ bushels of Barley. I was enabled to grind this much because some person went to the upper mill and pulled up the gates, thereby giving me the benefit of their whole head of water. Roberta came up but did not tarry long. weather clear & hot, with indications of rain. Ther: 95°. At midnight the wagon arrived from Huntsville, with the things obtained there by Sam. It had very good success in the homeward trip.

The boards were needed "to cover some cabins" (Monday, July 27).

Thursday July 30th 1863. Today the boys are still at work pulling fodder in the lower field. I assisted the little woman in pealing [peeling] *peaches to dry for winter's use, thus "making hay while the sun shines." Sam and Nellie drove my horse and buggy down to Mother's and while there Sam paid over to Father the balance in Money that he obtained from the sale of two bales of cotton to the Penitentiary after the 150 yards of cloth was deducted. These two bales of cotton I loaned to Mother, and are to be by her paid back to me and delivered to me at the mills, they weighed 905 lbs gross. In consequence of the low stage of water in the pond, I was unable to grind any corn. weather changeable and hot: Ther: 94°.*

These passages indicate that cotton was the medium of exchange even within families.

On Friday, August 14, Hall noted, "In consequence of a continued dispute and argument between Father and myself in relation to the distance from the mill to his house, I concluded to measure it. Sam assisted me; we commenced at the mill door[.]" They conducted the survey in *varas*, a Spanish unit of length, usually interpreted to be about 33 inches.[15] By the end of the day, they had measured 5,125 *varas* from the mill to the gate at Joshua's home, a total distance of approximately 2¾ miles. The distance had previously been estimated to be two miles. Thus the "vexed and disputed point" was settled.

Work on the mill and the levee continued intermittently. As if the repairs and maintenance were not enough, Hall wrote on Tuesday, September 1, that a "drove of about 600 beeves got into the mill pond and done considerable damage to the levee, tearing away a portion of it, and utterly destroying my boat." A week later (Tuesday, September 8), he bought three beef steers "that are now bogged down in the mill pond[.]" They bore C.S.A. and "other brands not now recollected" (Tuesday, September 8).

Both Hall and Sam Sharp ground corn and wheat, but for several days the mill pond contained too little water, and work stopped. The hands pulled and stacked fodder and hay, worked on the road from Hall's Bluff to the mill, chopped and hauled logs for a cotton storehouse which they then built, and collected pine to be burned in a tar kiln. Bill Hicks built two kilns; the first was unsuccessful, but the second worked very well.

Illness described as chills and fever passed through the family and the slaves, and both Hall's son James (Friday, August 14) and Sam (Sunday, August 23) suffered from cholera. Because of so much illness and repeated bouts of fever and chills, little James, called Jimmy, looked "very bad" (Wednesday, September 2). Even Florence was "very much reduced from her sickness" (Friday, September 11). By the time of Jimmy's first birthday (Thursday, October 8), because of his continual illness, Hall wrote, "he is not as well grown or as forward as Fawn [Florence] was at his age. I am thankful however that he is as well as he is." A few days later (Monday, October 19), Florence turned three years old, and Hall noted that "she is very well grown for her age." Sam and Nellie's son James, "the little Major," also suffered from chills and fever (Wednesday, August 26). Illness spread among the slaves as well. Carroll and Clara, both around age nine, were so sick that Hall sent for Dr. Murchison, and Fawn again had fever (Thursday, September 10). All three recovered, but Jimmy had another chill and fever (Monday, September 14). The children and several of the slaves continued to be sick with chills and fever, probably malaria, throughout the fall.

Hall owned at least nine slaves: Bill (Tubbs), Bill Hicks, John, Rachael, Conny (sometimes spelled "Conney"), Jemima, and the children Carroll ("Wolf") and Clara. There were two women named Louisa, but one may have belonged to Joshua. Within his own family were himself and Margaret, their children Florence and little James, plus Sam and Nellie Sharp and their son. Hall was responsible for the health, work, and well-being of all of them.

On Wednesday, September 9, Hall rode his horse Ratler "to Crockett and back in order to get released from Conscription, but did not succeed[,] in consequence of which I got on a slight bender." Hall returned to Crockett on Saturday, September 12, to get a discharge, but his old acquaintance L. W. Cooper "had been removed" and the new enrolling officer, H. W. Beeson, refused to take action until the following Monday. Although traveling to

Crockett had been a waste of time, while there he bought tobacco for $82.50 and one dollar's worth of pink root, which was thought to clean parasites out of the intestines. Hall and Sam Sharp tried to obtain discharges on the following Tuesday (September 15), but failed. Two days later, Margaret began making clothing for Hall to take to the army "in the event that I am conscripted and have to go." On Saturday, September 19, however, Hall received his discharge from conscription because he was a miller, an occupation exempted from military service, and Sam Sharp received a discharge as assistant miller.

Although Hall objected to military service, he did not seem to object to paying taxes. He and Sam submitted their lists of taxable property to James T. Heflin, the war tax assessor (Wednesday, September 23 and Thursday, September 24). On Friday, November 27, Hall "rode up to the school house and while there paid my war tax of $1213—and Sam's tax of $9.50." He neither commented on nor complained about the amount.

Throughout the fall months, crops were gathered, and corn and wheat were ground at the mill. Hall, Sam, and the hands built two corn cribs and made repairs to the mill. Hall continued to buy cotton and to store it in his new "cotton house."

Visitors occasionally interrupted the work flow. On Tuesday, October 13, a Mr. Ramsdale "stopped at the house for his breakfast, he is on his way home from Waco and walked the whole distance in eight days making 25 miles per day, this is pretty good walking for a man

Born in Tennessee, James T. Heflin (1816-1900) settled in Houston County in 1846. Before the war, he had served as justice of the peace, county judge, and sheriff of Houston County. In May 1862, Heflin was elected captain of Company E, Gould's Battalion, made up from men from Leon, Houston, and Madison counties. Robert S. Gould was elected major. The battalion of five companies and about 525 men was originally attached to Burnett's Thirteenth Texas Cavalry. (The battalion later served in Randal's Brigade, Walker's Division, and participated in the battles of Mansfield and Pleasant Hill, Louisiana, and Jenkins' Ferry, Arkansas.) Heflin, however, was soon discharged from Company E due to illness. Appointed Confederate tax assessor for Houston County, he held that position throughout most of the war. He was re-elected sheriff in 1867. In 1886, Heflin moved to Austin to be near his family, where he died in 1900.[16]

65 years of age." One night (Tuesday, October 20), "a strange woman came to the house and remained all night, who she was or what she was doing I could not learn, but as she behaved herself[,] I let her depart in peace."

Friday October 23rd 1863. Today the boys were compelled to stop working in the mill field [preparing the field to sow barley and wheat] *to haul cotton from Mr. Leaverton's gin, he wanting the use of it for his own crop. They made 3 loads. I ground 18½ bushels of corn & killed two fine ducks. Weather changeable and cold, with a strong wind blowing from the North, at night there was a hard frost which killed nearly all kinds of vegetation.*

The field hands transported cotton back to Hall's on two additional days, making a total of ten loads. The cotton remained in storage for months, while Hall concentrated on growing food crops and tending to the mill. He did not express anger or disappointment about the cotton, since Corley's and McElroy's gins were nearby if he wanted to arrange for their use.

Winter weather began with the hard frost on October 23, followed by a norther with "drizzling rain" (Thursday, October 29) and another hard frost and freeze (Friday, October 30), which formed ice one-half inch thick. The rhythms of autumn continued with the hunting of ducks, geese, and deer, and Hall branded several calves. The family and the slaves made excursions to collect chinquepins (a type of chestnut), hickory nuts, and walnuts. Sam, who was almost barefoot according to Hall, made himself a pair of shoes. Hall re-built, painted, and lettered two signs for Mr. Cox, a business owner from Crockett.

On Thursday, November 5, Joseph Keen (see Chapter 1), Thomas Keen, and Sam Sharp "went out fire hunting at night and succeeded in killing one fine buck, they got separated in the woods, and Mr. Keen carried the deer home with him, so I lost the venison steak that I so much hungered after, better luck next time." Although disappointed, Hall was too fond of the elderly Joseph Keen to be angry with him. (Thomas Keen was most likely one of Joseph's eleven children.)

On Monday, November 23, Hall "marked and branded eleven calves, the mark being a crop and two splits in the right ear and a swallow fork in the left ear, and branded thus AE A. & E. united." Such marks and branding were necessary since livestock were not fenced.

While Margaret was away visiting Mrs. Bird (Wednesday, November 25), Florence "fell from the house gallery and dislocated the Radius bone of the right fore arm at the elbow joint." Hall sent for Dr. Murchison, who came to the house and spent the night and most of the following day. Fortunately, her arm healed without further incident.

Another unfortunate event occurred on Saturday, November 28, after a night of hard rain and freezing temperatures:

> In the morning early the ground was covered with sleet and when I went down to the stables I found my horse <u>Gladiator</u> had seriously hurt himself some time during last night, he died about 10. o'clock A.M. from the injury, thus perished the finest horse that was in the County, and one that I had refused twelve hundred dollars for. '<u>Poor old horse let him die</u>' and he has now ended his labors on earth. . . . I had the skin taken off of Gladiator, and intend keeping the same to remind me of him.

Friday December 11th 1863. Today the boys finished putting up 3 stalls in the stable and got them partially covered in. John is at work hauling wood. Sam is at work mending a fiddle for Martin. I ground 10 bushels of corn. Capt Peacock arrived from Parker's bluff on his way to the City of Houston. He remained all night with me. Weather cloudy & rather cool.

Martin, as noted earlier, belonged to Joshua Hall.

On the following day, Hall wrote, "Capt Peacock and I had a settlement for the rent of my house in Liberty which is he occupying. I paid him the freight bill on my furniture from Liberty to Hall's bluff, which was brought up on the steamer Alamo while he was commander of her. The freight bill was 183$ but I deducted 50$ from it for lost articles. He then paid me $167 balance on rent and I receipted him in full for the current years rent of said house, which expires on the 31st inst."

Parker's Bluff, a steamboat landing on the Trinity River in Anderson County, lay approximately eighty-seven river miles north of Hall's Bluff and a few miles above Magnolia. The small port included a ferry and cotton landing. In the fall, citizens from counties on either side of the Trinity came to Parker's Bluff to gather native pecans.[17]

Captain Tom Peacock, born in Pennsylvania, lived in Galveston in 1850. At the time, his age was given as thirty-three and his occupation recorded as "engineer." He owned real estate worth $3,000. Also listed are his wife Mary C. (age twenty-nine), born in Kentucky; and his children: Sarah M. (age nine), Mary A. (age seven), Charles (age four) and Anna (age four), all born in Tennessee. During Peacock's career, which spanned some thirty years, he "probably captained more Trinity River steamboats than any other person[,]" according to steamboat historian W. T. Block. In addition to the *Alamo*, two of his vessels mentioned by Hall were the *A. S. Ruthven* and the *Orizaba*. In 1860, the highly respected Peacock traveled to Pittsburg, Pennsylvania, "to build a new boat for the Liberty and Galveston trade." Throughout the Civil War, he collected and transported supplies to Confederate troops along the Texas coast. Beginning in November 1870, Peacock, who lived in Galveston, received a pension of $4 per month for a gunshot wound to the right hip sustained during the war. It is not clear what Tom Peacock's relationship was to Isaac Peacock, or to other Peacock family members living in Crockett and Houston County.[18]

Hall's family continued to grow. On Tuesday, December 15, Margaret gave birth to a daughter at 11:30 in the morning. Mrs. Bird, Mahala Hall, Nellie Sharp, and James Hall, with the help of the slave woman named Rachael, were present at the delivery. Hall notes that he sent for Dr. Murchison, "who came but as usual too late to be of any service in his profession, he remained for dinner and then left for home." Two days later, they (Hall wrote "we") named the baby Josephine Martha. Mr. Keen came to see "the little new responsibility," and Joshua also came to see "the little stranger" (Friday, December 18).

As Christmas drew closer, Sam and their neighbor Mr. Keen killed six hogs, which the slaves cut up and salted down (Saturday, December 19). On the same day, Sam killed two turkeys, and Hall bought two bushels of pecans at $6 per bushel and exchanged flour for them at 50 cents per pound, but does not say with whom he made the trade, although it may have been with Mahala, since she was there to help Margaret.

In Crockett two days later, Hall bought one gallon of whiskey for eighty dollars, one ounce of oil of sassafras for $5 per ounce, and one pound of candy for three dollars. "I record these prices for the benefit of those that come after me, in order that they may see some of the benefits that war brings upon the Country and people." Dated Monday, December 21, the journal entry clearly expresses Hall's frustration with the price increases.

He also left "15 pairs of russet brogans" with L. E. Downes for him to sell. Hall did not say where he obtained so many pairs of brogans, but such heavy duty work shoes were generally worn by slaves and were also used for military footwear.

In preparation for Christmas, Hall sent John "across the Trinity river with Father to Rives' still after some whiskey, but they did not get any, they left my demijohn and wallet over there, which will cost another trip." Two days later (Thursday, December 24), Hall again sent John "over to Rives' still after the demijohn & wallet also for some whiskey but he did not get any in consequence of the still house having been robbed the night before."

Although Hall did not mention it in the journal, John must have returned with the demijohn and wallet. "Times are quite brisk at the house preparing for Christmas dinner."

Friday December 25th 1863. Today being Christmas, all order of business was suspended, and we all went in for a regular jollification. I had with me to partake of our Christmas dinner, Father, Mother, Capt Peacock [on his way from Liberty to Parker's Bluff], *Mrs Bird, Mr Leaverton, and sundry others besides the home folks, the egg nogg flowed freely and all went off as merry as a marriage bell. To close the scene at night the negroes had a ball in the yard by moonlight, they touched the light fantastic toe and were as happy as happy could be. If Lincoln should succeed in his mad project and for which he is now prosecuting his unholy war, for their emancipation, he will only plunge them into abject missery* [misery] *from their now happy condition. Weather changeable & cool.*

Many Southerners deplored the institution of slavery even as they needed black men and women to work the land and handle domestic chores. As part of this interdependent relationship, Southerners took responsibility for the welfare of their slaves, who relied upon them for housing, food, medical attention, and safety. Unfortunately, because slaves were purchased, they were still considered property. Yet sometimes strong personal relationships developed between whites and blacks, and men like Bill Hicks, who became Hall's miller, escaped the drudgery of field work.

Hall's statement shows that he understood how emancipation could cause hardships for the former slaves. As would be seen after the Civil War, the lack of education, training, and experience beyond that of field or domestic work, plus unfamiliarity with working for wages left the newly freed blacks vulnerable to depredation, mistreatment, and poverty. Hall did not acknowledge the slaves' natural desire for freedom, but he did recognize the interdependence of the two races. Hall worked side-by-side with his slaves on a daily basis. He knew them as individuals and worried that they would not be able to thrive on their own if suddenly thrust into the world. At the end of the war, however, Hall accepted the new reality, and several of the former slaves remained with him and his family until his death.

On Saturday, December 26, Hall gave everyone a holiday until the following Thursday (December 31) and allowed Bill to ride one of the mules "across the river to see his old mistress Mrs Tubbs." Bill returned two days later (Monday, December 28) with a bell that had been stolen from one of Hall's oxen while the ox had been "running over there." (Mrs. Tubbs may have been the widow of Elisha Tubbs or the wife of Jesse Tubbs.)

Joshua, Mahala, Nellie, and Bill Hicks rode to Crockett (Tuesday, December 29) "to purchase some of the goods imported by Capt. Stubblefield from Mexico." Hall worked at the mill, while Sam stayed at the elder Halls' homestead to be "Company and protection for the children." Everyone returned the next day, soaked with rain, and that night "a hail and snow storm passed over, leaving the ground covered with a coat of snow two inches deep, the surface of which was hardly frozen over." They all stayed overnight at Hall's.

Thomas Sharp also arrived on Wednesday, December 30, bringing eighty-four bushels of wheat to the mill, "he too was soaked both internally and externally . . ." In 1870, Sharp was enumerated in Rusk, Cherokee County, as a farmer, age forty, born in Alabama. His wife Martha (age twenty-one) was born in Missouri. James (age twenty-one) and Frank (age nineteen) were born in Tennessee. If her age is noted correctly, Martha was a second wife. Thomas Sharp was related to Mahala Hall through her late husband John Marshall Sharp.[19]

Thursday December 31st 1863. This morning the ground was covered over two inches deep with snow. Father, Mother and Mr Thomas Sharp all left, the two former for home, and the latter for the wheat region. Sam and I ground 6 bushels of corn & 10 bushels of wheat. In the evening the boys commenced work after their Christmas holliday. Weather clear and bitter cold, the mill pond being frozen entirely over one inch thick, and it continued to freeze all day even in the sunshine. At night it froze all the little woman's eggs in my room, although I kept a large fire in it throughout the entire night. It is decidedly the coldest spell of weather that I have ever experienced in the State of Texas, after a residence of 28 years.[20]

Thus closes my notes for the month of December and also for the year 1863, just passed and gone and now numbered with the things that were, whether the Almighty will spare me to chronicle the daily events of the incoming year is more than I know, but trusting in Him, I shall enter upon the pleasing task, which is useful as a reference and may be profitable to those who have an interest in me.

Chapter 5

1864

At the beginning of 1864, the Union Army occupied Brownsville and planned to move upriver as far as Laredo. The Federals also held Matagorda Island and the mainland opposite the island, as well as the town of Indianola, and naval vessels shelled military posts along the coast as far northward as Caney Creek and the Brazos and San Bernard rivers. A Union invasion of Texas appeared imminent and unstoppable.

Friday January 1st 1864. This being the first day of the current year, I commence my notes of the events that take place immediately around me, and in which I have any interest. The boys are at work chopping and hauling wood, which is very essential during the present cold spell. Sam & I ground 17 bushels of corn and 10 bushels of wheat. Weather clear and bitter cold. I think somewhat colder than yesterday. I thought I would freeze at night although I kept a fire in my room the whole time.

Work continued the next day, in spite of the bitter cold; the millpond was frozen an inch thick. On Sunday, January 3, Hall remained indoors "writing up this note book and hovering around the fire, it being a cloudy, dark, gloomy and misty day, so uncomfortable as to prevent one from stirring about. I weighed my daughter Josephine, who weighed 9½ lbs.[,] rather light compared with the other children."

Hail and snow followed (Monday, January 4), and the millpond remained frozen one inch thick through Saturday, January 9. The hands worked "covering in" the stables (Tuesday, January 5 through Saturday, January 9), and resumed after cutting up and salting down pork (Thursday, January 14 and Friday, January 15). One of the hands, whom he did not name, kept the fires going, a full time job (Friday, January 8). Hall ground wheat and corn at the mill. Sam and several of the men hunted for their free-ranging hogs and drove up six, then killed and cleaned them (Sunday, January 10 and Monday, January 11). Mahala sent one hog to James on Saturday, January 9, and Joshua sent two on the following day. After finding three more hogs, which belonged to Joshua, Sam was given half the meat "for his trouble in hunting and killing them[,]" (Tuesday, January 12).

Captain Tom Peacock, on his way from Parker's Bluff to Houston, spent the night of Sunday, January 10, with Hall. The next day, James gave him twenty dollars in gold to buy a gutta percha "band" (today termed a belt) for the flour mill. Gutta percha was the rubbery sap of an evergreen tree found only in the islands of Malaysia, and its waterproof quality made it ideal for industrial use. Captain Peacock returned on Friday, January 29, with a secondhand gutta percha "band" he purchased for $12 per foot; "just think of it," Hall wrote, "when in good times or before the war, it could have been purchased new for 50 cents per foot."

When the Civil War began, patriotic Confederates sincerely believed that the war would be a short one, their philosophy of states' rights would prevail, and they would create a new nation. Many Confederate officers, such as General Robert E. Lee, had spent their careers in the U.S. military and were effective and popular leaders. Southerners, defending their home territory and led by experienced officers, believed their honor, tenacity, energy, and devotion to their cause would make them truly invincible.

In 1861, Texas men could choose whether to enroll in the Confederate Army or the Texas State Troops (state militia). Among the thousands who enrolled, many chose the Confederate Army, while others joined the militia in order to remain close to home. Generally, the men who signed up for the militia were motivated by the desire to protect their families and personal or economic interests, to guard the state from invasion, or to serve on the Texas frontier.[1]

During the 1850s, the U.S. Army created a line of forts along the Western frontier of Texas to protect settlers from attacks by Indians. The soldiers from these forts were withdrawn as part of the surrender agreement between Brigadier General David E. Twiggs and Texas Ranger Ben McCulloch, representing the Texas secession convention's Commission on Public Safety. That left approximately fifty thousand frontier settlers without any military protection from raids that resulted in kidnappings, injuries, and deaths. The Confederate government failed to understand the depth of the need for frontier troops. Indeed, the Confederate secretary of war in 1861, Leroy P. Walker, authorized only one cavalry regiment to guard the entire Texas frontier, a large geographical area extending the length of the state. To save Texas the cost of supplying and maintaining these troops, Governor Edward Clark in 1861 recommended their transfer to the Confederate military, who would pay the costs but allow the troops to remain on the frontier.[2]

Fearful that the Confederate military would remove the cavalry regiment from frontier service in 1862, the Texas Legislature formed a Ranger company called the Frontier Regiment, which would be state-supported. The legislature was willing to allow the Frontier Regiment to be transferred to the Confederate military, with the understanding that the Regiment would remain on the frontier. Although the Confederate Congress approved the measure, President Jefferson Davis vetoed it. In April 1862, Davis called for the conscription of men between the ages of eighteen and thirty-five for three years of military duty. The law was amended in September of that year to include men up to the age of forty-five. The Texas Frontier Regiment remained state-supported and in active service until early in 1864.[3]

Texas State Troops served on the frontier and along the coast. Governor Francis R. Lubbock maintained the desire to transfer the troops to the Confederate Army, but keep them posted in Texas. However, the Confederate government would not guarantee these troops would remain in Texas, and Lubbock permitted them to be assigned to Confederate service. More state troops had to be recruited. This caused a great deal of confusion and placed "the state militia into a position of disorganization . . . By 1863, resistance to military enlistment was very strong in many parts of Texas . . . Desertion ran high in many parts of the state, and in many areas new recruits refused to travel outside the state, even to Louisiana." Reasons for difficulties in conscripting troops varied. From a dislike for military life to increasing unhappiness with or distrust of Confederate policies, men sought ways to avoid conscription.[4]

On July 4, 1863, Union forces captured Vicksburg, Mississippi, thereby gaining control of the Mississippi River and dividing the Confederacy into two separate parts. Leaders in Confederate states west of the Mississippi could no longer depend upon support from or even communication with the government in Richmond, Virginia. In some of the Western states, men whispered of secession from the Confederacy. To prevent this, the Confederate government in Richmond intensified the power of the Trans-Mississippi Department. When the Department was created in May 1862, initial commanders Brigadier General Paul O. Hébert followed by Major General Theophilus H. Holmes subdivided the Western states into ungainly districts and subdistricts. In February 1863, President Jefferson Davis appointed General Edmund Kirby Smith to head the Department. Kirby Smith reorganized the Department into three military units: the Ordnance Bureau, the Subsistence Bureau, and the Quartermaster Bureau. The Department became known as "Kirby Smithdom."[5]

Governor Pendleton Murrah, who took office in November 1863, recognized that there was a great deal of confusion in regard to conscription. "What bothered them [Texans] is that when their initial stint in the state militia ended, they were often transferred into the Confederate army. This move was made without their consideration, and troops were left without the opportunity to decide whether they wanted to return to state service or actually serve in the Confederate army." Greater than Murrah's concern for the war was his intention to protect the people and interests of the state. As the war continued, "enrolling officers, company captains, and citizens" wrote to Governor Murrah to reiterate "that the troops they raised were strictly for home protection and were not to be transferred into Confederate service or taken out of the state."[6]

Governor Murrah was not as willing as former Governor Lubbock had been to conscript men or send militia troops to the Confederate Army. Murrah wanted to keep the militia troops an additional six months past their enrollment time for duty within the state, and on December 16, 1863, the state legislature passed the "Act to Provide for the Defense of the State," which authorized him to do so and empowered him to call up the militia "now remaining at home." Among other provisions, the Act called for men currently enrolled in the militia but not "in the field" to join their units and to have a reorganization of company and field officers when the current enrollment term expired. The Act defined how three-month furloughs were to be organized. And the Act allowed the governor to place the militia under the orders of the Confederate military in Texas and to be paid and equipped by the Confederate military, but the militia would not be sworn into Confederate States service. The militia would, in fact, remain in the control of the governor, who could withdraw or disband the militia at any time. This act was to remain in force until the end of the war.[7]

The Defense Act incensed General John B. Magruder, in charge of the Military District of Texas, New Mexico, and Arizona, who was especially upset about the provision for rotating, three-month furloughs. Having convinced the state legislature in 1863 to approve a militia enrollment of some ten thousand men, who could be transferred to Confederate service if needed, Magruder could not abide the loss of one-third of them to furloughs. In January1864, Magruder stated his objections to Murrah in a letter composed by Magruder's judge advocate general, Colonel John Sayles. Murrah replied that Magruder should consider the militia a "volunteer aid." General Edmund Kirby Smith informed Murrah that only President Jefferson Davis had the authority to "suspend" Confederate conscription laws, even for frontier defense.[8]

"An Act to Provide for the Protection of the Frontier" established the frontier organization that remained in place until after the war. The first of the Act's thirteen sections stated that citizens of the frontier counties were liable for military duty and were to be organized into companies of twenty-five to sixty-five men. The second section permitted the governor to divide the counties into three districts, with each one commanded by a major of cavalry. Every soldier had to be a citizen of the district in which he served and would have to provide his own horse, gun, ammunition, and ten days' worth of provisions. During field rotation, at least one quarter of the men in each county would be in the field at any one time. Subsequent sections dealt with desertions and with payment from the state "at least once in every four months." Section 12 provided that the governor could turn the Frontier Regiment over to Confederate States service, but "only after the Confederate Commander accounts for the value of property being turned over." Finally, Section 13 gave the governor the authority to keep these troops on the frontier if there was an invasion. The act passed on December 15, 1863.[9]

These two acts placed Governor Murrah and the state into conflict with Confederate conscription laws and the two generals, Magruder and Kirby Smith, who met with Murrah early in 1864 in order to come to an understanding. Murrah held firm, maintaining state authority over conscription, but anyone who wanted to join the Confederate Army could do so.[10]

Due to a shortage of manpower after the huge losses at Vicksburg and Gettysburg in 1863, and the imminent Red River Campaign, on February 17, 1864, the Confederate government again modified the age requirement to include men between seventeen and fifty, who were to serve in their home states. In early April, as Union generals Frederick Steele in Arkansas and Nathaniel Banks in Louisiana led armies toward the Texas border, Governor Murrah relented. Texas State Troops not posted on the frontier were transferred to Confederate service.[11]

Even before the new conscription law took effect, Hall once more faced being drafted into the Confederate Army. On Thursday, January 14, he rode his horse Rob to Crockett "and while there was again arrested by the conscript officer, when they will get through conscripting me God only knows, for one set of officers pulls down as fast as the others set up. I however after much difficulty obtained another discharge, but how long it will last I cannot say." When Hall returned home, he found Dr. Murchison and Mahala "in attendance upon Nellie, whose symptoms [of miscarriage, begun the day before] are more aggravating."

Friday January 15th 1864. Today the boys are still at work on the stables. In the evening while Sam & I were running the mills a file of soldiers rode up and arrested us, and forthwith shut up my mills and marched us off to Crockett like common felons, when we reached Crockett we were imprisoned in the Court house and a guard mounted over us. We were not allowed any fire or food, neither were we permitted to converse with any person. So we were kept, without any charge against us but upon mere suspicion that we were liable to conscription. So much for our boasted rights as Southren [*sic*] *gentlemen and for the causes which led us to sever our connection with the old government. Had I been thus treated by the Yankees I could have borne it all without complaint for I could not have expected any thing else, but coming from those who ought to be our guardians instead of our oppressors comes exceedingly hard, and not well calculated to make good and true soldiers to the Confederacy. I predict that it is but the beginning of the reign of military despotism and will brake* [break] *down our once happy land of freedom. I was again discharged late in the night but how long before I am again arrested God only knows: Sam however was kept in close confinement all night. Weather clear & cold.*

Saturday January 16th 1864. Today I am still in Crockett and Sam is still in confinement, and as I said in yesterday's notes on no charge, but mere suspicion that he is liable to conscription. The reign of military despotism is now complete, and a man not in the army dares not say that his life is his own or that he owns one dollars worth of property. I left Crockett late in the evening after having failed to obtain Sam's release, upon my arrival at home I found as I had previously expected that Nellie had miscarried, this catastrophy was hastened by the cruel and brutal arrest of her husband. If the agents of the Government think this is the proper way to make good soldiers for its armies by dragging husbands from wives, who are almost at the point of death, I must humbly beg leave to differ with them. Dr. Murchison and Mother were in attendance upon Nellie. At night Sam came home to see his wife[,] *having been released upon his parole to return on Monday next. Dr. Murchison & Mother remained all night. Weather changeable & cold, with a hard frost at night.*

The following day passed quietly. Nellie began to improve, and Dr. Murchison left.

Hall rarely expressed such rage on paper, and he had barely calmed down on Monday, January 18, when Sam returned to Crockett on Ratler and "was conscripted and put into the army of the Confederacy Sans Serimonia." Hall gave him one hundred dollars that day and sent Bill Hicks to Crockett with another one hundred dollars plus Sam's clothing on the following day. Sam left for Marshall in northeast Texas on Wednesday, January 20.[12]

Nellie soon recovered, and work became routine at the farm. Margaret kept her garden, and with Sam away, Hall spent his days at the mill. Mahala sent two shoats and three turkeys to Margaret and, in apparent exchange, Hall gave Mahala thirty pounds of lint cotton (Friday, January 22). The next day, Hall noted that the men had finished "covering in" the stables, a project that began on Tuesday, January 5. For a week in late January, the weather turned warm and pleasant, and the men began to prepare the bottom field for spring planting. While Bill Hicks was busy "covering in" the corn cribs (it is unknown how many there were), Hall ground wheat and corn at the mill. The men assisted Hall with repairs to the mill by raising the runner stone (Wednesday, January 27) and helped clear the road between Hall's Bluff and the mill (Saturday, January 30).

On Monday, February 1, they had to raise the "mill stone" again so that Mr. Keen, the blacksmith, could repair the "mill irons." (The men would have used a hoist with a block and tackle to raise the stone.) According to milling expert Daniel Seifu, the "irons" were most likely the vertical shaft through the millstones and/or five to seven iron parts that worked adjacent to each other beneath the bed stone. Since the mill had stood idle for several years, rust may have damaged the shaft, or the parts may have simply worn out. Until they were repaired, Hall could not grind any corn, but he did grind seven bushels of wheat. Mr. Keen made the repairs, but when the runner stone was placed in position, the millstones did not perform well and the runner had to be raised again (Wednesday, February 3). Hall and Bill Hicks worked on the mill and "got it in pretty fair running order" (Friday, February 5).[13]

When Margaret was not working in her garden or taking care of her chickens, she made (or supervised the making of) clothing. At times she got help from other women in the neighborhood. For example, Mrs. Bird brought Margaret "the piece of Jeans" she had been weaving (Wednesday, January 27), and Margaret went to her mother's "to get some thread sized and warped" (Saturday, February 6). ("Jeans" here refers to cloth rather than to the denim pants called "jeans" today.)

Visitors also came to the farm. Captain Tom Peacock and Mr. H. Fitzsimmons "arrived from Liberty on their way to Magnolia" (Friday, January 29). Although they left the next day, Fitzsimmons returned in March, and he would permanently change the family structure. Mrs. Beale, Nellie's mother, arrived for a visit on Tuesday, February 2, but two days later, Hall drove her in the buggy to Crockett, where she joined Dr. Stanwood who was also returning to Liberty. He did not tarry or spend the night with friends. "Having become perfectly disgusted with the military rule that is now prevailing in Crockett I left for home and reached there late in the evening[.]"

Hall's anger continued to simmer. On Sunday, February 7, Joshua informed James that he had sold James's horse Rat, "for which I do not thank him and require him to furnish me another horse [as] good." No further explanation followed.

While Hall maintained order, safety, and stability on the farm, his notes indicate an undercurrent of anxiety about events over which he had no control.

Monday February 8th 1864. Today the boys are at work plowing in the bottom field. Hicks is at work getting logs to build the little woman a hen or chicken house. The little woman rode up to Mrs Beazly's to get some weaving done. I ground 19½ bushels of corn. In Crockett there was a negro man by the name of Sam the property of Dr. J. A. Corley hung for attempting to commit a rape upon the person of Mrs Billy Moore. Weather clear & pleasant, but cold at night.

Mrs. Moore may have been the wife of W. E. Moore, assistant marshal and the 1860 census enumerator for the Elkhart District, according to census pages for 1860.

The next day, Mr. Hansel Coburn "passed on his way to Magnolia with a gang of impressed negroes in the government service."

Although Hall turned forty-five years old on Monday, February 22, he continued to be eligible for conscription. Whether or not he wanted any part of the war, it seemed to be coming ever closer to him.

Four soldiers with "Lane's Regiment of Texas Volunteers" spent the night of Thursday, February 11, with Hall. Walter P. Lane (1817-1892), a storekeeper from Marshall, enlisted with the Third Texas Cavalry and rose to the rank of lieutenant colonel. After the Third Texas Cavalry was dismounted in May 1862, Lane organized a new regiment, the First Texas Partisan Rangers. The four soldiers mentioned by Hall would have been members of Lane's Rangers, which fought in Louisiana in 1863 and in the Red River Campaign of 1864. Lane received a promotion to brigadier general on March 18, 1865. After the war, he returned to Marshall, where he was a merchant, and later served as a deputy federal marshal and as treasurer of Harrison County. He never married.[14]

A combination of anger and anxiety kept Hall on edge. On the day following the visit of the four soldiers (Friday, February 12), Hall asked Mr. Keen to come and "examine" a sow and some shoats (young pigs). The sow bore Hall's "mark," but the shoats bore that of J. H. Leaverton, whose property lay adjacent to Hall's (see Chapter 1). As critical as plowing the bottom field was for spring planting, Hall "kept the boys at home" the next day to help him mark "some pigs." On Sunday, February 14, he wrote, "Today Mr Leaverton came over and had the impudence not only to claim the shoats spoken of in my notes of Friday last, but to claim the sow too, and as a matter of course I will be compelled to prosecute him for hog stealing."

Still furious, on Monday (February 15) Hall rode to Crockett "for the express purpose of indicting Jim Leaverton for hog stealing before the

District Court, which commenced its session there today, but was persuaded out of it. I will now have to rely upon a [civil] suit to recover my property, which I can prove beyond the shadow of a doubt."

Hall did not mention the proposed lawsuit again.

In his entry for Saturday, February 20, Hall wrote, "Five soldiers stopped for dinner and 7 more stopped for the night." A week later (Saturday, February 27), Sam Sharp "arrived home on a furlough from the army, he is a member of Capt. Nunn's Company of Cavalry." During Sam's return, which he spent mostly indoors because of harsh weather, he visited with friends and family, he made shoes for Margaret, Nellie, Florence, and himself, and he paid an unidentified person at Hall's Bluff five dollars "for the mere knitting" of gloves after providing the materials (Sunday, March 6). Hall had Ratler shod by Mr. Keen for Sam "to ride to the Army."

Sam left on Wednesday, March 9, to rejoin his company, which was then at Crockett. As winter passed into spring, Sam returned for occasional visits, and more soldiers passed through the area in anticipation of the Red River Campaign. In April, Confederate victories at the battles of Mansfield

David Alexander Nunn (1836-1911) was born in Mississippi, attended law schools in Tennessee and Louisiana, and was admitted to the bar in Mississippi in 1857. Soon after his marriage to Helen Williams in 1858, he and his bride settled in Crockett, where Nunn was elected the city's first mayor in 1859. He organized a company of cavalry from Houston and Madison counties in 1861, and his Company I, Fourth Texas Mounted Volunteers, served under General Henry H. Sibley at Val Verde and Glorieta Pass, New Mexico. Unpopular with his men, Captain Nunn resigned after the Battle of Val Verde. Returning to Crockett, he organized a new cavalry company, which was assigned to Walker's Texas Division. Elected captain, Nunn remained with Walker's Greyhounds until the war ended. Nunn returned to his legal practice, and he served as a delegate to the 1875 convention that drafted a new Texas constitution.[15]

and Pleasant Hill, Louisiana, and Jenkins' Ferry, Arkansas, prevented the Union Army from taking control of the Trans-Mississippi area, including Texas.

After working with Bill Hicks on the mill irons (Thursday, February 4 and Friday, February 5), Hall taught him how to dress the mill stones. "Hicks is attending the mill," Hall wrote on Saturday, February 13, "I not being able to do so in consequence of a hurt I received on my fingers, he ground 12 bushels of corn." Two days later, Hicks ran the mill while Hall went to Crockett, but afterward Hicks returned to unfinished projects such as building a hen house for Margaret and "clearing up the yard" (Friday, February 19). He again helped Hall at the mill on Saturday, February 20. More and more often, Bill Hicks worked at the mill, usually assisting Hall, and during March, Hicks regularly operated the mill alone.

Hail, sleet, snow, and freezes occurred at night, requiring the slaves to do "nothing but make fires" (Monday, February 29). "At night it clouded up and rained very hard, which was attended with considerable thunder and lightning, and hail fell as large as a partridge egg" (Monday, March 7). Heavy rains swelled the creek. On Wednesday, March 9, Hall wrote that he took Joshua's and his own hands "and opened a new road to [Joshua's] residence from the mill. The rain having rendered the old road impassable." The following day, while Bill Hicks re-grooved the millstones, Hall joined the men to finish the new road (Thursday, March 10).

Mr. H. Fitzsimmons of Liberty arrived from Parker's Bluff (Wednesday, March 16) and stayed with Hall, helping him at the mill for about a week (until Thursday, March 24). After a brief trip to Magnolia, Fitzsimmons returned on Saturday, March 26. He and Hall went hunting and killed a deer (Sunday, March 27). Two days later (Tuesday, March 29), Fitzsimmons "deposited in the mill 3 sacks of flour for safe keeping and subject to his order." Fitzsimmons "left for his home in Liberty" on Wednesday, March 30. Although Hall did not explain the circumstances, months later (Monday, July 18), he wrote that Margaret "rode down to Mother's in the evening and brought up Fanny Fitzsimmons with her who has been entrusted to my care by her father to raise and take care of." Fanny Fitzsimmons would remain with the Halls for many years.

Although a Union invasion seemed imminent in January, almost all of the Union troops at Matagorda and Indianola left in March. About 1,200 remained at Brazos Island in South Texas near the Rio Grande. General John B. Magruder sent Colonel John S. Ford with 1,800 men to retake South Texas. After a skirmish with Union pickets at Las Rucias in June, Ford occupied Brownsville in July. A fight at Palmito Ranch in September resulted in a Confederate victory. Juan Cortina, military governor of Tamaulipas, Mexico, had previously closed Matamoros (opposite Brownsville) to the cotton trade. Cortina hated *gringo* Americans in general and Texans in particular, including Ford, who wrote, "One of Cortina's projects, set forth in some of his proclamations, was the reconquest of Texas." It is not clear when Cortina's hatred of Americans began, although Ford suggests it could have been at the end of the war with Mexico in 1848, when Cortina worked as a teamster for the U.S. Army's quartermaster department. However, throughout the 1850s, he and his followers conducted raids on South Texas ranches, killed residents without compunction, stole livestock, and escaped across the Rio Grande. By 1859, U.S. troops and Ford's Rangers forced Cortina away from the river and deep into Mexico. Even so, Cortina favored the Union effort to defeat the Confederates, and according to Ford, the Union Army offered Cortina a commission as brigadier general, which he declined. (Cortina was a supporter of Mexico's President Benito Juárez, who was also supported by the United States.) In September 1864, Cortina gave up Matamoros to a combined Imperialist (Mexican) and French army commanded by General Tomás Mejía. A consummate opportunist, Cortina quickly joined the Imperialists. General Mejía, a faithful adherent of Emperor Maximilian, was described by Ford as "an Indian of rather rugged features who had fought his way up from a low position to the top of the ladder. He was honest, sincere, and truthful. . . . In battle he was represented to be fearless, quick to perceive, and prompt to execute." Ford's friendly diplomatic relations with Mejía helped to restore the Rio Grande cotton trade, a desperately needed outlet for commerce. "He [Ford] had been on good terms with General Tomás Mejía, the Imperial commandant of the line of the Bravo [Rio Grande], a man of character and of distinguished bravery." Between September 1864 and May 1865, this area remained a calm, quiet Confederate stronghold.[16]

In the meantime, Texans and Southerners were fighting their own battle of supply and demand. The Confederate Congress passed a tax-in-kind act on April 24, 1863, which was revised on February 17, 1864. The tax-in-kind required farmers to give one-tenth of their crops to the Confederate Army. This included grain, rice, potatoes, sugar, molasses, bacon and salt pork, hay and fodder, wool, cotton, and tobacco. However, farm families were allowed to keep sufficient rations for subsistence. The amount of tithe due was determined by a local tax assessor. (If a farmer thought the amount too high, a third and even a fourth party could be called in to determine a fair assessment.) The farmer took his produce to a depot, to be located no more than eight miles away, within sixty days after the assessment. (If he failed to meet this deadline, the penalty would add up to fifteen percent of his crop.) If a farmer failed to pay the tithe, the district tax collector could issue a distress warrant to sell the farmer's property in order to collect the tax. Farmers turned over cotton, wool, and tobacco to Confederate Treasury agents for sale. Food and forage gathered as taxes were distributed to the military. In Texas, the produce was forwarded to state and regular troops, as well as to the Texas Cotton Office, which transported wagonloads of cotton to delivery points on the Rio Grande River. In 1864, food and forage from East Texas made its way to troops engaged in the Red River Campaign. The tax-in-kind remained in force until the end of the Civil War.[17]

Although Hall stated any no objection to the tax-in-kind, he held onto his cotton. He also used the mill to support the Confederate effort. On Tuesday, March 29, he "delivered upon the order of Capt. Peacock 4 sacks of flour weighing 386 lbs, which was put on a Government wagon." Peacock delivered corn and other provisions to Texas troops at Liberty and along the coast.[18]

In addition to providing his tax-in-kind to the Trans-Mississippi Quartermaster's Department (the Houston County post quartermaster was in Crockett), Hall sold or bartered cornmeal and flour with family and friends.

On Friday, April 8, a Mr. Bowman "came down from Parker's bluff with two Government wagons after corn. He brought me a demijohn containing 3 gallons of whiskey." Both Mr. Bowman and his whiskey were no doubt welcome. The next day, Hall loaded the wagons with "eighty bushels of shelled corn" and Mr. Bowman left for Palestine in Anderson County, just north of Houston County.[19]

A frost on April 9 destroyed Hall's corn crop. While the hands replanted the corn in the "lower field" (Monday, April 11), Bill Hicks and Hall ground five bushels of wheat. During the evening, however, "a hole broke in the levee, and carried away about one third of the same, in consequence of which I lost my entire head of water." Without steady water pressure, the mill could not operate.

Tuesday April 12th 1864. Today I was compelled to stop the boys from planting corn and put them to work on the levee. I succeeded in getting the hole stopped, when I ground 4 bushels of wheat & 3 bushels of corn. Nellie & Burt [Roberta] *came up and I vaccinated Pet, also the negro children. Three soldiers stopped for the night. Weather changeable & cool.*

Hall never explained how he had the knowledge and the means to vaccinate the children.

The men spent two days repairing the levee and returned to the lower field to replant the corn (Thursday, April 14).

Hall's friend W. A. (Billy) Stewart (see Chapter 4) "came out from Crockett with his wagon" (Wednesday, April 13), and Hall "let him have 5 bushels of corn and 4½ bushels of meal." He also gave Stewart one hundred dollars to repay a note signed by Sam Sharp. The two men "went fishing with fine success." Hall and Stewart were close friends and visited each other often.

On the same day, Sylvester Hall arrived with his wagon and "camped near the house, he is bound for the wheat region after flour." Sylvester Hall was the son of Mrs. Lavinia L. Hall, "hotel keeper" in Crockett. His father, John L. Hall, died in 1857. In 1860, Sylvester was twelve years old; by 1864, he would have been about sixteen.[20]

On Monday, April 18, he "rode up to the school house and paid Mr. Bodenhamer the war tax Collector my taxes also those of Sam Sharp." Franklin Douglas Bodenhamer (1813-1877), from North Carolina, had also served as sheriff of Houston County (1852-1854).

Others passed through Hall's farm, frequently heading to Magnolia, a steamboat landing on the Trinity River in Anderson County, about ten miles from Palestine and some fifty-six river miles above Hall's Bluff. Founded during the 1840s, the town was named for a large magnolia tree growing there. The town's greatest population, in 1863, numbered 800, with thirty-three blocks of homes and businesses that included cotton gins, the Haygood Hotel on the river, a livery stable, a warehouse, a general store, a blacksmith shop, and a ferry to take travelers across the Trinity. When the river measured too low for riverboats, flatboats carried cotton bales downstream to Liberty, where the goods were placed on steamers and transported to Galveston. In the spring, when the river ran deepest, steamers came all the way upstream to the Magnolia landing. The arrival of a steamboat was an exciting occasion, and people as far away as Palestine hurried to Magnolia to greet the travelers, salesmen, and entertainers who stopped there. Like many small towns, Magnolia declined with the coming of the railroads, and when the International and Great Northern Railroad bypassed the town during the 1870s, Magnolia disappeared.[21] In 1864, Magnolia was a significant destination point.

Among the most unexpected visitors Hall noted in his journal were Coushatta Indians, who passed through on the night of Sunday, April 17. Hall neglected to state their purpose, only that he "had to take care of four Coshatti indians."

The Alabama-Coushatta Indians originated in what is now the state of Alabama, which they began leaving in 1763. After a brief period of settlement in Louisiana, they drifted westward into Spanish Texas during the 1780s, adapting quickly to the area around the Big Thicket. Over time, they formed three communities along the Trinity River. At the request of the Alabamas and of local citizens, the State of Texas bought over 1,000 acres for a reservation in Polk County, where they began settling during the winter of 1854-1855. The Coushattas joined the Alabamas on that reservation in 1859.[22]

During the Civil War, the Alabama-Coushattas served in Company G, Twenty-Fourth Texas Cavalry at Arkansas Post, but did not participate in the fighting. They returned to Texas and reorganized into a cavalry company by Captain William H. Beazley (1837-1919) of Smithfield in Polk County, though they remained unattached to a regiment. In 1862, Captain Beazley and the Alabama-Coushattas assisted in the placement of obstacles in the Trinity River to block Union gunboats from ascending the river. In 1864, the company was attached to the Sixth Brigade, Second Texas Infantry. The Alabama-Coushattas built flatboats at Magnolia, then served as crewmen on the boats. They floated downstream, collecting produce and supplies from plantations along the Trinity. At Liberty, they turned over the produce and supplies, as well as the boats, to the Confederate military. Sons of the flatboat crewmen rode overland, bringing the crewmen's horses to Liberty for the return trip.[23]

Hall's reference to the Coushatta Indians meant that he looked after them (if they were tired or ill), fed them, and gave them directions to Magnolia, where they most likely built flatboats or worked as crewmen.

During the spring, friends from Crockett as well as a large group of ladies and gentlemen came to fish at the millpond. Hall himself "caught the largest trout that has ever been caught" at the pond, but did not state the size or weight of the fish (Monday, May 2). On Thursday, May 12, Hall "left home with John, the little wagon & mules and drove up to Parker's Bluff a distance of 27 miles," where he stayed overnight with a friend. While there, he bought two pairs of cotton cards for $150 and a barrel of whisky for $20 per gallon. He returned home the next day (Friday, May 13). A visitor who would have long-term involvement with the Halls was Captain B. F. Cameron, who stayed with the Halls that night and then left for "his quarters at Magnolia" the next day.

Captain Cameron appears frequently in later journal entries. He joined the Sabine Pass Guards, Second Brigade, Texas State Troops in Jefferson County as a private on April 20, 1861. This was one of the early military companies protecting the coast in and around Galveston.[24] Captain Cameron visited Hall again (Friday, May 20), stopping for dinner on his way down from Magnolia.

In between visits from friends and passing strangers, Hall built a loom and made a spool frame for Margaret and a lounge chair for himself so he could sleep outdoors, and he ground corn and flour at the mill. He sold Mahala one pair of cotton cards for seventy-five dollars, the same price he had paid for them at Parker's Bluff (Monday, May 16). Hall and Nellie drove to Hall's Bluff (Tuesday, May 17), where they visited with Mr. Stubblefield, and from whom Hall bought twenty pounds of sugar "in exchange for 1 Gal of whiskey."

William M. Stubblefield (age twenty-nine in 1860) was a farmer born in Tennessee. His wife "L. S." (age thirty) was also born in Tennessee. Stephen Stubblefield (age seventy-three) and his wife Elizabeth (age sixty-four) lived with them and their three children. William may have been a brother of steamboat Captain Thomas Stubblefield, who lived at Hall's Bluff. It is not clear which "Mr. Stubblefield" Hall meant in his May 17 entry.[25]

He wrote of other transactions as well. He "let Dr. Murchison have two Gals. of whiskey" (Friday, May 20), but did not mention whether it was in payment for medical treatment for his family or in friendship. He traded his father cornmeal for fourteen hams, weighing 192 pounds, "at the rate of one bushel of meal for four pounds of hams" (Monday, May 23). He had paid $150 for "10 plugs of tobacco or 5 lbs." in Crockett (Thursday, April 21) "or $15 per plug." These entries recorded the rising prices of everyday goods.

Sunday June 5th 1864. Today I rode my horse hawk up to Mrs Bird's & remained there for dinner. I learned from her the death of Silas E. Keen, who was wounded at the battle of Mansfield. Nellie and Burt came up to see the little woman, they did not remain long, as they left Mother sick and had to return to wait upon her. Burt rode hawk home, because the pony she rode up

[on] *became refractory & would not be governed by her. Weather cloudy and warm, with occasional showers of rain. Ther: 82°.*

Hall went to see Joseph Keen the next day, commenting that the elderly man was "very sick. . . ."

Illness again filled Hall's notes. Florence and Jimmy suffered briefly from fever, and Josephine for about a week beginning Monday, May 23, from "Cholera Infantum." Hall remained close to home, while Dr. Murchison attended to Josephine. Even Mahala became sick, and although Hall does not describe her symptoms, he obtained medicine for her from Dr. Murchison (Monday, June 6). When Hall delivered the medicine to Mahala that evening, he found her already improving.

Billy Stewart, Thomas Stubblefield, and W. E. Wingfield visited with Hall to go fishing (Monday, June 6 and Tuesday, June 7). Wingfield frequently visited Hall and fished at the millpond. On Tuesday, June 7, Hall noted that he "sent to Captain Waul the post quarter master at Crockett 120 lbs of bacon by Mr Wingfield, it being my tax in kind on bacon, to be used for the benefit of the army of the Confederate States." The tithe on hog meat was sixty pounds of cured bacon for each 100 pounds of salt pork. The revised tax law of February 17, 1864, permitted farmers to submit salt pork instead of the bacon, but it appears that Hall was paying the tithe according to the 1863 act.[26]

Although busy with gardening and making clothes, Margaret rode down to her mother's on Saturday, June 25, to visit Mahala's nephew and Margaret's cousin John Connell, Jr. (spelled Connelly by Hall), who had "just returned from the army." Connell's mother, Matilda T. Roberts, a daughter of Elisha Roberts, was an older sister of Mahala. In 1830, Matilda Roberts married John Connell, Sr., who died in 1834; she next married Samuel T. Allen, who died in 1838; and she married Thomas J. Allen about 1847. In 1850, she conveyed the land to Bell County that became the county seat, Belton. John Connell, Jr., born about 1833, became a successful farmer and stockman in Bell and Williamson counties.[27]

James Hall, along with Margaret, the children, and Nellie visited with Connell the next day (Sunday, June 26) at the home of Mahala and Joshua and reported, "while we were there, Toby went in swimming, and came near being drowned." (Toby, born in 1854, and his sister Roberta, born in 1852, were the children of Mahala and Joshua and therefore the half-brother and half-sister of James.) Connell left "for home riding Father's little mule pompy."

After a peaceful few days in which Nellie, Joshua, and Roberta attended "an instrumental & vocal concert" in Crockett (Wednesday, June 29), and friends from town came to visit the Halls, James began noting illness again. Little James, called Jimmy, suffered from "a hard chill & severe fever" (Tuesday, June 28), followed by "a severe attack of bilious fever" (Saturday, July 2). Dr. Murchison "came to see Jimmy professionally" (Saturday, July 2) and returned each of the following four days to check on his progress. Dr. Murchison gave Margaret two bottles of paregoric, an opium derivative with an additive of camphor. Morphine was the primary constituent. Dispensed as syrup, it was used for coughing and for diarrhea. On Monday, July 4, Hall wrote that Jimmy was "still very very sick and sinking rapidly under his disease." Obviously very worried, he "kept the boys home to attend around the house." The next day, however, Hall thought the "crisis of the disease" had passed and he now had "some hope of his recovery." Even so, Hall again "kept the boys home to attend around the house." Mrs. J. H. Leaverton and Mrs. Bird came to help in whatever way they could. Jimmy improved slowly.

Within a few days, Bill Hicks, Louisa, Conny, Wolf (Carroll), and Clara fell ill with fevers, followed by Florence, Josephine, John, and Bill (Tubbs). On Tuesday, July 12, Hall moved the family from "the mill place" to "the King house" for the rest of the summer because of so much sickness. He and Bill drove the wagon back and forth to transport their belongings to the house. When John and Bill grew sick, Hall drove the wagon himself. Bill Hicks worked at the mill. Hall and those who were able spent several days making the house "a little comfortable" (Wednesday, July 13). In late August

(Monday, August 29), Hall and the family cleaned the mill house, and on Thursday, September 1, the family moved home for the winter.

On October 13, 1860, Hall surveyed forty acres of land for Dr. Abner G. King, "out of the Sam Chairs headright & wrote for him the deed for the same, which was executed by Joseph Keen." On June 14, 1863, Hall bought from Dr. King "his place near Mr. Keen's, consisting of forty acres of land with the improvements thereon, for which I paid him 300$ and took his deed." The house was one of the "improvements" on that property. [28]

While at the King house, on Monday, July 18, Mrs. Bird "came up and spent the day. I cut all the hair off of her head as close as I possibly could in order to cure the tetter." Tetter was a type of skin disease, such as eczema, which caused a great deal of itching.

On the same day, Hall stated that Margaret "rode down to Mother's in the evening and brought up Fanny Fitzsimmons with her who has been entrusted to my care by her father to raise and take care of." Hall did not provide information about how or when she had arrived nor did he refer to any arrangements for formal adoption or financial assistance from her father. She blended smoothly into the family and remained with Margaret until 1870. How long she may have stayed with Margaret after that time is unknown.

Four days later (Thursday, July 21), Hall borrowed a horse from Mrs. Bird and rode to Crockett. There he bought one ounce of quinine for $300; one ounce of blue mass for forty-five dollars; five combs for fifty dollars; and two pounds of black pepper for sixty dollars. Quinine was used to treat malaria. Blue mass was a pill that combined mercury and chalk, in common use for a variety of illnesses, including depression. The high amount of mercury, however, could cause violence and aggression, due to mercury poisoning. Aggressive behavior stopped when the patient ceased taking blue mass. It appears that Hall was trying everything he knew to do to treat the cycles of illness. Hall could not prevent accidents, however, and on Friday, July 29, almost eight months to the day after the first injury, Florence "fell from the top of the fence and again fractured her right arm. . . ." Cared for by Dr. Murchison and Mahala, Florence soon recovered.

Hall frequently used the expression "missed his/her fever" indicating that sickness was so prevalent it became commonplace. There seemed to be no end to the cycles of ill health.

As it was for so many Southern families, adequate clothing remained a concern for the Halls. James built Margaret's large floor loom at the mill and had it brought to the house on Friday, July 22, and set up the next day, "ready for work." He also made a bench for her to use at the loom, which was powered by foot treadles. Mrs. Keen "came over and drew the thread in the harness and sley (a reed or comb-like device) of the little woman's loom and wove about ¼ yd of cloth."[29] Mrs. Keen returned the next day (Wednesday, July 27), and several times thereafter. Both Margaret and Nellie learned how to weave cloth.

On Sunday, July 24, Hall drove Nellie to Mrs. Keen's so that the women could go together to the Baptist church to attend the "funeral sermon of Silas E. Keen preached by the Rev. Mr Nash." On Thursday, July 28, Hall gave Mr. Keen fifty pounds of flour. Two days later, Hall gave the older gentleman one and one half bushels of meal, and he sent John to help Keen stack his fodder (Saturday, August 6). Keen had repaired Hall's rifle (Saturday, July 16) as well as an iron cook stove and a buggy spring (Monday, July 25) in return. Reliance on the barter system worked well among friends such as the Halls and the Keens during these hard times. It may also be that some of the activity at this time was a way to provide emotional support to Mr. and Mrs. Keen.

Margaret quickly became adept at weaving, and on Thursday, August 25, she removed twenty and one half yards of cloth from the loom. The next day, Mahala helped Margaret make a dress "to visit Crockett in." Margaret and James traveled to Crockett on Saturday (August 27) to buy "a few articles." Although Hall did not describe the town, it had been severely damaged by a fire on Tuesday, August 2. Not knowing about the fire, on Wednesday, August 3, Mahala and Nellie went to Crockett (where Nellie bought a saddle for Hall), and the slave John also went there to buy sugar and to deliver meal, flour, and eggs to Billy Stewart. When they returned, they brought news of the fire. In his journal entry for that day, Hall wrote, "I learned that Crockett was nearly consumed by fire on yesterday. The fire broke out about 10. O'clock A.M. and burnt until 2. O'clk P.M. consuming in all about 25 houses." By the time they traveled to Crockett in late August, the town must have been busily rebuilding.

On Monday, August 22, Hall wrote that he sent John "with his wagon & 3 yoke of oxen to the saline after salt." The Saline, in Anderson County, was a salt-producing area near Palestine (the Grand Saline was in Van Zandt County).

Salt had many more uses than to flavor food. It was necessary to preserve food such as "meat, fish, eggs, and butter. It was not limited to human need, but was also vital for animals, especially horses, to prevent foot and mouth disease." Salt was also necessary to cure hides for leather (shoes, saddles, harness, and other equipment). In December 1863, the Texas Senate authorized the state military board to set up saltworks in various salt-rich counties, and it authorized a budget of fifty thousand dollars. "Due to Texas's success in the salt venture, the Trans-Mississippi Department relied on the state to provide an adequate supply for its needs."[30] Even though Texas had more salt than other states, there was yet a shortage. Before the war, a great deal of salt used by Texans had come from Saltville, Virginia, which fell to the Union. Another primary source of salt had been discovered on Avery Island, Louisiana, but Union occupation of the area and transportation difficulties limited salt distribution from there. In South Texas, salt production was increased at two lakes, where salt had been collected for centuries, but a Union Army detachment destroyed the workings there in 1863.[31]

Salt was required in large amounts "to cure the thousands of barrels of meat destined for the troops in battlefields throughout the South and East. As the demand for salt increased, the price increased proportionately." Commodity prices from the *Houston Tri-Weekly Telegraph* and the *Galveston Tri-Weekly News* show the price of salt rising from .06 cents per pound in 1861 to .28 cents per pound in 1864.[32] James Hall was fortunate in that he could acquire salt so close to home.

Wool and thread were additional necessities, easier purchased than made at home. From merchant L. E. Downes, Hall retrieved (Thursday, August 11) some fifty-six "balls of thread being a part of what I left with him for sale." Hall gave Mr. Silas Morgan twenty dollars in specie to buy wool for Margaret's use (Monday, September 12).[33] Morgan, a fifty-six-year-old farmer from Huntsville, was traveling to the Saline for salt. He returned on September 19, bringing twenty pounds of wool. Hall paid him $3.50 per pound. After obtaining thread from Mahala (Tuesday, September 20), Margaret began to weave surcingles, bands that went around the body of a horse to hold blankets and saddles in position. She became ill with fever, however, and Hall finished the surcingles (Friday, September 23), then "warped and beamed and drew in a set of bridle reins, and commenced weaving them." He finished making the bridle reins the next day. While Margaret remained ill with fever for several more days, Hall wove a pair of suspenders for himself (Wednesday, September 28). Before the war, each of these items had been commonly available through merchants and saddlers.

On January 11, 1862, Governor Francis R. Lubbock and the Texas Legislature authorized the creation of the Texas State Military Board, composed of Governor Francis R. Lubbock, Comptroller C. R. Johns, and Treasurer Cyrus H. Randolph. Like the Confederate government, Texas had leapt into the war with insufficient financial strength. The purposes of the Board were to sell or trade state bonds for arms and powder, as well as equipment, clothing, and supplies such as coffee; to establish a foundry at Austin to make cannon; and to authorize factories to make percussion caps and small arms.[34]

To pay and equip state militia needed for defense of the frontier and the coast, as well as troops fighting in the war, the Military Board attempted to sell U.S. bonds, dating from 1850 in Europe. When that failed, the state began to purchase cotton, which had a ready market in Europe. The Military

Board created twenty-eight districts, with agents in sixteen, who contracted for the cotton, which would be purchased with bonds at eight percent interest, or "cotton certificates" that would be redeemable in bonds. If a planter insisted upon specie, the agent would have to purchase the cotton out of his own pocket. The cotton would be collected at depots and then transported overland to Brownsville.[35]

Cyrus Randolph

The Military Board also bought and sold cotton for equipment, arms, and powder and, as the war progressed, for medicines such as quinine and chloroform. Clothing was made at the penitentiary, but the machinery was wearing out and could not be replaced. With commercial cloth unavailable, spinning and weaving cloth became household industries. Orders from the Board for hand-held cotton and wool cards were continuous.[36]

During the early spring of 1863, the Confederate Congress passed bills that attempted to define the circumstances or conditions that permitted the impressment or the outright destruction of cotton by military officers. Impressed cotton would be paid for. Nevertheless, these restrictions upon their personal property rights offended many Southerners, and the military continued to impress cotton, as well as the labor of slaves. In March 1863, Lieutenant General Edmund Kirby Smith took command of the Trans-Mississippi Department, which included Texas, Arkansas, and Louisiana, in an overall reorganization of the military district in general and of the quartermaster's department in particular. Conflicts between Kirby Smith and Governor Pendleton Murrah soon developed.

On August 3, 1863, Kirby Smith "through illegal general orders established the Cotton Bureau to supervise the purchase, collection and sale of cotton within the Trans-Mississippi Department." The purpose was to sell the cotton for arms and supplies. Officials in Richmond, who knew the Cotton Bureau was not officially sanctioned, allowed it to continue. In late August, governors from the Trans-Mississippi states met with Kirby Smith at a conference in Marshall, Texas, and approved his authority over the cotton trade. Although the departmental office of the Cotton Bureau was in Shreveport, Louisiana, Kirby Smith authorized the establishment of "branch offices" in Houston and Monticello, Arkansas. The purpose of the Houston office "was to place Texans in control of the office to gain the trust of Texas planters. He gave orders for the Houston office to obtain, through either purchase or impressment, all cotton necessary to meet the demands of the army, . . ." He also had the authority to use military force, if necessary, to impress cotton. All of the field agents were instructed to report to Colonel William J. Hutchins.[37]

Kirby Smith and the Cotton Bureau established new rules for acquiring cotton. The Bureau would buy half a planter's cotton and exempt the remainder from impressment in exchange for Confederate specie certificates, redeemable later. The planter could sell the other half however he wished or he could obtain a permit from the Cotton Bureau to export his cotton. At the same time, the Confederacy passed laws to control cotton speculators in an effort to induce the planter to sell to the Bureau instead of to the state. However, planters had to bear the cost of transportation of the cotton to a depot, which they resented, along with the fear of impressment, and they lost faith in the financial management of the Confederate government.[38]

Although threatened with impressment, Texas planters held onto their cotton. Hutchins, however, did not blame the planters. In an open letter to the newspapers in December 1863, he stated the lack of cotton was due to "the various and conflicting orders issued by Kirby Smith and the government, the numerous government agents engaged in acquiring cotton, and the exorbitant rates stemming from the intense competition."[39]

Governor Murrah countered Kirby Smith and the Cotton Bureau with the "State Plan," in which the Texas Loan Agency would buy cotton with state bonds at seven percent interest. The state would transport the cotton to Brownsville, and since the state owned the cotton, it was exempt from impressment en route. At Brownsville, half of the planter's cotton would be returned to him, which he could then sell, and the other half would be bought by the state for bonds (guaranteed by land) at the prevailing price less the cost of transportation. Planters responded to the "State Plan" and by March of 1864 had sold almost half the total crop to the state.[40]

During the spring of 1864, cotton "was worth fifteen cents a pound [with a permit] and only eight cents per pound without the permit." Magruder, before the Houston office opened, restricted cotton exports across the Rio Grande, and after the office opened, he continued to issue orders regarding the trade in cotton, which conflicted with those of Kirby Smith or Hutchins. Confederate General Hamilton Bee, commanding in Brownsville in 1863 and lacking enough cotton to sell for supplies, "levied a 20 percent contribution stipulation on all cotton in Brownsville. Once the owner turned his cotton over to the government, he received a certain price in Confederate Treasury notes." However, Bee had the power to exempt "his loyal contractors" from this fee. Military officers "disregarded Confederate law prescribing the mode of impressment, and often confiscated cotton from individuals without proper remuneration and without proper evidence for claims." The plan offered by Kirby Smith "only complicated matters as military and Cotton Bureau officials all operated under their own legal and extralegal guidelines."[41]

Kirby Smith next issued new regulations to gain control of the cotton. After further disagreements, primarily based upon Murrah's insistence on state sovereignty, Kirby Smith met with Governor Murrah in July 1864 to resolve the matter. On July 19, Governor Murrah announced his acquiescence to Kirby Smith's argument, based upon the need of the army to sell cotton to procure supplies, and Murrah asked planters to sell their cotton to the Cotton Bureau's agents (but would no longer protect cotton en route to the border). On October 3, 1864, Kirby Smith ordered business relating to cotton to be placed under the umbrella of the new Trans-Mississippi Treasury Department. However, cotton continued to be exported under the "State Plan" through the winter of 1864-1865.[42] Chaos between the Texas and Confederate authorities continued.

The Texas State Military Board, created in 1862, became subject to harsh criticism, and a committee appointed by the legislature to investigate the records of the Board found that it had made many mistakes, but agreed that they were due to poor judgment rather than to any intent to defraud the state. Because of the heavy workloads of the state treasurer and comptroller, the Board asked to be on reorganized, and on April 12, 1864, the New Military

Board took office. Governor Pendleton Murrah remained on the Board, with two additional members to be appointed by him. The Board remained in office until the end of the war. An 1865 audit showed that the records of the Board were missing or destroyed; significant amounts of property and funds could not be found, and only a small part of them were ever recovered.[43]

On Wednesday, August 3, Hall stated that he with Margaret and the children "drove down to the mill & while there Mr. Miller the Govt. agent called upon me for one half of my cotton, which I declined to let go." The agent may have been T. D. Miller, a Confederate Treasury Agent from Washington, Louisiana (near Lafayette).

Hall "declined" to sell his cotton to the Confederate Cotton Bureau, in spite of the possibility that the cotton might be impressed, nor did he sell it through the "State Plan." He needed it to barter for commodities and services. In addition, the Union Army controlled Brownsville between November 1863 and July 30, 1864, and on this day Hall probably did not know that the Union Army had abandoned Brownsville, thus reopening Texas for cotton exports through Matamoros. Confederate currency and bonds continued to depreciate in value, and although the price of cotton continued to rise, Hall did not want to take payment in Confederate certificates. At this time, the state paid between 8 and 10 cents per pound, depending upon the grade of the cotton, but without a secure means of transporting the cotton to Brownsville, if Hall had wanted to send it there, he risked losing it to unscrupulous speculators and even army officers. Hall not only possessed his own cotton, but also bought and stored cotton for Frank Hitchcock according to their arrangement.[44] Perhaps Miller did not impress the cotton because Hall planned to take some of it to the penitentiary to trade for cloth.

On Wednesday, September 7, John "left for Huntsville, with the wagon, three yoke of oxen and five bales of cotton." The next day, Hall left for Huntsville and rode his horse Rob about twenty-five miles before stopping with a Mr. Brown for the night, which cost him twenty dollars. The day after (Friday, September 9), Hall caught up with John and the wagon about ten miles from Brown's. That day, he "fell in company with Mr White," with whom he traveled as far as Nelson's Creek, "where we camped for the night having crossed the Trinity river at Wyser's for which I paid 10$."

Saturday September 10th 1864. Today we left our camp at Nelson's creek and drove to Huntsville, where I exchanged at the Penitentiary my five bales of cotton which weighed 1958 lbs. for 198½ yards of osnaburgs and 141 yards of cotton Jeans; after which we left Huntsville in route for Home, with the wagons and drove 8 miles where the wagons camped at Nelson's creek for the night. I however rode to the river 13 miles and stopped with Mrs. Wyser for the night for which I paid her 10$. Mr. White and myself having parted company at Huntsville. Weather changeable & hot[.] Ther: 94°.

Hall rode forty-one miles on the following day to reach home, and John arrived from Huntsville with the wagon "all safe and sound" on Monday, September 12. This relatively uneventful interlude represented the effects of the Civil War on the Texas home front.

Hall rarely complained about the hardships in his journal, only noted the scarcity and inflated cost of goods. He soldered "some old tin vessels" for Margaret (Wednesday, September 14), "sold" a bale of cotton for forty-seven pounds of coffee (Thursday, September 29) and "gave" one bale to merchant Thomas P. Collins in exchange for fifteen pounds of coffee (Saturday, October 1). He also bought sixty-two pounds of wool with 310 pounds of flour (Tuesday, October 4) and rendered a list of taxable property to the "War Tax Assessor" (Monday, October 3). He made repairs to the house, collected seed cotton from neighbors, and provided food and lodging for soldiers who passed through the area.

Margaret rode down to her mother's to take clothing "to be sent" to Frank Stewart (Tuesday, September 13). Stewart was serving in Waul's Brigade, Walker's Division, in Arkansas and Louisiana. Hall and Nellie traveled to Crockett and back in one day (Saturday, October 8) "in order to fix up and send forward Sam Sharp's clothing."

Acquiring shoes for the family occupied several days in October.

Tuesday October 11th 1864. Today Mother & I drove in the buggy up to the tan yard in order to get some leather, and have some shoes made. Tubbs with the little wagon & mules drove up with us, hauling 18 beef hides. We were compelled to stop with Mr Prewitt for the night. John is at work digging potatoes. Hicks ground 3 bushels of corn. Weather clear & very hot for the season of the year.

This was the first reference to Bill Tubbs' last name. Prewitt owned the tan yard. The next day, "after getting some leather from Mr. Prewitt, for which we had to leave the little wagon & Tubbs, as it was not ready for delivery & will not be until tomorrow, Mother & I left in the buggy for home, where we arrived about sun down, too late for Mother to go home, therefore she remained all night." Bill Tubbs brought the leather home on Thursday, as projected by Hall. John retrieved the shoes from Prewitt's tan yard on Friday, November 18.

Hall became sick on Thursday, October 13, although he failed to mention his symptoms, and he remained ill until the following Tuesday, October 18, when he noted his state was "much improved." Florence turned four years old on Wednesday, October 19. For the next several days, Hall remained close to home, making a bridle and three surcingles. The slaves plowed fields, sowed barley and rye, chopped and hauled fire wood, hunted and slaughtered cattle, and stored cotton. Bill Hicks worked primarily at the mill. Mrs. Keen "warped and beamed a piece of jeans" on the loom for Margaret (Monday, October 24). The next day, Hall spent time "drawing the thread through the harness[,]" and on Friday, November 25, he "received [his] new jeans pants[,] they being made of the cloth that I wove for myself." Clearly, he took pride in his newly found skill.

Hall, with his family, several slaves, and a group of neighbors traveled to the Trinity River bank (Wednesday, October 26), where they camped for two nights and spent a day and a half gathering pecans at a place called Barnes Prairie. Altogether, the group collected about five bushels of pecans. For two days in November (Tuesday, November 8 and Wednesday, November 9), he allowed the men (except Bill Hicks, who remained at the mill) to go to Barnes Prairie to collect pecans, in effect giving them a small holiday. (On Friday, November 11, he wrote that he "assisted Hicks to repair the fore bay floor.")

Illness among those at the farm filled many journal entries for late October and early November. On Sunday, November 13, Hall mentioned that he was "quite sick." He stayed at home, suffering from rheumatism (Tuesday, November 15) and two days later wrote that he was "still sick with the sore mouth." Even so, he traveled to Crockett (Thursday, November 17), staying with L. E. Downes overnight, and the next day he received his "detail as a miller." Upon returning home, he found little Josephine ill "with a fever." Josephine, who had been struck in the head by a windblown door (Wednesday, September 14), again recovered. Hall suffered from "the sore mouth" until early December.

Although he felt ill, on Monday, November 28, Hall "rode around to see the families of soldiers and take an account of what they require for their next year's supply." He reported his findings to Joseph Keen and to Mr. Dailey (he does not say which one but most likely T. R. Dailey) the next day. During the war, counties authorized committees to visit the families of soldiers and find out what they needed in the way of food and clothing for the coming year. With their menfolk gone off to war, many of the families became indigent, and these families needed help from others in the county to survive.[45]

Regular chores continued. The hands split and hauled rails for fences around the garden and the house yard. Bill Hicks made an axletree for the "little wagon" and ground wheat and corn at the mill. They killed five hogs (Monday, December 12), weighing a total of only 738 pounds, then cut up and salted the meat. Hall made shoes for Jimmy, Toby, and for Sam and Nellie's son James, and he half-soled a pair of shoes for himself; he "paid" thirty-five pounds of flour for tallow already purchased (probably for candles); and he helped Margaret thread the loom so that she could make linsey, a coarse cloth of wool and linen (or wool and cotton).

Saturday December 17th 1864. Today the boys are at work hauling wood. Hicks ground 20 bushels of corn, and 3 bushels of wheat. Sam Sharp arrived home from the army on a 40 days furlough. He looks quite well but is sorely troubled with the itch. He lost my horse Ratler, which is a heavy loss on me at this time particularly as another cannot be procured. Weather cloudy & warm, with a hard rain at night.

While the hands "went out hog hunting" (Tuesday, December 20), Hall rode to the school house, where he paid his and Sam Sharp's taxes, loaning Sam $256 to cover the amount due. He also borrowed $370 from T. R. Dailey "in old issue, which I am to pay back in new issue, with a discount of one third, or rather I am to pay him $246.66 in new issue."

When the Civil War began, the Confederacy had no money and borrowed funds from the state government of Alabama and from bankers in New Orleans. Confederate legislators hesitated to issue a direct tax upon Southerners, who were unaccustomed to such a tax and whose loyalty might suffer under the strain. A new law passed on April 24, 1863: levied a graduated tax on incomes of more than $10,000; taxed licenses for bankers, auctioneers, liquor dealers, physicians, peddlers, and photographers, among others; and established a tax-in-kind consisting of one-tenth of a farmer's or planter's crops. Farmers east of the Mississippi strongly opposed the tax-in-kind; west of the Mississippi, farmers expressed fewer objections and complaints. On February 17, 1864, the Confederate Congress revised the tax law and allowed taxes to be paid in rapidly depreciating notes. Congress again tried to improve the tax laws on March 11, 1865, but by then it was too late.[46]

The Confederate government encountered a little more success with loans, especially during the early years of the war, when enthusiastic bankers and planters subscribed to the loans with a combination of specie (coin), paper money, and cotton. Planters gave their cotton to the government in exchange for bonds, which in turn, were redeemable for specie. In 1863, the Confederacy attempted to borrow money in Europe with bonds secured by cotton, but the French financier named Erlanger, orchestrating the arrangements of the loan, benefited the most due to his large commission.[47]

With neither loans nor taxes generating sufficient capital, the Confederate Treasury began printing paper money, or treasury notes, redeemable at a specified amount two years after the Confederate and United States governments signed and ratified a peace treaty. Because of the proliferation of these notes, people held onto their coins. Businesses printed illegal "shinplasters," or paper money in small denominations, and a great deal of counterfeiting occurred. As more paper money was printed, its value dropped: notes worth 90 cents (in gold) in 1861 were worth only 4.6 cents by early 1864.[48]

On February 17, 1864, the Confederate government passed a law mandating that treasury notes be exchanged for four percent bonds by July 1 (west of the Mississippi) and by April 1 (east of the Mississippi). After those respective dates, large bills depreciated until they were worthless, while smaller bills could be redeemed at two-thirds of their face value. New notes, recently printed and valued much higher, were the "new issue" mentioned by Hall. The Confederacy continued to print paper notes, however, and by early February 1865, the treasury notes were worth only 1.7 cents.[49]

Christmas, which fell on a Sunday, passed quietly, with the entire family gathered at Joshua and Mahala's home. "We had a fine dinner & a good egg nogg." The weather, Hall noted, was "cloudy & rather warm."

On Monday, the men "rode out hog hunting and succeeded in getting one." Two days later, John again went hog hunting and "was arrested by Mr Malone" and the hogs were "taken away from him." Although Sam Sharp and John "rode down to Stubblefield's mill to see Mr Malone in relation to his conduct on yesterday," they were unable to retrieve the hogs (Thursday, December 29).

While Sam and John were gone, McNeill's Regiment and Waller's Battalion "passed by the mill and camped about 3 miles below on the Elkhart creek, at what is known as the Pridgeon field. I was troubled a great deal by the soldiers & 4 remained for dinner."

Henry C. McNeill, a West Point graduate from Mississippi, served as lieutenant colonel of the Fifth Texas Cavalry Regiment during the New Mexico Campaign of 1862. Survivors of the campaign, which included McNeill and the Fifth Texas, took part in the Battle of Galveston on January 1, 1863, and at several battles in Louisiana that year, before returning to Texas, where General Magruder assigned the regiment to coastal defense at Galveston. In March 1864, McNeill and the Fifth Texas, among others, traveled to Louisiana to join General Richard Taylor at the battles of Mansfield and Pleasant Hill, part of the Red River Campaign.[50]

Early in 1863, Lieutenant Colonel Edwin Waller's Thirteenth Texas Cavalry Battalion had been assigned to General Tom Green's brigade, which included the Fifth Texas Cavalry. Edwin Waller, Jr., previously served as a major in the Second Texas Cavalry in New Mexico.[51]

Upon the death of General Tom Green at the Battle of Blair's Landing, Louisiana, on April 12, 1864, Major General John A. Wharton took command of Confederate forces in that area.[52] Although the Union Army failed to capture Shreveport, Louisiana, the headquarters of Confederate General Edmund Kirby Smith, commander of the Trans-Mississippi forces, the Federals continued to conduct smaller campaigns in Louisiana and Arkansas. During the early months of 1865, the Trans-Mississippi Department would be reorganized, leaving the Fifth Texas in the eastern part of the state. McNeill's and Waller's troops, camped near Hall's farm in late December, awaited reassignment. The soldiers probably harassed Hall for not joining the Confederate military.

Hall ended his journal notes for 1864 on Saturday, December 31. He paid "K. Murchison 310 lbs of flour for 62 lbs of wool" bought from Murchison last fall. Bill Hicks ground "20 bushels of corn and 5 bushels of wheat." The weather was "clear & cold, with a frost & freeze at night." He concluded the year in his usual manner: "Thus I close my jottings for the month of

December and for the year 1864, which has just passed & gone, and now numbered with the things that were. Whether the Almighty will spare me to chronicle the daily events of the incoming year is more than poor mortal man can foresee or know, but trusting in his goodness, I shall enter upon the pleasing task, which to me is useful as a book of reference and may hereafter be profitable to those who have an interest in my affairs, after I shall have shuffled off this mortal coil and been reaped to the bosom of my ancestors."

Chapter 6

1865

By early 1865, the Confederate defeat in Tennessee, rumors and fear of widespread insurrection by slaves and conspiracies by Unionists, and Indian attacks on the frontier, kept Texans dispirited and edgy. Taken altogether, one can sense in Hall's journal the nearing of the end of the Civil War.

Sunday January 1st 1865. Today I commence my notes of daily events that may happen immediately around me during the current year just began, Though they are of no interest to any one save my own family, Nevertheless I cheerfully enter upon my task. We all left home and rode down to Mother's where we spent an agreeable day, returning home in the evening. A sick soldier stopped [with] *us, for the night. Weather clear and rather warm for the season of the year.*

Everyday pursuits continued without incident. The men split rails "to reset the fence around the bottom field." Margaret wove one yard of linsey. Bill Hicks ground wheat at the mill. And Hall "sent Billy Stewart his negro woman America & her child Claudine, who have been staying with me some time." A few weeks later (Sunday, February 5), Hall purchased America and Claudine for ten bales of cotton.

With Bill Hicks now working fulltime as miller, Hall noted on Wednesday, January 4, that "the mill" had ground ten bushels of wheat for "the Government[.]" Hall wrote on Friday, January 6, that "the mill was broken open" during the night, and "two sacks of flour [were] stolen out by the soldiers belonging to [Colonel William P.] Hardeman's brigade." The two sacks weighed about 150 pounds. Although General Edmund Kirby Smith, in charge of the Trans-Mississippi Department, was an able administrator, the soldiers remained poorly provisioned.

On Saturday, January 7, Hall wrote, "Sam & I are engaged [in] trying to ferret out the persons who broke into & robbed the mill last night, but without any success." The two stood guard at the mill. "At night four soldiers made another attack upon the mill to rob it again, but we detected them in the act, not being successful at the mill, they rode over to Mr Leaverton's and robbed Mr Mitchell's negro man of a sack weighing about 160 lbs.[,] so much for the soldiers of the Confederacy."

If Hall's disillusionment with the Confederate military remained firm, so did his sense of obligation to those in need. On Thursday, January 12, he "rode 28 miles, gathering up pork for the families of soldiers, having taken with me the little wagon & mules." The weather had turned clear and very cold, ideal for slaughtering hogs and preserving the pork.

Ten days later (Saturday, January 14), Hall wrote that another "gang of soldiers broke into the mill and stole therefrom about 350 lbs of flour."

Sunday January 15th 1865. Today Sam Sharp & I tracked the flour that had been stolen from the mill last night into Company K. of the 5th Regt. of Texas Cavalry. I made complaint to Col. Waller, but got very poor comfort, in fact it amounted almost to an insult, thus a citizen must be treated by a lawless armed rabble called soldiers, his property stolen and him insulted for presuming to ask about it. Weather cloudy & cold, with showers of rain throughout the night.

On Monday, January 16, Sam Sharp left for Liberty, and Colonel Waller sent two soldiers to guard the mill. Their names were John Burrows and E. P. Baugh, and no more thefts occurred. The two guards were relieved on Wednesday, February 1, and replaced by Thomas Hill and Edward Graham. However, on Thursday, February 9, Hardeman's Brigade "that has been camped on the Elkhart for the past 6 or 7 weeks, left for Tennessee Colony in Anderson County. The guard stationed in the mill in consequence of the removal of the soldiers were relieved from duty in the mill & ordered to join their commands."

Hall may have been relieved that trouble with the soldiers had ended, but more problems at the mill lay ahead.

On Friday, January 20, Hall attended a fundraising ball given by steamboat Captain Stubblefield at Hall's Bluff and "danced one cotillion for which I paid 10$. This closed my dancing." The next day, three soldiers stayed overnight with Hall, and two days later, two more soldiers "stopped for the night, who are very shabby fellows to say the least of it." On the other hand, Mahala's nephew James C. Roberts and a Lieutenant Barlow "came up from the camp" at Magnolia to visit with Hall (Tuesday, January 24). James Roberts and his brother William visited often during the spring.

On Thursday, January 26, Hall placed Bill Tubbs "in the service of the Government for the space of two months and 12 days, to work in the flat boat yard at Brookfield's bluff." Brookfield's Bluff was about twelve miles below Hall's Bluff on the Trinity. He turned Bill Tubbs over to Captain J. T. Smith (Friday, January 27) at Stubblefield's Mill. Bill Tubbs came home for a visit on Monday, February 6, and helped repair the mill levee. He returned to work at the flatboat yard, but he ran away and came home on Friday, March 3. The following day, Hall noted, "Mr. Hays came up from the boat yard and took Tubbs back with him." Hall did not mention Bill Tubbs again, but Tubbs settled in Liberty after the war.

Tuesday January 31st 1865. Today James Roberts left for camp. Mr Cameron from Jasper County came to see Fanny [Fitzsimmons], *it appears that he has possession of Fanny's brother, and in my judgment is a very shabby fellow. The boys done nothing in consequence of the rain. It rained all day and all night. The weather was very cold. Thus I close my notes for the month of January.*

By the following day, with Elkhart Creek "booming high[,]" Hall feared the mill levee would collapse, but it held. Then, on Saturday,

February 4, the mill levee "commenced giving way and God only knows whether we will be able to save it." On the same day that Bill Tubbs arrived from the boat yard (Monday, February 6), the levee "gave way in part and required the labor of all hands to save it." Hall waited for the water to fall before beginning to repair the levee (Thursday, February 9), work that was completed a week later (Friday, February 17). More rain fell, and by Saturday, February 25, the creek was so full that the mill could not be used, "the wheels being some 5 or 6 feet under water." Two days passed before enough water drained out so that the mill could be used again.

Although the temperature remained very cold at night, the days grew warmer, and more work could be done outdoors.

Saturday February 11th 1865. Today early in the morning I went out to the Pidgeon roost, having found it the evening before, and succeeded in killing 30 of them. The boys are still at work on the mill levee and got it repaired sufficiently to raise a small head of water, when Hicks ground 12 bushels of corn. I washed and put out to dry 8 bushels of wheat, and then made myself a good bridle. Weather clear and cold.

During these days, Margaret "planted english peas" (Thursday, February 14) and "irish potatoes" (Friday, February 17). Hall repaired his saddle (Tuesday, February 14 and Wednesday, February 15) as well as Margaret's rocking chair (Friday, February 17) and the next day he "set out about 25 young peach trees."

Monday February 20th 1865. Today I rode my horse Rob in company with James Roberts to Crockett and back, and while there, I paid Mr. Duglass the Assessor & Collector my state & County taxes, which amounted to $235. Hicks done nothing in consequence of the mill machinery getting out of running order[.] *Weather cloudy and cold, with a rain at night.*

Hall repaired the mill machinery, and Bill Hicks resumed his work as miller.

Wednesday February 22nd 1865. Today John is engaged [in] *hauling fire wood. The little woman is engaged in gardening. I sent to Billy Stewart by his boy Harry 80 lbs of flour, which makes 100 lbs that he now owes me for. I this day attained the 46th anniversary of my birth day. Hicks ground 20 bushels of corn and 8 bushels of wheat. weather cloudy & warm, with a rain throughout the day and night. The Elkhart creek is booming high.*

It is noticeable that Hall made no mention of any kind of birthday celebration.

Journal entries for most of March recorded the usual events. Hall noted the work done by John (plowing and helping Margaret with the garden) and Bill Hicks (continuing as miller). James and William Roberts, camped with the army at Magnolia, came to see Hall several times, and visits with family and friends occurred regularly. Sam came home on a furlough from March 9 until March 13. Hall spent several days making a loom for Mahala and attempted to distill whiskey, which "signally failed" (Saturday, March 11).

At times, Hall sold cotton and flour. For example, on Tuesday, March 7, he "let Mrs. Wortham have 100 lbs of flour at $6. which she paid." He also sold two bales of cotton for 6 cents per pound (Wednesday, March 22).

The most tantalizing journal entry, dated Tuesday, March 14, stated, "At night Tom Neely & 5 other men, attempted to assassinate me. The men who were with Neely were unknown to me." The Neelys were neighbors. Hall did not describe the circumstances or offer a reason for the attack, nor did he refer to it again.

As March drew to a close, Hall described several unusual events. "My poor old horse Hawk after a lingering illness of several months laid down and died," he wrote on Monday, March 27, "he had been a faithful and serviceable horse to me while living, poor old horse, I regret his death but as all must die, let him go."

Thursday March 30th 1865. Today I am still in Crockett [since the previous day] *and stopping with Billy Stewart*[.] *My mule broke out of the lot last night and made his escape. Billy Stewart's negro boy York robbed my pocket book of 250$ in new issue of Confederate Money and 1$ in specie. Cols. Gregg, Jones & Crawford took dinner at Billy Stewart's. Weather clear & cool.*

Friday March 31st 1865. Today I am still in Crockett and cannot get away as my [mule] *has not yet been found. Billy Stewart tried to get my money from the negro boy York which he had stolen and succeeded in getting 30$ in new issue. The balance he had disposed off. At the mill, Hicks ground 41 bushels of corn. Mother got 13 lbs of cotton. Weather changeable & pleasant. Thus closes my notes for the month of March.*

Saturday April 1st 1865. Today I left Crockett in company with Mr Haden [a merchant (see Chapter 1)] *and drove in his buggy out to the mill and thence down to Father's, where I let Mr Haden have 15 B/C.* [bales of cotton] *which weighed 7161 lbs for which he is to pay me 6¢ per lb. Mr Driscol also went down with us & assisted in weighing the cotton. We then returned to the mill. I found the little woman and Roberta had gone to Crockett to see me, but we took different roads & therefore missed each other. Billy Roberts rode over to Mr Lacy's and found my mule, that had escaped from Crockett*[,] *and led him home. The little woman & Roberta returned home at night pretty well worn out from fatigue. Hicks ground 17 bushels of corn. Weather variable & pleasant. It clouded up at night however and rained hard nearly the whole night.*

These events took place during the final days of the Civil War, marking the passage of an iconic Southern culture that would become romanticized in song, literature, film, and theater. The dark days of Congressional Reconstruction lay ahead, cementing Southern pride and anger into cultural and political monuments that affected the course of the twentieth century. And James Hall recorded this transitional moment in American history in his journal.

At Point Isabel (now Port Isabel) in South Texas, on March 16, Colonel John S. Ford and Brigadier General James E. Slaughter, both Confederates, met with Major General Lew Wallace of the Union Army to discuss terms for a cessation of fighting on the Rio Grande. Major General John G. Walker, commanding the District of Texas, New Mexico, and Arizona, and headquartered at Houston, rejected the agreement they reached. (General Magruder had been transferred to the District of Arkansas, but returned to Texas in March 1865.) No more fighting occurred in South Texas until May.[1]

In the meantime, Joseph E. Johnston replaced John Bell Hood as commander of the Army of Tennessee. Hood wanted to be relieved from command, and President Davis complied. The diminished Confederate Army, unable to prevent Sherman from sweeping through Georgia, now tried to stop his advance through the Carolinas toward Virginia. Desperately short of men, the Confederate Congress in March passed the Barksdale Bill, which authorized the recruitment of black slaves into the army, but this emergency measure came too late. On April 1, the Union Army defeated Confederate troops at Five Forks, near Petersburg, Virginia. General Lee and the remaining forces could not hold Richmond and began a retreat. On April 9, Lee surrendered to General Ulysses S. Grant at Appomattox Court House, Virginia.[2]

For reasons he did not explain, Hall hurried to Liberty in early April 1865. Through his network of friends or from newspaper reports, he may have learned of Sherman's destructive sweep through Georgia and northward through the Carolinas toward the Confederate capital at Richmond, Virginia. He may have heard about the fall of Columbia, South Carolina, to Sherman's Army on February 17, and Sherman's order to grant land along the coast of Georgia to the freedmen. It is possible that he learned about the Thirteenth Amendment to the Constitution, then making its way among the states, that would abolish slavery. He may have read in a newspaper about peace overtures between Marylander Francis P. Blair and Jefferson Davis, which would lead to further talks, or about President Abraham Lincoln's inauguration for his second term of office on March 4. Although it is not likely he would have known about the surrender of Richmond on April 3, he seemed aware that the war was about to end.

On Sunday, April 2, he mentioned Frank Stewart for the first time since May 1863, when he left to join the army. Frank had gone hunting and killed "a fine turkey and a deer." Hall does not state when Stewart returned from military service, but he undoubtedly shared news of the war with Hall.

After helping Margaret "in warping and beaming some thread, in order to weave out a piece of cloth[,]" (Monday, April 3), Hall left home on Tuesday, April 4, "on my mule John in company with Billy Roberts in route for Liberty." At Crockett they "stopped for dinner with Billy Stewart. We then rode down to Dan Dailey's where we stopped for the night." The distance to Dailey's was twenty-five miles. They continued the next day and stayed overnight at Mr. Alderman's, a distance of twenty-nine miles (Wednesday, April 5). They reached John F. Carr's place on Thursday, April 6, a further twenty-eight miles. Roberts left Hall at Carr's and turned back toward Crockett, taking Hall's mule with him (Friday, April 7). That same day, Hall helped Carr "in loading his flat boat with cotton." Between showers, the loading continued until Sunday.

Monday, April 10th 1865. Today John F. Carr, John Beazley & myself with 6 negro fellows, left Smithfield on the flat boat in route for Liberty, we dropped down the river 30 miles and tied up for the night. At home Hicks ground 5 bushels of corn. The little woman let Mrs John Wortham have 50 lbs of flour. Weather cloudy & cool, with a rain throughout the day, & very disagreeable at night.

During his absence, Margaret kept records for him, which he incorporated into the journal.

Tuesday April 11th 1865. Today we dropped the flat boat down the river 45 miles and tied up for the night at the plantation of Dr. Baldwin. at home Hicks ground 13 bushels of corn. Weather cloudy & cool, with occasional showers of rain.

Wednesday April 12th 1865. Today after taking Dr. Baldwin on board, we dropped the flat boat down the river 32 miles, and arrived at Liberty at 1. O'clk P.M. & tied up above the rail road bridge. I went up to and stopped with Capt. Peacock. I found all my friends in Liberty well. Weather cloudy and cool, with occasional showers of rain throughout the day.

Thursday April 13th 1865. Today I am still in Liberty and visited the town in company with Capt. Peacock. Weather variable & cool with rain.

At exactly the same time, the nation was propelled into a new crisis. President Abraham Lincoln, shot by John Wilkes Booth on April 14, died the following day, and Vice President Andrew Johnson became President.

Friday April 14th 1865. Today I am still in Liberty and stopping with Capt. Peacock. As yet I have not concluded what to do. Weather cloudy & cool with occasional showers of rain throughout the entire day.

This provocative statement suggests that he was trying to decide whether or not to return to Liberty on a permanent basis. He may have been wondering if Lund and Wrigley planned to reopen their store and, if so, whether he might return to work for them. He may have been referring to the shipment and sale of the cotton he had been storing, his own plus Frank Hitchcock's, since his daily notes refer to the passage of steamboats up and down the Trinity and their cargos of cotton. In any case, it seems that he traveled to Liberty with expectations beyond visiting with friends, but since he brought no cotton with him to sell, he may have meant only to gather information about the war and the status of the cotton market. He apparently did not intend to make a quick trip to Liberty and a rapid return home. For the next several weeks, he remained adrift in the uncertainty of the times.

The Confederate troops in Virginia, paroled by General Grant and permitted to travel by military wagons and railroads, headed home. Those who could reach ports took ships and sailed home. Few horses or mules remained, and most of the former Confederates walked. Without money, food, or equipment, the ex-soldiers traveled in groups, for companionship and protection.

Although Southerners thought that General Edmund Kirby Smith, headquartered in Shreveport, Louisiana, would hold the fighting forces together and continue the war in the Trans-Mississippi, the capture of President Jefferson Davis on May 10 left the Confederacy without a civilian government. Even troops who had remained loyal to the cause lost hope when General Richard Taylor surrendered to Union General E. R. S. Canby in Alabama on May 4. At the same time, inflation raised prices for basic goods while the paper money became worthless; Confederate soldiers had not been paid for up to sixteen months, and discipline began to collapse.[3]

Hall's journal entries indicate his own lack of focus. He wrote about the steamer *Mary Hill* from Houston (Saturday, April 15), the first steamboat that had come to Liberty since Hall's arrival. He tried to go downriver to visit his friend Richard Cole (Sunday, April 16), but the river was too high, so he waited until the next day. After traveling downriver in a "batteaux" to Cole's residence, he remained overnight, and they drank lager beer, a novelty and a luxury. He returned to Liberty the next day (Tuesday, April 18). Hall had little to do and was "loafing around generally" (Wednesday, April 19). The *Ruthven* came downriver loaded with 300 bales of cotton (Friday, April 21), and on Saturday, Hall accompanied "the Misses Peacock & Mrs. Bolling" in a hunt for dewberries, which was "partially successful." (Hall was staying with Captain Peacock and his family, and Carrie Bolling was the wife of merchant James Bolling.) The *Lone Star* and the *Mary Hill* arrived from Houston on Wednesday, April 26, and the *Lone Star* left for Houston with 300 bales of cotton the following day. These rather disjointed notes reflect the restlessness of Hall's days in Liberty.

On Friday, April 28, Hall and Captain Peacock sailed down the Trinity on the *Mary Hill* and crossed the bay to Galveston, where they landed at one o'clock in the morning.

Saturday April 29th 1865. Today I am in Galveston and after having finished what little business I had to do, I strolled around the City and fortifications in Company with my old friend Col Jim Wrigley, whom I have not seen before since the summer of 1862. We had a pleasant time together and I found him the same old Jim, he seems to be enjoying excellent health, and may his shaddow never grow less. At home Hicks ground 15 bushels of corn. Weather clear & warm.

Hall's joy at reuniting with James Wrigley sparkles on the page.

Hall and Captain Peacock left for Liberty on Sunday, April 30, and arrived early in the morning of the following day (Monday, May 1). Hall received his first letter from home the same day. Still at loose ends, on Tuesday, May 2, he attended a picnic given by a Captain Harrison, which he termed "a brilliant affair[,]" and he returned to Richard Cole's to visit and probably play cards with various friends (Wednesday, May 3). The *Ruthven*, loaded with 500 bales of cotton, tied up at Liberty (Friday, May 5). Hall boarded the *Ruthven* for a visit to Houston (Saturday, May 6), and the steamer made "a pleasant run down the river, but got aground in the canal, where we remained all night."

Sunday May 7th 1865. Today the Steamer is still hard and fast aground in the canal. I went on shore and visited the late residence of Genl. Chambers, which is a very desirable place to live. I saw the place where the assassin must have stood when he fired through the window & killed Chambers [March 15]. *Weather variable & warm, with rain.*

Monday, May 8th 1865. Today the steamer is still aground with very little prospects of her getting afloat. The Steamer Orizaba came down from Liberty and tied up waiting for the "Ruthven" to get out of the canal. Weather changeable and cold with a hard rain and a keen norther blowing, making it very disagreeable.

Tuesday, May 9th 1865. Today after taking nearly all the cotton off the steamer, she floated and we got out of the canal and over the bar, then run to Chamber's [sic] *wharf and commenced taking in our loading again. The Steamer Orizaba also run over the bar and proceeded on her voyage to Galveston. Weather changeable & cool, with a light shower of rain.*

On Wednesday, after reloading the cargo at Chambers' wharf, the *Ruthven* "had a pleasant run across the bay, and up the San Jacinto river and Buffalo bayou." Arriving in Houston early in the morning on Thursday, May 11, Hall "found all kinds of business prostrated." He stayed at "a private boarding house" owned by a Mrs. Farrow. Hall did not describe his activities in Houston, but left there on the *Ruthven* "late in the evening" of Friday, May 12, "bound for Liberty, via of Galveston. I had a very sick night being attacked with Cholera Morbus."

Saturday, May 13th 1865. Today the Steamer Ruthven arrived at Galveston, I found our troops, mutinous and determined to give up the ship. I saw my old friend Jim Wrigley, who has no idea of surrendering if it can be avoided. Weather clear & pleasant.

The last battle of the Civil War took place that same day, when Confederates defeated Union troops at Palmito Ranch, not far from Brownsville, in South Texas.[4]

As more and more Confederate troops surrendered, it became clear that the fighting was over. Events that followed, alluded to by Hall, were generally known as "the breakup." Confederate soldiers in the Trans-Mississippi states, still commanded by Kirby Smith and Magruder, who had not surrendered, began to desert, and only determined persuasion by superior officers kept them at their posts. After the near-mutiny of about 400 troops in Galveston on May 14, Kirby Smith ordered the soldiers to evacuate the city and regroup in Houston, where he planned to make his headquarters.[5]

Sunday, May 14th 1865. Today I am still in Galveston, with very small prospects of getting off. Col Jim Wrigley with several other gentlemen & I had a conviviality, we pass[ed] *the time very pleasantly. The blockade runner steamship "Wren" left for Havana. Weather cloudy, but pleasant, with strong indications of rain.*

Monday, May 15th 1865. Today I am still in Galveston. The "Ruthven" run down to battery "Scurry" and over to Pelican spit, and brought over to Galveston 150 soldiers and 120 negroes. I went over on the excursion. Weather cloudy and warm.

Hall remained at Galveston until Thursday, May 18, when he took the *Ruthven* back across the bay and up the Trinity River to Liberty, arriving "late in the evening." There he found his house "in a wretched, dirty, and filthy condition, more like a pig pen than a gentleman's residence." The following day, he wrote, "Today I am in Liberty and as it is my home I shall not note my whereabouts unless I leave the place. I commenced boarding with John Booth." This entry was his first reference to Liberty as his home. The boarding house owned by Booth, a Mississippian, stood adjacent to the home of James Wrigley.

For something to do, on Saturday, May 20, Hall helped Charles Lund "in checking off some freight."

Sunday May 21st 1865. Today I am still at John Booth's and loafing around the river. The Commissary & Quarter Master's departments, [were] *broken up, and the officers ceased to discharge the duties of their offices. Weather clear and hot.*

Monday May 22nd 1865. Today I am still at John Booth's. A part of the disbanded soldiers passed through this place and stole every thing they could get hold off [*sic*], *Every person is hiding their horses, mules and wagons from them, and considerable excitement prevails here. Weather clear and very hot.*

While Kirby Smith was en route from Shreveport, soldiers rioted and broke into Confederate warehouses, taking whatever they could find. For example, at Hempstead, northwest of Houston, troops and citizens raided a Confederate supply train. Forced to "make do" throughout the war, citizens needed and took whatever they could grab. Riots occurred in other Texas cities such as Austin, where looters raided the state treasury; San Antonio; La Grange; and even Camp Ford, the prisoner-of-war camp near Tyler.[6]

Tuesday May 23rd 1865. Today I am still at Booth's. The steamer Orizaba arrived from Galveston, with Spaight's Regiment on board. The soldiers of this command upon coming ashore immediately proceeded to sack Col. Wrigley's warehouse, stealing every species of property they could find, both public and private, some one of the party, stold [*sic*] *my fine double barrel shot gun, saddle, bridle and blanket out of the ware house. May my eternal curse rest upon the scoundrel who done it. The reign of terror is now complete in the land, our own soldiers are doing worse than the enemy . . . under any circumstances could do. The Steamers Ruthven & Orizaba left in order to seek a place of safety from the soldiers. At night Col. Wrigley arrived from Houston perfectly disgusted with the opperation of our soldiers, and the disgusting lawlessness of our Citizens. Weather clear & hot.*

Ashley W. Spaight, an attorney and planter from Liberty County, raised and commanded the Moss Bluff Rifles, comprised of men from southeast Texas. When the Eleventh Cavalry and Infantry Battalion mustered in (March 1862), Spaight became lieutenant colonel of the battalion, which consisted of cavalry, artillery, and infantry. Assigned to defend the coast from Galveston Bay to Louisiana and initially camped on a hill called Spindletop, Spaight's Battalion took part in several skirmishes with Union troops, burned a Union ship, and captured two blockading vessels, the *Velocity* and the *Morning Light*. After service in Louisiana in early 1863, Spaight's Battalion returned to Texas in the fall and was stationed at Sabine Pass. During the spring of 1864, Spaight's Battalion again saw action in Louisiana and again returned to Texas. In November 1864, the battalion was incorporated into the Twenty-First Texas Infantry Regiment, part of the Second Texas Infantry Division, and Spaight received a promotion to colonel. The Twenty-First Texas Infantry spent the remainder of the war engaged in routine duties. After word of Lee's surrender reached Texas, military protocols dissolved. Many troops simply left their stations and went home. Others plundered the towns where they were garrisoned. Soldiers in Galveston threatened an insurrection, noted above, and rumors swirled that the Twenty-First Texas Infantry planned to take a train and escape to the mainland, which did not occur.[7] Hall's description of events in Liberty following "the breakup" corresponds to those happening elsewhere.

Wednesday May 24th 1865. Today I am still at Booth's. The soldiers who destroyed and carried away all the property they could find left on the cars for Beaumont, in order to sack that place. Be it remembered that Genl. E. K. Smith surrendered to Genl. Canby the Trans-Mississippi department, which finally winds up the war ingloriously to the South. Weather clear and very hot.

Kirby Smith sent envoys to New Orleans to meet with General Canby to negotiate surrender details for the Trans-Mississippi, and by the time Kirby Smith reached Houston on May 27, the Confederate Army in Texas had evaporated.

On Thursday, May 25, a second party of soldiers stole what they could find and then left on the railroad for Beaumont. Hall and several friends went downriver to Richard Cole's "and found him gone to parts unknown." The next day, James Wrigley and "a large party of old confederate soldiers left on the train for Houston." This was probably an effort to help provide law and order there. By Saturday, May 27, excitement over the "lawless acts of the soldiers" began to subside. Although he neglected to state when he sent for Margaret, Hall expected her soon, and noted that without news from home or the arrival of his family, he was "beginning to grow restive under the trial" (Sunday, May 28).

Monday, May 29th 1865. Today I am still at Booth's. Capt Harrison and I took a long hunt after squirrels. In fact I am willing to hunt all the time in order to occupy my mind, and keep it from dwelling all the time upon home. A large party of gentlemen came over on the cars from Beaumont and put up at Booth's, entirely crowding us out. Be it remembered that the President of the United States (Andrew Johnson) issued his proclamation, liberating and freeing all the negro slaves in the south and by this high handed and unlawful act, I am deprived of nearly all my property that I have been working for, for the past 30 years, nearly all the Capital that I had being invested in that species of property. Weather clear and hot.

The "crowd" left for Houston on Tuesday, May 30, "giving us a little more room." Hall and Captain Harrison went fishing, "with very poor success," but killed some squirrels.

Thursday June 1st 1865. Today I rode up to José bayou, in company with Capt. Harrison & John Booth, on a fishing excursion, but was rather unsuccessful. We however killed some fine squirrells. Capt Cameron & Miss Adelia Wrigley were married at night. Nothing yet from home. I am still at John Booth's. At home the little woman went down to Mothers to spend what time she remained up the Country, and consequently quit keeping the opperations of the mill. As this is the first day of summer, I shall give the state of the thermometer, noting it each day at 3 O'clock P.M. Weather clear & hot: Ther: 90º,

Adelia Wrigley was the fifteen- or sixteen-year-old daughter of John and Sarah Hardin Wrigley.[8]

Still "loafing" around Liberty and waiting for Margaret with growing impatience, Hall noted the arrival of the train from Houston, the first train to cross the bridge since the bridge had been "repaired," and the sinking of the *Orizaba* "on a snag" about "one mile below the residence of Dick Cole" (Friday, June 2). The following day, an "extra train came over from Houston and brought a part of Hoods' old Texas brigade." Friends Jim Wrigley and George Gordon took the *Ruthven* to Galveston on Sunday, June 4. The Texas and New Orleans Railroad began making "regular daily trips" between Houston and Beaumont (Monday, June 5). These journal entries indicate the return to dependable transportation in this area.

On June 2, Confederate generals Kirby Smith and Magruder, together, signed the formal surrender agreement with General Canby aboard the steamer *Fort Jackson*, which also ended the naval blockade.

Wednesday June 7th 1865. Today the train arrived from Houston, with the news that the yankee troops had reduced Galveston island into formal possession, and were treating the Galvestonians with marked respect, I don't know how long this treatment will last. I am still at Booth's. Weather clear & hot: Ther: 90°.

After a great deal of destruction to by ex-Confederates and others, federal troops re-established law and order. Civil government resumed. Galvestonians who had left the city returned. Buildings and homes were repaired, businesses reopened, and the city began a rapid recovery from the war. Federal troops maintained a positive relationship with the citizens until they left the island in May 1870.

Hall continued to hunt squirrels with Captain Harrison, read books, and visit friends in Liberty. On Friday, June 9, he received a letter from home "which gave me much pleasure in learning that all were well, yet it produced some sorrow that the little woman & children had not as yet left to join me at this place. However it will not be long before they come & I must be patient." By the next day, however, his feelings were "rather gloomy & desponding," and on Wednesday, June 14, he noted that he was "becoming home sick . . ."

Major General Gordon Granger took command of U.S. soldiers in Texas on June 17, and two days later, on June 19, he issued a proclamation freeing all slaves in Texas and Louisiana. "Juneteenth" remains an important celebration among African Americans today.

To keep busy, Hall picked blackberries with "splendid success" (Thursday, June 15) and went fishing "with pretty fair luck" (Friday, June 16). His entry for June 19 did not mention the announcement of emancipation, only that he had been "boarding" with John Booth for a month. On the following day (Tuesday, June 20), he sent a letter to W. P. Leaverton at Crockett and enclosed one for Margaret, "urging her speedy departure from the mill to join me here." He attended a fish fry at Gum Lake (Wednesday, June 21) followed by a bridal party at Richard Cole's that night.

Thursday June 22nd 1865. Today I am still at John Booth's. Nothing as yet from my little woman and I am becoming quite anxious to see her, but must wait yet a little longer. If she does not come down by the end of the current month, I have resolved to go up after her. Weather clear & hot. Ther: 91°.

Saturday June 24th 1865. Today I succeeded in stopping the diarrhea, from running on me [since the previous day] *and am consequently much better. The little woman, with Fanny Fitzsimmons & Josephine in my buggy drawn by my horse Rob, arrived safe and sound in Liberty. Frank Stewart, with the little wagon & mules also arrived safe, bringing down in the little wagon Florence and Jimmy, also Louisa, Jemima, Conny and Wolf* [Carroll], *with sundry provisions, etc. We all upon the invitation of Col Jim Wrigley, stopped at his house, of course I left John Booths* [boarding house]. *The little woman passed my wagons on the road, they having left on the 16th inst.* [instant: this month]. *Jemima was taken down at the residence of my old friend Dan Dailey & safely delivered of a female child on the 17th inst.* [,] *both mother & child are doing well. Weather clear & hot*[.] *Ther: 92°.*

Sunday June 25th 1865. Today Billy Roberts arrived with the wagons all safe and sound, without breaking any of the furniture. Hicks & John [are] *looking very well.—My family are all still over at Col. Wrigley's. Weather clear & hot. Ther: 92°.*

Monday June 26th 1865. Today I am at work getting thinks [things] *arranged in the house, and putting the furniture up, assisted by Frank Stewart & Billy Roberts, and after partially arranging the house, I moved my family over from Col. Wrigley's and can now say, that we are once more at home. Weather clear & hot. Ther: 90°*

With the family and servants now at home with him in Liberty, Hall's daily activities became more focused. He and James Wrigley took the railroad to Houston and stayed at the Fannin House (Tuesday, June 27). The next day, Hall purchased bagging and rope to "rebale the cotton, that is now up at the mill." Charles A. Leaverton arrived in Houston from Crockett, on other business, and they met by accident (Thursday, June 29). Leaverton, who was staying at the same hotel, informed Hall that his friends in Crockett were well. Hall returned to Liberty with Charles Leaverton by rail the following day. Leaverton and Frank Stewart went "up to town in the buggy" with him on Saturday, July 1, where he bought a pair of shoes for Roberta that cost

$2.50. He also set the men to work "hauling wood." Mr. and Mrs. Charles Lund spent Sunday evening with Margaret, but Fanny Fitzsimmons and little Florence were both "sick with fever."

Monday July 3rd 1865. Today the train came over from Houston, and brought my bagging & rope[,] *also a barrel of sugar. I had the wagons loaded up, and after dinner, they left in route, for the mills. Frank Stewart & Charles Leaverton* [are] *going along in charge of them. I purchased from Charley Lund, 100 lbs of bacon at 10¢ per lb. I borrowed from Charles Leaverton 25$ and gave him a draft for the amount on Sam H. Sharp. Weather clear & hot. Ther: 90°.*

Margaret and Louisa next became ill with fever. The regularity of the episodes of illness suggests they were suffering from malaria.

Nellie Sharp's mother, Mrs. Beale, came from her home in Danville to visit. Danville was a small town in northern Montgomery County, a few miles west of New Waverly. (Most of the residents moved to Willis in 1870 due to the arrival of the railroad there.)[9] Mrs. Beale gave Margaret "a cow & calf and sent several articles of furniture over to be taken care of" (Thursday, July 6). On Saturday, Hall "drove Mrs. Beale up town and while there loaned her six dollars to purchase two pairs of shoes and one bottle of whiskey, She left sundry articles of furniture with us, for safe keeping." Then she left her home in Liberty and took the train to West Liberty, now Dayton, en route for Danville.

After a quiet Sunday (July 9) spent reading, Hall "rode up town in the buggy" with Jim Wrigley on Monday (July 10), although he did not say why. Important because of later events, Hall also mentioned that Captain John Redman "took dinner" with him that day.

Hall became ill with diarrhea and fever the same day (July 10) and did not recover completely until Friday, July 14, when he again "rode up town in the buggy" with Wrigley. The next day, he and Wrigley "remained at the depot, until the cars came in, on which I found William Leaverton, who has just come down from the mills, and who informs me that all my relatives up there are well." Leaverton was on his way to Houston. Hall again went to town on Sunday (July 16) "in order to mail some letters."

Monday July 17th 1865. Today the Yankees reduced this point (Liberty) into possession and established head quarters at the Court house, they also opened a Provost Marshal's office, to enforce the amnesty oath down the throats of the Southern people. Mr Perkins [Henry E. Perkins, an attorney and land agent] *came over from Houston on the train, I drove up town in my buggy to see the grand display of the infernal yankee troops. Weather variable and hot with a shower of rain. Ther: 92°.*

Two days later, Hall "let Jemima go down the river on the Steamer Lone Star, to see her mother." Jemima returned with her mother (Thursday, August 3), and Hall wrote, "I suppose I will now have to support [her] in order to keep Jemima with me."

One by one, the family and the former slaves all became sick with chills, fever, and diarrhea. Hall pulled and tied fodder and noted the comings and goings of the *Ruthven* and the *Mary Hill.* He bought four pounds of "star candles" from James Wrigley (Saturday, July 22) and "made a couple of cribbage boards" (Wednesday, July 26).

Friday July 28th 1865. Today I drove out to Rick's mill after some meal, but did not succeed in getting any. Fanny & Jimmy are still sick, but slowly improving. My negro woman Louisa became refractory and I drove her off the premises, she having been freed by the President's proclamation, began to feel her oats too strong, and hence the rupture between us. The little woman is now doing her own house work. Weather changeable and hot: Ther: 94°.

While Hall did not elaborate on the disagreement between himself and Louisa, it is clear that social tensions had developed.

The following day (Saturday, July 29), Margaret continued with "her own house work which goes pretty hard with her, but she works at it very cheerfully." However, a gust of wind caused the dining room door to shut, and it struck Josephine on the forehead, knocking her down. A large bump formed on her head, "which instantly threw her into fever." By Sunday (July 30), with Josephine still suffering from fever and Fanny also sick, it was evident that Margaret needed help.

Hall hired a black woman named Ophelia on Monday, July 31. She was to work for one month and to be paid three dollars "in greenbacks" to help Margaret in the kitchen. One month later (Thursday, August 31), he "paid off and discharged" Ophelia, "having no use for such worthless free negroes." It would be helpful to know what Hall's expectations of Ophelia were in order to understand why she became a disappointment to him. New roles were being defined on a daily basis. The newly freed were learning to be independent and self-supporting; the white employers were learning to modify old rules of society and create new management practices. The resulting tension affected everyone, and the emerging patterns strained patience on both sides. No one knew quite what to do.

William Leaverton arrived on Wednesday, August 2, and reported that Hall's family was well and the mill "in successful opperation." He brought Margaret "some apples and a package of letters." Two days later, Leaverton "left on the train for Sour Lake." Served by the Texas & New Orleans Railroad, Sour Lake was a popular spa, with sulphur-laden mineral waters believed to be restorative. There were numerous hotels; however, visitors complained of "mosquitoes and hard beds." There were no clean cups, no candles over an inch long, and the towels were too small.[10] When Leaverton returned after a brief trip to Houston, Hall gave him a packet of letters to take to the family at Hall's Bluff (Friday, August 11).

The steamer *Lone Star* brought three companies of federal soldiers to Liberty (Saturday, August 5), and as soon as the "infernal rascals" landed, they "commenced plundering through the premises of all the Citizens who lived on their route, in hunt of mellons, peaches, etc. They were very insolent and rude. I drove up town in company with Col. Jim Wrigley in hopes of seeing the Federals leave, one company left on the train but 3 others came in their place. The Lone Star left in the evening for Galveston and thank God, one of the Companies named above left on her." The remaining companies in Liberty left on the train to Houston (Thursday, August 17), and Hall wrote, "I sincerely hope no more will be stationed here."

It is very likely that circumstances honored Hall's wish. Although troops remained in Galveston until 1870, federal soldiers left Houston in August 1865, and because Houston did not require military rule, the provost marshal's office closed in November. Liberty and the surrounding county remained calm and quiet during Reconstruction, and it is likely that the presence of troops was minimal.[11]

With so much confusion in social roles, and so many of the freedmen destitute or seeking a new start as laborers, farmers, or small business owners, white families who needed the help of servants offered contracts to former slaves to keep them from leaving. Planters offered contracts to black laborers in order to grow and harvest crops, and in some instances, the black laborers worked for shares of the crop. The practice of contracting with blacks, usually for one year at a time, began months before the Freedmen's Bureau, designed to protect the rights of the freedmen, was set up. The newly freed men and women, illiterate and unaccustomed to legalities such as contracts, may have been conflicted by the lure of new opportunities versus the security of known employers and responsibilities. In Liberty County many freedmen, like Bill Hicks, continued working for their former owners. Others sought work in cities such as Liberty, Galveston, and Houston.[12]

Hall noted on Monday, August 7, that he "drove over and locked up Mrs. Beale's house." Susan, Mrs. Beale's "negro woman, who occupied her house, having refused to go to Mrs Beale in accordance with her written Contract, I sent her adrift." His assumption that Mrs. Beale would approve of his action indicates he knew her well enough to do so, but it also shows his frustration with the freed woman.

Even though Hall had very little cash, he nevertheless had to provide food for his family and those in his employ. From his friend Richard Cole, he "borrowed" six bushels of corn (Sunday, August 6). The following day

Hall bought fifty-five pounds of bacon for $7.30 from merchant James Skinner "on a credit." He owed Mr. Jackson "for 60 pounds of beef at 4¢" per pound (Thursday, August 10). He bought another fourteen pounds of beef and five chickens on credit from Mr. Jackson (Thursday, August 17), and the next day, he bought two dollars' worth of sugar, three dollars' worth of flour, and one plug of tobacco at six cents from Mr. Richardson, again on credit.

At the same time, Margaret, Jemima, Conny, and Wolf, as well as Fanny and Florence, all suffered from chills and fever. On Sunday, August 13, Hall wrote that he "remained in the house to waite upon the sick" and to write entries in his journal "in the intervals[.]" As the others recovered, Margaret remained ill, and Hall took the buggy into town to get (unnamed) medicine for her on Wednesday, August 16. Then he "remained at home pretty much all day to attend on the little woman & children." The fever passed the next day, but left her and Florence each with "a very sore mouth." Other health matters followed relentlessly. Hall suffered from "the itch[,]" which made his "getting about perfectly painful" (Monday, August 21), and a few days later (Friday, August 25), "a large boil on [his] posterior" as well as the itch, kept him at home. Just after his first boil healed, a second boil formed "just opposite where the first one came." The discomfort became so great that he remained at home, working in the new garden when able. Hall did not mention the boil again after Tuesday, September 5.

Saturday August 19th 1865. Today the little woman again missed her fever, and I now think she has entirely recovered from her late indisposition. I went up town to attend a meeting of the City Council and was by said Council elected Mayor of the City of Liberty. [A]*fter a full organization & election of all City officers, the Council adjourned until the next regular meeting. I purchased from Mr Bristley one pound of candles at fifty cents, and for which I yet owe him. Weather clear & hot: Ther: 92°.*

Hall served as mayor of Liberty until his death.

In the midst of his discomfort from "the itch," Hall conducted a mayor's court on Wednesday, August 23. "Today I walked up town to try a negro boy, who broke into the store of Mr Skinner, but the parties not being able to identify the negro under arrest as the one who committed the offence, I discharged the negro." Hall's respect for the law and his sense of fairness were among the attributes that served him and Liberty well during his term of office.

Hall continued to note his purchases, debts, and debt payments. He borrowed fifteen dollars from Charles Lund (Saturday, August 26) and "had a settlement with him for hauling some things up the country for Mr. Green. In said settlement I paid him for the bacon, lard and soap" bought earlier. Hall purchased five pounds of candles from Mr. Bristley (a merchant), paying cash, and also paid fifty cents for the candles bought on credit on August 19. On the same day (Saturday, August 26), Margaret bought seventeen pounds of beef from Mr. Jackson on credit. Hall visited with Charles Lund, who sent Margaret "a nice present of some peaches" (Sunday, August 27). A few days later (Wednesday, August 30), Hall paid Clay Stone 15 cents per pound for forty-three pounds of bacon and one dollar to Mr. Jackson for chickens purchased on August 17.

Planning ahead, Hall bought "garden seed" (Monday, August 28), and Margaret planted "eschalots" in the garden (Tuesday, August 29). Hall pulled corn out of a small patch to free up land for a pasture for his horse Rob (Saturday, September 2), and on Tuesday, September 5, he hired a black man named Ned Smith to plow the garden "in order to sow some turnip & raddish seeds." Whether bought or grown, the food supply continued to be uppermost in their activities.

On Friday, September 1, Hall visited with Frank Hitchcock, who "came over from Houston in company with Col Jim Wrigley" on the train. Once

Wrigley, who was ill, reached his home, Hitchcock and Hall discussed their "cotton matters."

Though Hall does not detail these "matters" it is likely that Hitchcock sought information regarding the $15,000 he gave to Hall to buy cotton: how many bales he had purchased, current market prices, whether they would sell the cotton directly to a textile mill or through a merchant or factor, and transportation costs. They may also have discussed the purchase and sale of cotton held by planters from previous crops as well as cotton crops still in the field. With Northern and European merchants paying as much as $1.80 per pound, anyone with cotton to sell could make a fortune. The next day, Hall drove Hitchcock to the railroad station in the business district to catch the train back to Houston.

Hall received letters from the family (Tuesday, September 5) advising him that his wagons were about to leave the farm (dates of the letters unknown). To his great relief, the wagons reached Liberty on Saturday, September 9. Bill Hicks drove one and John the other, "with 3 yoke of oxen attached to each wagon. They brought down some provisions, 22 chickens, 4 bales of Cotton and a small lot of furniture, and have been on the road 10 days. They however brought everything safe."

Hall sold the four bales to Colonel Jim Wrigley, now recovered from his illness, at 16 cents per pound, and he collected one hundred dollars of the sale price (Monday, September 11). With the money, he paid debts to grocers, and Margaret bought "a very pretty Calico dress for Roberta, which she is to send up by the wagons" (Tuesday, September 12). Charles Leaverton arrived on the mail stage (Thursday, September 14), en route to Sour Lake, bringing letters and $255 "in specie." During the next week, Hall paid what he owed to John Booth and bought food items. He noted the prices as a reminder of the high costs of these commodities.

Sunday September 10th 1865. Today I remained at home arranging my books & other things about the house. Hicks took Wolf off with him, and carried him up town to waite upon that old she devil Louisa. Weather variable and hot.

Wolf, whose formal name was Carroll, was only a boy and may have been attached to Louisa at the farm. Perhaps he and Bill Hicks missed her. Hall may have feared her influence would encourage Hicks and Wolf to leave him, but they went to visit and returned home.

Always busy, Hall spent much of September in making the house more attractive and comfortable. He wallpapered the dining room, hall, and parlor, and he placed carpet on the floor of the parlor and other rooms. Work on the house continued intermittently.

A popular man, as well as being mayor, Hall attended numerous social events. Serving as her chaperone, he drove Lelia (also spelled "Lela") Wrigley, the teenaged daughter of James and Ann Wrigley, to a surprise party at a private residence "given there by the young gentlemen of Liberty. We had plenty of dancing and so far as I am individually concerned spent a very pleasant evening." Hall did not state why he accompanied Lelia instead of her father (Tuesday, September 12). He also attended a party given by Mrs. John Wrigley (Monday, September 18).

After a party held at the home of Colonel Frank Hardin "given by the young men of Liberty" (Thursday, September 28), Hall stated that he "passed a very pleasant evening among the girls." Benjamin Franklin Hardin (1803-1878) came to Texas from Tennessee in 1826, settled in the Liberty area in 1831, and fought in the Texas Revolution in 1835 and 1836. Through the years, Hardin was a surveyor, colonel of militia, postmaster, and state legislator. Hardin County, initially part of Liberty County, was named for the extensive Hardin family.[13]

Hall did not always go to social events alone. On Wednesday, October 4, he and Margaret "attended a dancing party given at the residence of Mr A. B. Trowell. There was a large concourse of people in attendance, and the amusements of the evening gave general satisfaction to all participating. In fact it was a brilliant affair and reflected credit upon its projectors." He had made a cribbage board for Trowell (Thursday, September 14), and the two spent evenings playing the card game whist in company with others.

Abraham B. Trowell (age twenty-seven in 1860), the son of a schoolteacher also named A. B. Trowell, was an attorney, born in Alabama, with real estate worth $500 and personal property valued at $1,500 in 1860. When the census was taken, he was unmarried and living in the home of another attorney. Trowell opened his practice in 1858, specializing in claims collection, and was one of the speakers at the raising of the Texas flag on the square in Liberty in January 1861. He joined Waul's Texas Legion in 1862, served under Lieutenant Colonel James Wrigley in the Second Infantry Battalion, and was captured and released after the fall of Vicksburg in 1864. He returned to Texas to guard the coast at Galveston. Both before and after the war he served as a city councilman, and in 1866 he was elected to the second district of the Texas Legislature, representing Liberty and Polk counties.[14]

Clearly, Hall circulated within the upper society of the region.

Saturday September 16th 1865. Today I drove up town in my buggy, and while there I purchased from Mr. Bristley one barrel of flour at 11$, one half barrel Mackerel at 11$, one ½ barrel Sugar at 18$, and two decks of cards at $1. I done nothing in the way of papering. Charles Leaverton arrived on the train from Sour Lake, and left immediately on the same train for Houston, and as said train attempted to pass over the trestle work in the river bottom, the work gave way and precipitated the Locomotive, tender and one of the platform cars into the bottom, although it was a smash up among the cars, it mercifully happened that no person was hurt in the least. A special train came over from Houston after the passengers, and they all left on it. Weather changeable & hot, with occasional showers of rain.

Sunday September 17th 1865. Today Col. Jim Wrigley & Mr Haggart left for the up Country, and to the latter I loaned my revolver & Bowie knife. The Steamer Mary Hill arrived from Galveston and after taking aboard about 80 bales of Cotton dropped down to Walnut bluff. Weather variable & warm, with occasional showers of rain.

Monday September 18th 1865. Today I am engaged in papering the parlor. Capt John Redman came and stopped with me for the night. Hicks & John are engaged [in] hauling with my big wagon Cotton from the ware house to the Steamer Mary Hill now lying at Walnut bluff, they made 4 loads carrying 8 bales at a load. At night I attended a party given at the residence of Mrs John Wrigley's. Weather variable and hot, with a light shower of rain.

Tuesday September 19th 1865. Today Capt. John Redman is still with me. My negro man John or rather freedman by the nefarious proclamation of the President of the United States, although indentured to me for one year, ran off and shipped on the Steamer Mary Hill and left for Galveston. I finished papering my parlor. The little woman drove up town, after sundry articles. Weather cloudy with a light shower of rain.

Wednesday September 20th 1865. Today I worked on the hen house for the little woman. Capt. John Redman is still with me. Hicks hauled the beef hides out of my carriage house and stored them in Wrigley's warehouse. The evening I spent over at Mr. Trowell's. Weather variable and hot.

Hall spent September 21st and 22nd papering the hall with the help of John Redman.

Saturday September 23rd 1865. Today the steamer Mary Hill arrived at Walnut bluff, from Galveston, with 300 sacks of salt on board, which were consigned to James Wrigley. I drove down there and got my freedman John from off of her. He having run away the trip before, and left here on said boat. He promised me upon his arrival home to faithfully remain out the time for which he entered into a special Contract. The Steamer Mary Hill left for Galveston. In the evening I drove up town in Company with James Wrigley, and we were both regularly registered as Voters of the County & State. My wagon driven by Hicks is engaged in hauling salt from Walnut bluff to the warehouse, and hauled 72 sacks at 10¢ per sack. Capt. John Redman left my house for parts unknown. Weather cloudy & hot with a very hard rain late in the evening.

Hardly had the Hall family settled into their home when riverboat Captain John Redman turned up, first on Monday, July 10, when he came for dinner, then for an overnight visit on Monday, September 11. He returned on the 18th, again for one night, but remained until the 23rd. Hall's relief that Redman had left again is unmistakable, but his visits became more and more frequent.

In order to vote, men were required to swear an oath of allegiance to the federal government. As decreed by President Johnson, the Southerners received amnesty and the restoration of all confiscated property except slaves. The oath of allegiance was not the hated "ironclad" or Test Oath later instituted by Congress to keep former Confederate civilian and military leaders out of office.[15]

Hall made frequent entries about the newly freed slaves who remained with him, those he hired, and even those he sent away. Bill Hicks and John both fell ill with "the chills & fever" on Wednesday, September 13, but the next day, Hicks was busy "hanging the garden and house yard gates." Four days later (Monday, September 18), Hall noted that Hicks and John hauled cotton from the warehouse to the *Mary Hill* downstream at Walnut Bluff.

During the summer, as more federal troops left and the Freedmen's Bureau had not yet been established in Texas, Lieutenant Colonel R. G. Laughlin, the provost marshal general, urged the freedmen to sign work-related contracts to protect their interests. Hall considered the contract a form of indenture. Bill Hicks and John signed contracts with Hall to work for a year, but on September 19, John left on the *Mary Hill* to go to Galveston. Bill Hicks remained in Liberty, where he hauled beef hides from Hall's carriage house to Wrigley's warehouse for storage (Wednesday, September 20) and brought sacks of salt from the *Mary Hill* to the warehouse (Saturday, September 23). When John returned on the *Mary Hill*, Hall drove to Walnut Bluff to get him and bring him home. No doubt John had been eager to explore the world at large without intending to leave Hall permanently.

Still adjusting to their freedom, black men and women were now required to understand contractual obligations and the status of "employee."

Hall, who thoroughly understood contracts and indentures, may have had difficulty explaining the documents in terms the uneducated freedmen could comprehend.

In contrast to John, Bill Hicks remained as dependable as ever. That may have been his nature. He may have been earning and saving as much money as he could toward future plans. And he may have been content with the new arrangement because it provided security.

Very few walked confidently in this shadowy land of transition.

The assassination of President Abraham Lincoln on April 14 placed Vice President Andrew Johnson in charge of the wounded nation. A Tennessean, Johnson had opposed secession and now he generally followed Lincoln's plan for Reconstruction. The late President had wanted a smooth transition in the return of the states to the Union. Johnson demanded loyalty, but he was not in favor of revenge, nor did he want to see control of the government held by a few vindictive individuals in Congress. "Like Lincoln, he viewed the restoration of the Southern states as an executive, not a legislative, function; but while his predecessor had moved with great adroitness and flexibility, Johnson was rigid, stubborn, and inept."[16]

At the time Johnson took office in April, Congress was in recess, and he refused to call a special session to deal with Reconstruction. A great deal of controversy regarding Reconstruction as a Congressional, as opposed to a Presidential, function followed, with Congress insisting upon maintaining its authority. Johnson's actions independent of Congress caused so much anger that when Congress reconvened in December, it threw out Johnson's plans for Reconstruction. Johnson was impeached by Radical Republicans in 1868, but he avoided conviction by a single vote.[17]

Presidential Reconstruction was designed to follow a combined military and political plan. On June 17, 1865, President Johnson issued a proclamation making A. J. Hamilton the provisional governor of Texas. Hamilton arrived at Galveston on July 22 and reached Austin on August 2, where he called for a new state constitution, to be written by those who had remained loyal to the

Union. Like the provisional governors in the other former Confederate states, Hamilton called for a convention of delegates to be elected by the voters, and both delegates and voters were required to take an oath of allegiance. This policy was designed to prohibit the re-emergence of antebellum political leaders and to strengthen the political power of Unionists. Once the work of the convention had been approved (passage of acts regarding the nullification of Confederate authority, permanent abolition of slavery, and repudiation of the Confederate debt), voters would ratify the convention's ordinances, elect a governor, a state legislature, and additional state officers. And after the Thirteenth Amendment to the U.S. Constitution, which abolished slavery, had been approved by the voters, the state would be restored to the Union. However, the election of January 8, 1866, returned many of the former Confederate leaders, who were Democrats, to political power, infuriating the Republicans. At the same time, a reduction of federal troop strength, as well as the political and social influences of the Freedmen's Bureau, led to continued chaos.[18]

Congress authorized establishment of the Bureau of Refugees, Freedmen and Abandoned Lands, an agency of the War Department, on March 3, 1865. The new organization was established to help white and black refugees, but it became identified with the newly freed slaves. The Bureau helped former slaves find work, acquire land and transportation to it, negotiate labor contracts, receive medical attention, open schools, and obtain justice in legal matters. The Bureau was intended to last until the end of the war and for one year after, but its tenure was extended in July 1866 for two more years, and a Civil Rights Bill was passed at the same time. The Civil Rights Bill established the citizenship of the former slaves and assured their rights in all states "to sue, to testify in court, to purchase, hold, and dispose of real and personal property," to have the full benefit of the law, and to bear arms. In addition, punishment for violation of the law was to be no different from that of whites. The purpose of the Freedmen's Bureau was to protect the new equality of the blacks, their legal standing, and their safety.[19]

The work of the Freedmen's Bureau in Texas began in September 1865 with the arrival of Edgar M. Gregory, the assistant commissioner. Gregory appointed subassistant commissioners, which included two civilians (Dr. J. O. Shelby and A. H. Mayer in Liberty), and made traveling inspections through as much of the cotton-growing area as he could. However, a great deal of the state had no Bureau agent, and there were too few troops to provide help to areas troubled by threats or attacks by groups such as Jayhawkers or the Ku Klux Klan. Gregory remained until May 14, 1866, and four more assistant commissioners served in Texas until the Freedmen's Bureau closed during the latter part of 1868. The educational element of the Bureau continued until 1872.[20]

Hicks and John repaired the wagons for a return trip to Houston County, and Margaret bought several items for them to carry to her mother (Monday, September 25).

Wednesday September 27th 1865. Today Hicks & John left with one wagon and four yoke of oxen in route for my mills. Mr Haggart arrived from Houston on the construction train, but he failed to procure me another bowie knife in lieu of the one he lost, so I presume I shall be minus my knife. I am engaged [in] *working around the house and put the carpet down on the parlor floor. Weather variable and cool, with occasional showers of rain.*

Friday September 29th 1865. Today my freedwoman Jemima and old Elsey left me, in route for Galveston, thus leaving me without a servant, and forcing the little woman into the kitchen to perform her own household work. I assisted around the house generally. I received a pair of shoes which Charley Lund purchased for me in New Orleans for which he paid $3.50 and which amt. I still owe him. James Wrigley and Mrs. Perkins arrived on the train from Houston. Weather changeable and warm, with occasional rain.

On the following day, Hall "drove over to negroville and up town in order to hire a servant but signally failed. The little woman is still performing her own household work." Conny, who suffered from "a chill and fever" on Tuesday, October 3, remained with the Halls, but her role was unclear.

Monday October 2nd 1865. Today I remained at home, writing up this note book. The little woman is still doing her own house work. Col James Wrigley dismissed his former slaves Charley and Rose for impertenance. I loaned my revolver to James Wrigley to go out to Mr Minters, for the purpose of arresting said Minter on a charge of an Assault to commit murder on the person of N. Lacour. The party went, but were unsuccessful. Weather clear and cool.

Nicholas LaCour (age forty-five in 1860) was a farmer. Born in Louisiana, he was one of the Creoles, along with the Gillard, DeBlanc, and Dugat families, who settled in Liberty County during the 1840s. LaCour and his wife had seven children in 1860. Hall did not explain the circumstances relating to the attempted murder.

On Wednesday, October 4, Hall bought Margaret a hoop skirt ($2.50), a belt ($2.00), two pounds of cheese (80 cents), and 1 pound of candy (50 cents). That night, he and Margaret attended a "dancing party" at the home of A. B. Trowell.

Perhaps to have something more to do, and to help James Wrigley, Hall began working at the warehouse each morning, first noting it on Tuesday, October 3. He returned to the warehouse on the morning of Thursday, October 5, but spent the evening at home, "being rather unwell from my disipation at the party last evening."

On Saturday, October 7, he noted, "Be it remembered that my little woman attained the 25th anniversary of her birthday." And little James "attained the 3rd anniversary of his birthday" on the following day.

It appears that most of the pre-war patterns of Hall's life were returning to normal.

Transitioning business matters also filled Hall's journal entries. Charles Lund arrived (Friday, October 6) in Liberty by train from Galveston, where he had "established himself in business." The next day, Hall repaid Lund a loan of fifteen dollars plus another loan of ten dollars for 100 pounds of bacon, and $3.50 for the pair of shoes from New Orleans.

Without explaining his purpose, Hall arranged with Captain Tom Peacock to meet the *Mary Hill* at Walnut Bluff and continue to Galveston (Sunday, October 8). The steamer had come from Galveston and loaded forty-five bales of cotton from the warehouse, then "dropped down the river to finish loading with wood." That night, "a few wild geese flew over southward, being the first of the season." Although he could have left on the *Mary Hill*, he remained at home so that he would not miss little James's birthday.

Monday October 9th 1865. Today about one hour before day break, Col Wrigley & I drove down to Walnut bluff in the buggy in order that I could get on the Steamer Mary Hill in accordance with my agreement with Capt Peacock, but she had dropped down the river and I was disappointed in my expected trip to Galveston, so we returned home in time for breakfast. Col Wrigley's wagon hauled me 47 bu. of corn, that I had purchased from Mr T. W. Key. Charley Lund left for Houston. Weather variable and rather cool.

Tuesday October 10th 1865. Today the little woman and children drove out in the buggy, in company with a party of ladies and gentlemen, on a chinquepin hunt. I spent all the evening at the warehouse assisting James Wrigley in marking and weighing cotton. I purchased from Mr Lindsey one bushel of pea nuts for which I paid him two dollars. Weather variable and warm, with occasional light showers of rain, and a very hard rain at night.

On Monday, October 16, he "commenced clerking for James Wrigley in his warehouse at a salary of $5. per day, or if I remain as much as a Month, then at 100$ per Month." That same day, he bought twenty-one bales of cotton for Wrigley from J. F. Carr and A. Drew at 23 cents per pound. Before and during the war, Hall purchased cotton for 6 cents per pound.

The average price of cotton in New York for 1864-1865 ran 83 cents per pound.[21]

By the end of 1865, however, the cotton held in storage during the war had been sold. While Northern merchants sent shipments of goods to Southern stores and provided some improvement for the South, it was not enough to offset the wartime ruin. And even the sale of some two million bales in 1865 was offset by costs such as commissions and transportation. According to historian Harold D. Woodman, planters still owed debts to merchants and factors, "debts which had gone unpaid and had been accumulating interest for as long as five years. Southern merchants in turn were deeply obligated to Northern firms. Both growers and merchants required new loans, but indebtedness had first to be eliminated, a difficult task for those who had not managed to save valuable commodities during the war."[22]

On his way to Sour Lake, William Leaverton brought Roberta from Hall's Bluff "on the stage" so that Roberta could live with the Halls and go to school (Monday, October 16). Leaverton also brought letters from Hall's family, and he took letters from Hall to the family when he returned to Houston County four days later.

Florence turned five years old on Thursday, October 19, and Margaret "made her a first rate birth day cake."

Hall hired a black man named Ike to dig potatoes (Friday, October 20).

Billy Stewart and Mr. H. Ballinger arrived from Crockett on Saturday, October 21, and Stewart stayed with the Halls. That evening, Hall attended a meeting of the city council. On Sunday, October 22, he worked at the warehouse in order to receive a shipment of cotton. He normally did not work on Sunday, but Wrigley had left for Polk County on Sunday, October 15, and did not return until the night of October 22.

Wednesday October 25th 1865. Today I am still at work at the ware house and finished loading the propeller Kate. In the evening Billy Stewart, Mr Ballinger & I left my residence and drove down in my buggy to the steamer

Kate and embarked on her for Galveston. Before leaving I hired a negro boy by the name of Stephen for two months, for which I am to pay four dollars per Month. I also got from Mrs Wrigley $150. We were compelled to remain on board of the Kate all night, The Capt. having refused to start until morning. Weather variable and cool.

Steamboats were usually powered by boilers and engines that turned paddlewheels, placed on both sides or at the stern of the vessel. However, after 1840, screw propellers were sometimes used to drive steamboats. Hall referred to the "propeller Kate" to distinguish her from the steamboat *Kate*, built in Algiers, Louisiana, for service in Galveston. The small steamboat (twenty-eight tons), not launched until 1866, continued in river trade service until well into the 1870s. The propeller *Kate* also remained in service for many years.[23]

Thursday October 26th 1865. Today we left Walnut bluff on the Steamer Kate in route for Galveston, and had a pleasant run down to the mouth of the river. Our vessel got aground in the canal and the steamer Ruthven coming along side of our boat, we left the Kate and took passage on the Ruthven for Galveston, we were compelled however to lay at the mouth of the river all night. Weather clear and pleasant until night, when a severe norther came out, rendering it very cold.

On the following morning, they left the propeller *Kate* "still aground in the Canal," and continued to Galveston on the *Ruthven*, for which Hall paid $2.75 "in specie." The three men stayed at the Washington Hotel once they arrived in Galveston. Ballinger "handed" Hall $61.50 "which he had collected for the warehouse at Liberty."

Billy Stewart became seriously ill with what Hall termed Cholera Morbus, and Hall sent for Dr. Stanwood, who treated Stewart on Saturday (October 28) and Sunday (October 29). Hall remained with Stewart, going into the city "but little" until Stewart improved by Monday (October 30), when they both went into town "for a short time." Hall purchased several items for Margaret, paying sixty-eight dollars "in gold." The weather remained very cold, with a strong "north wind blowing" each day. Hall and Stewart took the steamer

Arizona to Houston on Tuesday (October 31). Hall noted that his hotel bill amounted to eight dollars in specie, and his passage to Houston cost five dollars. In spite of the norther, Hall and Stewart "had a very pleasant trip across the bay and up Buffalo bayou[.]" They stayed overnight at the Rusk House, where Hall had to pay one dollar in specie for breakfast (Wednesday, November 1). Hall and Stewart took a freight train for Liberty, costing four dollars in specie, and arrived home about two o'clock that afternoon. They probably rode in the "conductor's van" (caboose).

Upon his return home (Wednesday, November 1), Hall found Fanny sick "and confined to her room." She did not begin to improve until Tuesday, November 7.

At the warehouse, Hall bought cotton, supervised the loading of bales and beef hides onto steamboats, bottled and shipped brandy to a merchant in Livingston, and stored incoming freight. As agreed upon earlier, Hall began working for James Wrigley "at a salary of one hundred dollars per month" (Friday, November 3). On the same day, James Wrigley took the stagecoach for Polk County, and Billy Stewart "also left in route for Crockett." Wrigley's destination may have been Livingston, the county seat of Polk County. He was probably buying cotton, collecting money for unpaid bills, and generating business for his store. Wrigley returned late on Sunday night. A few weeks later (Friday, December 8), Hall moved the office from the warehouse to the storehouse "in order to be more comfortable." Postwar business was booming, but tragedy lay ahead for James Wrigley and for James Hall.

On Saturday night (November 4), Frank Stewart "arrived in the little woman's buggy, drawn by my mules. He reports all my relatives up at my mills in good health and that my wagon is on the road coming down. Frank is in very feeble health." Stewart remained bedridden for days, and on Monday November 13, he "was attacked with a severe hemmerage [*sic*] from the nose, I finally got it stopped with the assistance of Col. Wrigley, by holding his arm perpendicularly for about 30 minutes." On Tuesday, November 21, Hall bought an "overshirt" for Stewart from Ed Jones, and Margaret bought a shirt for him from a merchant "up town." The next day, Stewart had recovered enough to walk to the warehouse for the first time since his return to Liberty. He made a second visit to the warehouse on the following Saturday (November 25). After a relapse in December and weeks of being bedridden off and on, Stewart left by stagecoach for Crockett on Thursday, March 8, 1866.

Monday November 6th 1865. Today my wagon and team driven by negro man Hicks arrived from the mills with 5 bales of Cotton, my desk, and sundry other articles on board. The negro man John having run off and left it on the road, and Hicks after turning out the oxen left, and I suppose my employment for good. The little woman drove up town in my buggy after some articles. Fannie is still sick. Col Wrigley & I drove up town in Maggie's buggy, after returning home, we all went over to Col. Wrigley's, where The little woman, Mrs Wrigley, Col. J. Wrigley and I all took a solemn vow, not to use any spirituous [*sic*] *liquor as a beveridge for the space of one year. Weather clear and cold, with a hard frost at night.*

Disappointed by the loss of John, and unaccustomed to the independence of the freedmen, Hall lamented the loss of Hicks. However, the very next day, Hall wrote, "Hicks drove my team making 3 loads from the warehouse to town." Bill Hicks continued driving the wagon for Hall and he also hauled goods for others, such as Ed Jones. (John may have gone to Galveston to find Jemima and their baby.)

The *Sunflower* arrived from Galveston with a barrel of onions, a barrel of potatoes, and fruit for Hall's children (Wednesday, November 8). Hall then "loaded her with 350 bales of cotton & 52 beef hides." On the same day, Bill Hicks "made one load with the big wagon to the public square." Hicks continued to work as a teamster, hauling corn from Dr. Coleman's to cribs owned by Hall and Wrigley (Friday, November 17).

On Thursday, November 9, Hall "drove up town in order to try and sell my buggy and mules to Col. Bethell, but did not succeed, he only offering me about one half of my price."

Hall sold his "large road wagon" to L. Jackson for eighty dollars specie on Monday, November 27.

Beginning on Sunday, October 1, Hall noted more of the activities of Ed Jones. On that day, Hall loaned Jones his horse and buggy "to drive out after chinquepins." On Thursday, October 12, Jones accompanied Margaret and the children along with her friends Mrs. Wrigley and Mrs. Bolling to collect chinquepins "and had tolerable success." He loaned his horse and buggy to Jones so that he could go duck hunting (Wednesday, November 22), and Jones "presented" Hall with "a fine duck of mallard." When Jones needed to go "up country" to Livingston on business, Hall loaned him his revolver (Tuesday, November 28). First mentioned in company with Sam Sharp on Saturday, March 23, 1861, and often thereafter regarding activities in the store, Jones was a loyal member of Hall's inner circle.

Edward Livingstone Jones was born in Liberty in November 1840. He served in the Ninth Texas Infantry Regiment under E. B. Nichols and after six months of duty, he re-enlisted in Waul's Texas Legion, serving in Company F, Second Battalion, as a second lieutenant, in 1862. Captured at Vicksburg on July 4, 1863, Jones was paroled on July 19 and remained in the service until the end of the war, when he was discharged at Galveston in May 1865. Ed Jones married James and Ann Wrigley's daughter Lelia.[24]

Journal entries for November include illnesses for the family and for Frank Stewart, dinner at the Wrigley home, and chess matches with James Wrigley. At the warehouse he drew off brandy and put it up "in cases" (Saturday, November 25). Hall shipped six dozen bottles of brandy and twenty-eight sacks of salt to D. Willis at Livingston (Monday, November 27), and on the following day, he "finished bottling off the brandy" and noted that he was afflicted with sores and "the itch."

The Hall family still suffered from a shortage of servants. The "negro boy Steve" left, and Hall paid him $2.66 "for the time he had been with me" (Tuesday, December 5). On Thursday, December 7, Hall wrote that Margaret was "still doing her own house work" and that he could not "procure a cook for any thing like reasonable wages."

Monday December 11th 1865. Today I worked at the warehouse & assisted in loading the Str. Kate & Sloop Luna, we put 126 Bales of Cotton on them, and they left for Galveston. [The *Kate* was towing the *Luna*, a sailing vessel.] *At night I drove up town, with the little woman, to the residence of Pryor Bryan, to witness the marriage ceremony of Mr W. D. Williams and Miss Laura Bryan, After which the Company took up the line of march to the old City Hotel, where they touched the "light fantastic toe" until the "wee sma" hours of the morn. Weather cloudy & rather warm, with indications of rain.*

Laura was a daughter of Pryor Bryan, who fought in the Texas Revolution. The Bryan and Hardin families were related. (For details about W. D. Williams, see Chapter 3.)[25]

Two days later (Wednesday, December 13), Hall noted that Billy Duncan returned from "his trip up the Country." William B. Duncan traveled to Sumpter on Saturday, December 9, to buy cotton and to collect money owed to James Wrigley. He returned to Liberty by way of Livingston, arriving home at half past three on Wednesday afternoon, December 13. The following Tuesday, he returned the money Wrigley had given him to buy cotton with, and "after deducting my wages & expenses—$113.60—paying him $1386.40. He gave me some letters & cotton samples to deliver to Houston. Got back to Depot just in time to get on cars."[26]

During 1845, a large party of Louisiana Creoles settled in Liberty County. Among them were Dr. Edward J. Gillard and his family. William Berry Duncan, born in Louisiana in 1818, very likely came with them or joined them soon after. In 1848, at age thirty, Duncan married Eliza Gillard, age fifteen. They had three children before her death of pneumonia in 1856. Two years later, Duncan married Celima DeBlanc, age twenty-six, a niece of Dr. Gillard. William and Celima had five children. Beautiful, black-haired Celima DeBlanc Duncan became the belle of the county. Invitations to her picnics, soirees, dinners, and dances were greatly desired. William conducted plantation business, bought and sold horses and cattle, and pursued the interests of a country gentleman. He stood 5'11" tall, and as shown in a photograph, he had a dark, perhaps tanned, complexion, dark brown or black eyes, and black hair.

For years Duncan kept a diary in which he described money won and lost at gambling, loans made and paid off, and items purchased for him and his family. During the Civil War, he wrote many letters to Celima, which read like continuing conversations. Duncan first served with the Liberty Guards, then in March 1862 he joined the Moss Bluff Rebels, a company of eighty-four men organized by Ashley Ward Spaight and named for the Liberty County community where Spaight lived. After reorganization in June 1862 as Spaight's Eleventh Battalion, Texas Volunteers, Duncan was elected captain of Company F. Spaight's Battalion guarded the Sabine and Neches Rivers, saw action in Louisiana, and completed tours of duty at Houston, Galveston, and Beaumont.

After the war, Duncan returned home to Liberty. A farmer and stockman, he worked hard to support his family. He hunted turkeys, gambled a little, supervised his black workers, and joined them in the work. Duncan ploughed ditches, planted cotton and corn, and traveled back and forth to Liberty to conduct business, visit friends, and collect or pay debts. Always a serious man before and during the war, afterwards he began to sound like a man suffering from depression. He wrote of his illnesses, which were frequent, as well as his frustrations with hired workers and with neighbors who would ignore contracts and "steal" his workers away from him. He made no political comments and apparently felt no resentment toward the freedmen. During the summer of 1867, he injured his thumb, and no amount of medical attention, except laudanum, eased the pain. He died of apparent blood poisoning in August 1867 and was buried at Liberty. The beautiful Celima did not remarry, but lived in Liberty with her family until her death in 1925. In 1976, descendant Elizabeth Bennett donated their house to the Texas State Library, and in 1980, the Gillard-Duncan House was moved to the grounds of the Sam Houston Regional Library at Liberty. Duncan's letters and journals are also at the Sam Houston Regional Library.

Although James Hall's reference to William Duncan was brief, his friendship with Duncan is important. Duncan's journal and letters provide a personal account of events in Liberty County, which corroborates those described by Hall, and it firmly establishes the date of Hall's death.

Although no details are given, Steve returned to work for Hall. On Thursday, December 14, Hall wrote that he "loaned negro porter Steve" $2.50 "to give a party with at his house."

The entire Hall family suffered from "the itch," which no medical treatment would relieve (Friday, December 15), and on the same day as that entry, he noted that Josephine turned two years old.

Saturday December 16th 1865. Today I am still at work at the warehouse. Jimmy missed the chill and fever. Frank Stewart has a relapse and is now very sick with diarrhea. At night Mrs Beale and her whole family with three servants and seven horses arrived from Montgomery County, and stopped with me, to be taken care of until she can arrange to go to housekeeping. Weather cloudy and cold, with light drizzling rain.

Mrs. Beale's three servants and six mules left the following day to return to Montgomery County, but the house remained full of people. Ed Jones, who was in and out of Liberty on business for James Wrigley, borrowed Hall's horse and buggy "to drive out courting" (Tuesday, December 19). On Wednesday, December 20, Mrs. Beale moved to her own home in town, and Jones left again on business. Only Frank Stewart remained with the Halls.

Friday December 22nd 1865. Today I am still at work at the warehouse[.] Hicks [is] *hauling for Mr Wrigley, he also made another load for Mrs Beale.*

I drove up town and finished trying the negroes [for burglary, the trial began the previous day], *one of them I discharged and the other I held to bail to answer the offence at the District Court. We received by express $15.000*[.] *The little woman drove up town and purchased a few articles for the children. Weather cloudy and cold.*

Hall did not state who sent the $15,000, to whom, or why. The amount suggests the money may have been part of Hall's arrangement with Frank Hitchcock for the sale of cotton he collected while living in Houston County. It may have been payment for a cotton consignment. Or it may have been funds with which to buy more cotton as it came down the river.

Sunday December 24th 1865. Today I am very busy at work at the warehouse[.] *We shipped 146 B/C* [bales of cotton] *by an extra train of the T & N.O. R.R.* [Texas and New Orleans Railroad] *for Houston. The little woman drove up town and purchased divers* [diverse] *and sundry toys, to be distributed to the children to night by way of presents from St. Nicholas, put into their respective stockings. Weather variable and cool.*

Monday December 25th 1865. Today I am very busy at the warehouse, loading the steamer Kate & sloop Luna, we put 135 B/C. on them, when they left for Galveston. The only thing I had in way of Christmas festivities, was a first rate dinner, which was gotten up in the little woman's happy style. Weather variable and warm, for the season, with occasional showers of rain.

(Hall is referring to the propeller-driven *Kate*, which towed the *Luna* up and down the Trinity River. Since the *Kate* was a steamboat, Hall used "steamer" as a general term.)

The festivities of the season came to a devastating end on the day after Christmas.

Tuesday December 26th 1865. Today I am still at work at the Warehouse. The propeller Royal Arch arrived from Galveston, with 500 Sacks of salt on board consigned to James Wrigley. The salt was discharged too late to attempt to put in the warehouse. At night between the hours of 12 & two, some infernal incendiary applied the torch to Col. Wrigley's large and very excellent warehouse, consuming the entire building with about 324 Bales of Cotton, besides a large lot of furniture & various other things. The loss by the conflagration [will] *be at least 50.000$. Thus sweeping from Col. Wrigley, the accumulation of years of toil. Weather variable & warm, with occasional showers of rain.*

Wednesday December 27th 1865. Today I am at work at the old store house, which we have converted into a warehouse, and had the 500 Sacks of salt, which came up yesterday on the Royal Arch, stored away. The Steamer Royal Arch left for Galveston, with a very small freight. Weather variable and cold.

Thursday December 28th 1865. Today I am still at work at the storehouse arranging papers etc. from the utter confusion into which they were thrown, by the burning of the warehouse. Jimmy had a chill and fever. Frank Stewart is improving slowly. Col Wrigley is confined to his room, from sore eyes and burns received at the fire which destroyed the warehouse. Weather variable & cold, rain at night.

With James Wrigley at home, recuperating from his injuries, Hall remained at the store house. He checked in freight delivered by the propeller *Kate* and the sloop *Luna* from Galveston, and he shipped out seventy-one beef hides and nine bales of cotton (Saturday, December 30). The same day, Hall attended "a meeting of the citizens to raise a police guard, but it all ended in smoke." His disappointment resonates from the journal entry.

Sunday December 31st 1865. Today I am engaged in making out bills of lading for the Steamer Kate & Sloop Luna, both of said boats are still here. Mrs. Beale came over and spent the day. Jimmy had another chill and fever. Frank is still improving. Weather cloudy with occasional showers of rain. Thus I close my notes for the month of December and for the year 1865 which has just passed and gone and now numbered with the things that were. Whether the Almighty will spare me to record the daily events of things passing around me for the incoming year, is more than mortal man can know, but trusting in his goodness and mercy, I shall enter upon the pleasing task, which to me is useful as a book of reference, and may hereafter be profitable to those who have an interest in my affairs.

His words seem tinged with sadness, as if he knew more tragedy lay ahead.

Chapter 7

1866

Even though the warehouse had been destroyed just the week before (December 26, 1865), Hall seems to have overcome his sadness to begin the year with enthusiasm and a sense of purpose, perhaps occasioned by his new partnership with James Wrigley. This arrangement gave him the authority to make decisions about the business, offered opportunities for renewed prosperity, and enhanced his status in the community.

Monday January 1st 1866. Today I commence my notes of events that may daily happen immediately around me during the current year. These notes are not intended to be of any service to any one, except myself as a book of reference and to my family as a faithful exposition of my daily transactions. I formed & entered into a copartnership with James Wrigley to carry on in the town of Liberty a general Commission and Warehouse business. The Steamer Kate & Sloop Luna, left for Galveston. The little woman had a fine new year's dinner, which reflected great credit upon her art as a house keeper. I entered into a Contract with negro man Albert to work for the year, at 15$ per month with board, he furnishing a negro woman to cook. I also employed my old servant Hicks for the year at 10$ per month. Weather cloudy & cold with incessant rain throughout the entire day.

Tuesday January 2nd 1866. Today I am work at the store house. The boys are at work around the house. Hicks hauled one load of wood for Mrs Beale.

I made Hicks a present of 10$. Weather clear & cold, with a hard freeze and frost at night[,] being the coldest night of the winter so far.

Wednesday January 3rd 1866. Today I am at work at the store house. The boys are at work around the house. Negro woman Rose came over and set in to work for the little woman, relieving her from cooking. Rose is the woman furnished by Albert under his contract. Col. Wrigley commenced opperations on the cotton shed. At dusk Ed. Jones arrived home from his up Country trip, bringing me some letters from my relatives. Weather clear & cold, with another freeze & frost at night.

Journal entries full of small incidents followed. Albert became ill and could not do any of the gardening Hall wanted for several days, but returned to work by Wednesday, January 17. Bill Hicks spent an entire day (Thursday, January 4) hunting for the horse Rob, escaping "through the negligence of some of the children leaving the yard gate open." Frank Stewart, who had been ill since mid-December, felt well enough to leave the house and he "succeeded in killing a couple of squirrels." The next day (Friday, January 5), Hall drove into town in the buggy to meet the train from Houston, which delivered "sundry papers and letters." Later the same day, Margaret drove the buggy into town to do some shopping, and Hall bought some "cups and saucers" from a Mr. Fontaine. Frank Stewart, Roberta, and Florence became "sorely afflicted with the itch" (Saturday, January 6), and Hall applied a mixture of lard and sulfur to the girls (Sunday, January 7).

Monday January 8th 1866. Today I drove up town to attend the election for a delegate to the convention for reconstruction, and while there, I voted for J. O. Shelby to be said delegate. I assisted Col. Wrigley in making a settlement with B. F. White. Mrs Beale took her horse away, which has been staying here, since her arrival from Montgomery County. Albert is still sick. Hicks however is at work in the garden. Weather cloudy & cold with occasional light showers of rain.

Dr. John Orville Shelby was a physician practicing in Liberty from 1850 until the mid-1870s. A brief notice in *The Liberty Gazette* announced a

Christmas Eve (1856) ball to be given in Livingston by the "young gentlemen of Polk county" and that "supper arrangements have been entrusted to our portly friend, Dr. J. O. Shelby, of the Kaleta Cottage, and we know that he has too much pride about him to get up anything in a half way manner."

Felix Smotridge, born in Poland, was a fifty-year-old physician in 1860, with real estate valued at $4,000 and personal property at $2,000. His wife Josephine (age forty-four) was born in Louisiana. Family members in 1860 included a twelve-year-old boy named Joseph Desrisenx (born in Louisiana), and two girls: Joanna, age nine (born in France), and Cecile, age two (born in Missouri).[2]

Dr. J. O. Shelby fought in the Civil War between 1862 and 1865, serving as a first lieutenant under E. B. Pickett in the Third Regiment of Texas Mounted Volunteers. After the war, Shelby received two special military appointments to serve as county judge (1865-1866 and 1870-1875). Between 1866 and 1868, he was a representative for the Freedmen's Bureau. In 1868, Shelby and Dr. Felix Smotridge shared offices in the latter's home. Shelby was county treasurer (1869) and postmaster, and he served on the city council (1870-1872). Dr. Stanwood later lived in Dr. Shelby's home in Liberty.[1]

Following President Andrew Johnson's directive for returning the South to the Union, Provisional Governor A. J. Hamilton called a convention for reconstruction. Delegates were to be elected by voters who had taken the oath of allegiance, and those delegates were also to have taken the oath. The purpose of the convention was threefold: to declare secession null and void, to eliminate slavery, and to repudiate Texas' Confederate debt. Once these measure were passed and ratified by the voters, a general election for governor, legislature, and other officials would follow.

Held on January 8, 1866, the election returned many antebellum leaders, such as Hardin R. Runnels, O. M. Roberts, and Thomas N. Waul, to public office. Delegates to the convention, which began in February, elected James W. Throckmorton president. As summarized by Carl H. Moneyhon, the convention "showed the reluctance of the majority to meet anything more than the president's minimum requirements for readmission to regular status in the Union." The delegates also validated "all laws of the state government during the war that were not in conflict with the United States Constitution, the state constitution prior to secession, or proclamations of the provisional governor," thus creating a controversy that lasted for several years.[3]

Wednesday January 10th 1866. Today the Steamer Kate arrived from Galveston with a heavy freight on board. Frank Hitchcock came up on her, and we had a full settlement in relation to the cotton, I purchased for him. I am very busy discharging the freight from the Kate. I received by her 2 Bbls [barrels] *potatoes, one for Mrs Beale, also 1 box of cod fish. Capt. Chandler presented me with a fine large red fish, which was a nice treat. F. M. Sansom came down the river with a flat boat & 110 bales of Cotton on board, a large portion of which was shipped by the steamer Kate. Weather cloudy and cold, with indications of rain.*

On the following day, the *Kate* was loaded with ninety-five bales from the flatboat and left for Galveston with Frank Hitchcock on board. Hall bought rails, planking, two skiffs, and a saddle blanket from Sansom, who was "in charge" of the flatboat. When the *Kate* next arrived (Sunday, January 14), Hall "received a new hat & one box raisons, keg lard & some butter." Hall had the *Kate* loaded the next day with cotton and gave Captain Chandler $10.60 in gold to give C. C. Lund & Co. in Galveston to pay for both barrels of potatoes and the codfish.

A few days later (Thursday, January 18), Hall wrote that the *Kate* "was burnt up on Red fish bar on her downward trip with 85 bales of Cotton." This event was corroborated by William B. Duncan. (This was most likely the propeller-driven steamboat *Kate*. The new, 28-ton *Kate*, built in Algiers, Louisiana, in 1866 for the Galveston trade, may not have been in service yet.)

While healing from injuries sustained during the warehouse fire, James Wrigley supervised the construction of the cotton shed near their steamboat landing (first mentioned on Tuesday, January 9). Wrigley "raised the second string or row of posts for the Cotton shed" two days later (Thursday, January 11). On

Saturday, January 13, the train from Beaumont "brought over the lumber to build the Cotton shed, and in the evening the wagons hauled it down to the river." Hall "sent over to Houston for some iron bars to brace the Cotton shed" (Thursday, January 18). For several days Bill Hicks and Albert hauled logs for "ground poles" to store cotton on (first noted on Saturday, January 20). John Cochran of Houston brought to Hall and Wrigley $10,000 in gold with which to buy cotton (Friday, January 19). Wrigley and the hands finished the cotton shed on Friday, January 26.

During this time, Wrigley "commenced digging a well at the convent" (Friday, January 19), which was completed on Monday, January 22. The Ursuline Convent and its school closed in June 1866 due to a lack of funds.

James Wrigley hired a Mrs. Buckley "to teach school for him until the 1st of July next" (Sunday, January 21), and they signed a contract the following day. He ordered a load of lumber from Beaumont, which was delivered by rail (Saturday, January 27) for construction of a school house. Two days later, Wrigley moved "the Smith house to a new location in order to convert it into a school house." With help from Albert and Bill Hicks, Wrigley "succeeded in getting it up to the new location and blocking it up" the following day (Tuesday, January 30). The men then remodeled the house for a school. Hall finished the interior with wallpaper, and on Friday, March 2, Hall pronounced the school house "now ready for business opperations."

Hall worked at the warehouse each day and continued to describe details of everyday life in his journal entries. Margaret hired a Mrs. Massie, who lived out of town, to sew clothing for the family. She stayed with the Halls for a week, earning "6 bits [75 cents] per day." She would return several times during the spring to continue sewing.

Work around the house included planting mulberry trees in the yard for shade, establishing a garden, and setting up a peach orchard with one hundred peach trees brought from Galveston. Fruit was a luxury. Hall's journal entry for Tuesday, January 30, listed "oranges, apples, banannas, and cocoa nuts" bought that day. The peach orchard would provide even more fruit for a longer period of time and presumably in such quantity that the family, servants, and guests could enjoy them.

Members of the family, including Fanny Fitzsimmons and Frank Stewart, suffered from unnamed illnesses. By Thursday, February 1, Hall himself fell ill.

Thursday February 1st 1866. Today I am so sorely afflicted, with a cough and cold as to render me entirely unfit for business. The little woman and Mrs Wrigley drove up town, to purchase a few articles. Hicks is still at work on the school house for Col. Wrigley. Albert worked in the garden, setting out onions. Mrs Massie, still here sewing for the little woman. Frank and Burt are no better. Weather variable and cool.

Hall remained at home with "a bad cold, cough and sore throat" on Friday, Saturday, and Sunday, which did not improve.

Monday, February 5th 1866. Today the steamers Indian No. 2 and Col. Stell came up to the landing from Walnut bluff and commenced discharging their freight. I walked down to the warehouse and made out the bills of ladings for 52 bales of Cotton, although I am quite feeble and suffering severely with a Cough and sore throat. Frank and Burt are still very sick. Fannie is better. Weather cloudy and cold with rain throughout the entire day.

After the steamboats left for Galveston (Tuesday, February 6), Hall continued to work at the warehouse. Although he was still suffering from "the cough & sore throat" on the evening of Wednesday, February 7, "there was a surprise party at Col. Wrigley's, to which the little woman & I was compelled to go. The party was a brilliant little affair, and passed off to the general satisfaction of all concerned."

Thursday February 8th 1866. Today Hicks & Albert are engaged [in] *hauling wood. I am at work at the Warehouse, although suffering greatly with bronchitis. Frank is still very sick. Burta is improving a little. I received from Thomas Haggart a bowie knife in lieu of the one, which I loaned him and which he lost, while on his tour through the Country. Weather clear and pleasant.*

Friday February 9th 1866. Today I worked a little at the Warehouse, and then drove up town, while there I paid Mr Brustley [Bristley] *every dollar I owed him, amounting to 26.50$ also all the little woman owed him. Hicks & Albert are engaged* [in] *getting wood. Mr Holley repaired my wagon, Mrs Beale paid me 10$ for keeping her horse, since the 16th of December last to the present time*[,] *she having sold said horse to Mr. Baldwin. Frank Stewart still very sick. My Cough and cold, no better. Weather cloudy, cool and unpleasant.*

Mr. Baldwin was probably J. W. Baldwin, who owned a hotel in Liberty. He was also a city councilman (1866-1867). Notices in *The Liberty Gazette* in 1866 and 1867 state "J. W. Baldwin & Co." was a consignee for goods delivered by the steamer *Alice M*, and Hall mentioned settling "in full" with him (Tuesday, February 27). The goods may have been for the hotel, or he may have also been a merchant, like Bristley.[4]

Hall worked at the warehouse on Sunday, February 11, and the next day Margaret "drove up town after some medicine for me." But Hall remained ill, and all of the children suffered from "sore eyes" and colds. In the midst of so much sickness, Captain John W. Redman, also spelled Redmond in some entries, paid a five-day visit beginning Thursday, February 15, which would not be his last.

Thursday February 15th 1866. The forenoon of today I worked at the warehouse and the evening I spent at home. I am still suffering with my cough and cold. Capt John W. Redmond arrived on the cars from Sour Lake and stopped at my house. Frank is still confined to his room. Hicks worked in the garden. Albert worked for Mrs Beale. [He was plowing.] *The children are still afflicted with the sore eyes. Weather variable and cold, with* [a] *strong norther blowing and hard freeze at night.*

Friday February 16th 1866. Today I am confined to my room at home, with the Cough and Cold, which is daily growing worse. Frank [is] *still confined to his room*[.] *Capt. Redmond* [is] *still here. All the children are still suffering with sore eyes & colds. I discharged the negro woman Rose, who has been cooking for me, since the 1st of January last, and whom I found to be a lying, deceitful & mean specimen of negro humanity, not worth the salt that she uses in her bread. Weather cloudy and cold with a strong north wind blowing & a freeze at night.*

There is no further explanation given for his discharge of Rose. The next day, Hall "spent the forenoon at the Warehouse and the evening at home." Margaret was "now doing her own cooking." His cough and cold were not improving, Burta and Frank were both still sick, and Captain Redman remained at the house.

Sunday February 18th 1866. Today I spent at home, not being able to get out, my cough and cold growing worse. The little woman [is] *still doing her own cooking. John Redmond* [is] *still here. The Steamer Indian No 2. arrived from Galveston. Weather cloudy & cold, with an incessant rain all day and all night causing the Trinity river to rise rapidly and filling up to overflowing all the ponds around town, In fact there is more water in the various ponds & lakes around town, than I ever saw before: with a hard frost and freeze at night.*

Hall returned to the warehouse on Monday, February 19, and attended a meeting of the city council that evening. The following day, most likely to Hall's relief, Captain John Redman left on the *Indian No. 2* for Galveston.

Wednesday February 21st 1866. Today I worked at the warehouse. The Str. T. J. Emery opened the draw of the railroad bridge, for the first time in 3 years and passed through the bridge, on the upward bound voyage. The Steamer Ruthven arrived from Galveston, with a small freight on board and left again for Galveston. My cold is no better. Hicks & Albert are at work hauling. Frank [is] *no better. The little woman drove out in the Country and brought Mrs Massie home with her, who commenced sewing for the family. I entered* *into a Contract with Henry a freeman of Color to cook for me, at 12$ per month gold. Weather variable & cool.*

Thursday February 22nd 1866. All the forenoon I worked at the warehouse and the evening I spent at home. My cough and cold being no better, and under which I am rapidly failing. Be it remembered that I attained the 47th anniversary of my birth day, and I had a magnificent birth day dinner and cake, gotten up in my cook Henry's happy style & with rich profusion. Mrs Massie is still here, sewing for the family. Frank [is] *still sick. The children's eyes are still sore. Weather variable and cold, with occasional showers of rain.*

On Friday, February 23, Margaret also became afflicted with "sore eyes." James Wrigley returned from Galveston that day (he had left with John Redman on February 20), and brought Hall "100 peach trees and two bales of hay." On Saturday night, Hall "sent for Dr. Shelby to visit me professionally, who came and administered some medicine, for my Cough, which is no better." That day Henry's wife came to live with the Halls "in order to be near her husband." Without explanation, a few days later (Thursday, March 1), Hall "paid off and discharged" Albert.

Saturday March 3rd 1866. Today I am at work at the warehouse, my Cough, however is no better. The little woman still has sore eyes. Capt. John W. Redmond arrived on the Str. [steamer] *Indian, and is now* [staying] *with me. Frank Stewart failed to get off in the stage* [to return to Crockett] *and is still at my house. Roberta & the children are all sick with colds. I am preparing to visit Galveston for Medical aid. Hicks is at work hauling with the little wagon. Mrs Massie is still here. Weather clear and pleasant.*

Mrs. Massie remained until Saturday, March 24, when Hall "paid her in full" for thirty-three days of work.

With a house full of so many people, and so much illness present, Hall may have needed a break as much as he needed medical attention.

Sunday March 4th 1866. Today I left Liberty on the Str. Indian No 2. in route for Galveston. We run down to the lower landing and took on board the 100 head of Cattle, and then proceeded on our voyage. I left at my house, in addition to my own family, Frank Stewart, who is still improving a little, and Capt John W. Redmond, also Mrs Massie, who is still sewing for the little woman. We run down to the mouth of the river and came to an anchor until morning. My Cough [is] *no better. Weather clear & cold, with a stiff norther.*

The vessel arrived at Galveston the next day at three o'clock in the afternoon, and Hall immediately went to see Dr. Stanwood, "placing myself under his medical treatment. My cough is no better." Hall did not mention medications the doctor may have given him, but each day he drove around Galveston or along the beach with Dr. Stanwood, and his cough soon improved. He shopped for "a few articles" to be shipped to Margaret by the *Indian No. 2* and bought two pairs of "fine gold spectacles" for himself and Margaret (Tuesday, March 6). The next day, he "drove out to the beach" with Charles Lund, where he "spent a very pleasant day." That evening, "Capt. J. H. Wootters called around to see me. . . ." Wootters was a friend from Crockett. L. E. Downes "arrived in Galveston direct from Crockett" and "put up with me at the Crawford house" (Thursday, March 8). Downes had come to Galveston to buy items to sell at his store in Crockett. By Downes, he sent a letter to Sam Sharp relative to his "up country business" (Friday, March 9).

On Sunday, March 11, he paid his bill at the Crawford House, "24$ for 6 days [of] very indifferent board" and moved to the Washington Hotel, where he "found much better accommodations for the same price of board." The next day, Captain John Redman arrived on the *Indian No. 2* with a letter from Margaret, "ordering some other things and in consequence of which I had to turn out and purchase them." He also noted that he drove out to the beach with Dr. Stanwood and that his cough was "much improved."

Tuesday March 13th 1866. Today after settling my board bill to the Washington Hotel, amounting to 8$[,] My medical bill 75$ and the various other bills, *which I had contracted amounting in all to 500$ in gold*[,] *I left Galveston on the steamer Indian No 2. in route for Liberty. We run across the bay and anchored at the mouth of the river for the night. My Cough is much improved. Weather cloudy and cool, with rain occasionally.*

John H. Wootters

Arriving in Liberty about sundown the following day, Hall learned that everyone was well, except Roberta, who remained ill but was nevertheless attending school; Frank Stewart had left on the stagecoach for Crockett the previous Thursday, and Mrs. Massie was still sewing clothes for the family.

The next day (Thursday, March 15), Hall returned to work at the warehouse, "making out bills of lading and shipping freight." On Monday, March 19, he "held the election in relation to the corporation tax" for the city of Liberty, and the district court for Liberty County began its session that day. Captain Redman returned, continuing his pattern of coming and going.

Although Hall's cough had improved, after attending a "dancing party" at Baldwin's hotel on the evening of Wednesday, March 21, he suffered a relapse. His cough would grow steadily worse.

Regardless of how he felt, Hall kept working at the warehouse, receiving and shipping cotton and freight, and on Monday, March 26, he held "a special Mayor's Court, for the purpose of trying Mr S. Baillio and a negro man for an affray."[5] He did not describe the circumstances or outcome. Hall sold two mules to attorney and land agent Henry E. Perkins for $300 specie, and James Wrigley took six mules, one horse, and ten sacks of corn by train to Houston, presumably to sell there (Tuesday, March 27). Hall also wrote letters demanding payment for goods purchased by various customers on credit, and he sent Ed Jones "on a collection tour up the Country." John Redman arrived on the train from Houston on Friday, March 30, and "put up at my house being quite sick." The same day, Hall noted that his cough was "rather worse than it has been for some time back."

Spring rains raised the level of the Trinity, first mentioned on Friday, March 23, and the following day, the *T. J. Emory* (also spelled Emery) arrived from upriver with 200 bales of cotton on board, bound for Galveston. Hall worked at the warehouse on Sunday, March 25, supervising the loading of the *Ruthven* with 500 barrels of freight. The steamer was bound up river, described by Hall as "rising slowly." The *Arizona* arrived from Galveston with freight for customers up river (Wednesday, March 28), and on Thursday, March 29, John Carr "arrived from Smithfield on a flat boat with 83 bales of cotton on board." He also "advanced Captain B. L. Taylor $150. on 2 bales of cotton" that day.

Saturday March 31st 1866. Today I am busy receiving and discharging 43 bales of Cotton, that has just came [sic] *down from Hall's bluff, on a flat boat belonging to A. J. Wolston, and for bringing which I paid him $172 gold. I received a* [letter] *from my relatives of the Country informing me that they were in good health. My Cough is but little if any better. At night the steamers Shreveport and Sunflower arrived from Galveston, bound up the river. Weather cloudy and cool. Thus I close my notes for March.*

Sunday April 1st 1866. Today the steamer Indian No. 2 arrived from Galveston bound up the river. I had to put on her 212 sacks of salt, which consumed nearly the entire day. She left about 4 o'clock for the up river. My cough is a little better. Weather variable and warm.

For the next week, flatboats continued to come downriver loaded with cotton. Hall marked the bales, then weighed and stored them at the warehouse prior to shipment to their consignee. John Murchison of Houston County brought a flatboat loaded with 300 bales of cotton (Wednesday, April 4), and three more flatboats "commanded" by Hall's friends John T. Smith, Wash Rose, and Mr. Brown arrived at the warehouse the next day. The cargoes were transferred onto the *Sunflower* and the *Arizona* and then shipped to Galveston. The *Col. Stell*, "loaded down to the guards with cotton . . ." brought twenty-eight bales for Hall plus his parlor furniture and one box of bacon. He paid $127 in specie for their delivery (Friday, April 6).

In early April a "raft" or "drift" of floating debris above the railroad bridge almost stopped all navigation on the Trinity, and steamers were stuck above the raft. Railroad "hands" worked to break it up (Wednesday, April 11). Hall continued to receive cotton and "landed all the flat boats, which [he] had purchased[,] on the flat in front of the Cotton shed" (Thursday, April 12).

Friday April 13th 1866. Today I am still at work at the warehouse. The Steamers Shreveport and Ruthven came down the river ladened with cotton and pretty well torn up. In consequence of the raft they were compelled to lay up [remain tied up at the landing]. *The river still continues to rise and I am fearful there will be a general overflow. Weather cloudy and rather cool with a very hard rain.*

Saturday April 14th 1866. Today I am still at work at the warehouse. The Steamer Indian No 2. came down the river loaded with cotton and landed with the other boats above the raft. The Steamers Emery and Royal Arch arrived from Galveston with some freight. Roberta and Florence are suffering severely with colds and coughs. Weather cloudy & cool with occasional showers of rain.

Sunday April 15th 1866. Today I discharged my cook Henry for stealing, In consequence of which the little woman was compelled to go into the kitchen and do her own housework. The Steamer Ruthven succeeded in opening her way through the raft to the rail road bridge when the hands belonging to said boat, cut the East span of the bridge and let the steamer through. The hands of the steamer Indian No 2. pulled down the west span of the bridge, but the boat did not succeed in getting through. The Steamers Emery and Ruthven left for Galveston. Weather variable & pleasant.

After such an optimistic beginning, Hall's disappointment with Henry must have been profound. He filed a suit against Henry on Wednesday, April 18, and a month later, the sheriff arrested Henry when he turned up on the *Indian No. 2*, which had arrived from the upper reaches of the Trinity (Friday, May 18). Hall did not say what Henry took, but on the evening of May 18, he "prosecuted" Henry "for theft" and "succeeded in binding him over to the District Court." He did not mention Henry again nor state what became of Henry's wife.

Ships and cargo continued to move regularly up and down the Trinity River.

Monday April 16th 1866. Today I am at work at the warehouse, loading the propeller Royal Arch, I sent forward to Frank Hitchcock 57 bales of cotton by the Royal Arch. The Steamers Shreveport & Indian No 2. worked their way through the raft and bridge and left for Galveston. The steamer Arizona arrived from Galveston and proceeded on up the river. The little woman is still doing her own housework. Pet [Florence] *is sick with fever. Weather clear & pleasant.*

Tuesday April 17th 1866. Today I am at work at the warehouse. In the evening I drove up town on business. Fawn [Florence] *is quite sick with high fever. Roberta is no better. The river has commenced overflowing its banks and is still rising. Weather cloudy, with occasional showers of rain.*

On Wednesday (April 18), Hall noted that the river was "overflowing all the bottom lands." The next day, he wrote that the river was "now on a stand." After cresting on April 19, the river began to fall and continued for several days. Hall noted the falling of the river as reported by steamboat captains arriving from the upper reaches of the Trinity River.

Each day Hall worked at the warehouse, loading or shipping cotton and other freight, and the steamboats struggled to get past the raft and the bridge. Although the river fell, the raft remained in place, and the steamers fought their way through the obstruction.

Perhaps Hall's concerns were lightened by visits from friends and colleagues. Mrs. Stanwood brought lamps, lamp oil, and a pocket knife she purchased for him in Galveston, for which he paid $12.50 (Saturday, April 28), and Ed Jones brought him three suits of summer clothing and a harness from Houston ($113 in specie) (Tuesday, May 1). Margaret hired a black woman named Winney to do the cooking and general housework for $10 per month (Tuesday, May 1). Misfortune, however, formed an undercurrent.

Florence broke out with measles on April 18, followed by Roberta, Conny, Jimmy, and Josephine. Treated by Dr. Shelby, each began to improve, and by Wednesday, May 9, everyone was well, but Roberta continued to suffer "from her nervous affection." By then, Hall's health had once more begun to deteriorate.

Thursday May 3rd 1866. Today I am engaged at work at the warehouse. Jimmy and Josephine are still recovering from the measles. Roberta & Florence are about well. The Steamer Col. Stell came down the river with 300 bales of Cotton on board and reports the river falling, she proceeded on her voyage to Galveston. The Steamer Kate arrived from Galveston, with some freight on board, which we stored except one load, which Col. Wrigley attempted to haul to town, but his horses became frightened, and run off with the wagon, doing considerable damage to the wagon, breaking up the harness and damaging the load of flour. Capt John W. Redmond is still with me. Weather variable and warm.

Friday May 4th 1866. Today I am still at work at the warehouse. The Str. Emery passed down the river with a full load of Cotton. James Wrigley is considerably [bruised] *up by his fall from the wagon, in the run away scrape last evening. Jimmy and Josephine are still recovering slowly from the measles. Capt John W. Redmond is still with me. Ed. Jones left for Houston on horse back. Weather variable and warm.*

Hall neglected to mention what frightened the horses, but this entry, in addition to his concern for James Wrigley, indicates there was a great deal of activity between the river landing and town.

Since Hall did not describe the *Kate* as the propeller-driven steamboat of the same name, nor mention the sloop *Luna*, usually towed by the *Kate*, the "Steamer Kate" named above may have been the new vessel built in Louisiana.

The large amount of cotton brought downriver for shipment to Galveston shows that many others besides James Hall held onto their crops during the war, knowing that the price would be high at the end of the war, when demand outweighed supply. Considering the destruction soon to come, they were wise to ship their cotton at this time.

Captain John W. Redman could not seem to find his way in life. After a trip to Sour Lake and a visit to his brother, who lived downriver from Liberty, he returned to Hall's on Wednesday, May 2. On the following Saturday (May 5), Hall put Redman to work painting his house, probably in exchange for room and board and to give him something constructive to do. By Saturday, May 12, Redman had finished painting the primer coat on the exterior, "except the door & window blinds." He continued with a second coat of paint, finishing on Saturday, May 19. Two days later, Hall painted "the gallery and steps." Redman rode off for the day but returned the next day (Tuesday, May 22), "having got on a drunken spree, lost his horse, saddle, bridle, blanket and coat and remained in the prairie all night." Redman sobered up, but Hall's patience with him wore thin.

Although the children were recovering from the measles, Hall suffered with "the itch." On Sunday, May 6, he wrote that he was "severely suffering from the itch, or some other infernal eruption of the skin, breaking out all over my body and producing considerable pain." He continued to work at the warehouse each day, but his sore throat returned and the itch remained severe; "between the two I am suffering greatly[,]" he wrote on Wednesday, May 9. The next day his sore throat had grown so much worse that he could "hardly swallow or articulate." After working all day on Friday, May 11, he "drove up town and had [his] throat cauterized or burnt with caustic." All of the children were well, except Jimmy, who had a fever and was "covered with sores" (Thursday, May 10). By Thursday, May 17, Hall felt "quite sick."

Even so, he continued to work at the warehouse, and at home he glazed "the sash door" and painted "the gallery and steps."

Saturday May 19th 1866. Today I worked at the warehouse in the forenoon. In the evening I walked up town in company with Col. Wrigley in order to attend a meeting of the City Council, which did not meet however in consequence of a very hard rain, which lasted all the evening. Capt. John W. Redmond finished putting on the second coat of paint on the house. Hicks is engaged hauling Cotton from the cars to the warehouse. Weather variable and pleasant after the rain.

Sunday May 20th 1866. Today I wrote a little in this journal and then walked down to the river. I am suffering with diarrhea. The river is rising very fast. John W. Redmond is still here and suffering with rheumatism. Weather cloudy and cool with occasional showers of rain.

During these days, Bill Hicks worked in the garden; hauled wood, cotton, and miscellaneous freight; and carried "two chairs and the centre [dining] table to the shop for repairs. He brought home the curtain frames for the windows" (Tuesday, May 22). (Mrs. Gayle had brought Margaret some drapes from Houston on Monday, May 14.) In June, he hauled bricks and sand for the blacksmith shop to be run by Captain Dawson, and shingles from Beaumont brought by rail.

Hall continued working at the warehouse during the day and in the evening he painted shutters for "the little room" (Thursday, May 24 and Friday, May 25). John Redman remained at Hall's, apparently doing nothing.

As mayor and a popular citizen, on Friday, May 25, Hall "attended a party given at the Court house, and remained there until late at night or rather early in the morning." Nevertheless, he got up the next day to go to work.

Saturday May 26th 1866. Today I worked at the warehouse. Hicks & Steve [a freedman hired by Hall the previous October 25 for two months and who continued to work for him] *are at work hauling Cotton from the cars. The steamer Ruthven came down the river, with all the crew of the steamer Col. Stell on board, the latter named boat having been seized by the government* *while up the river. My old friend John C. Zimmerman came down on the Ruthven and I loaned him 25$ gold, which he promised to return as he goes back home, or to deposit the same at Galveston to my credit with Mess.* [Messrs.] *Bolling, Spooner & Co. The Ruthven left for Galveston loaded with cotton. Capt Redmond is still here. Weather variable and warm, with light showers of rain.*

The *Colonel Stell*, named for a Trinity River plantation owner, was a sidewheel packet built at Pittsburgh, Pennsylvania, in 1860. The steamer was chartered by the Confederacy in 1861 and the Texas Marine Department in 1862 to carry military supplies and troops. During 1862 and 1863, the vessel held picket stations near Galveston. After an accident in Galveston Bay in February 1864, the steamer was raised and repaired, and she remained on cargo and troop transport duty throughout the war. In May 1866, the *Colonel Stell* carried what was reported as a large cotton cargo of 288 bales from Trinity River plantations to Galveston, although she had a capacity of 1,000 bales. Federal troops captured the vessel, as noted by Hall, and the U.S. Treasury Department sold her on July 12, 1866. Bought by investors, the *Colonel Stell* returned to the river trade until she sank in December 1867.[6]

Although Hall noted the weather in his journal, mentioning various rain storms, he did not describe the flooding which occurred along the Trinity River as far north as Dallas in late May and early June. *The Galveston Weekly News* for May 23, 1866, reported that cotton plantations along the Trinity were completely covered in water. Major John Smith of Houston County, a friend of the Halls, believed there would be "little if any cotton made on the Trinity plantations, most of which are overflowed." His own plantation of "4,000 acres under cultivation, is all under water except the portion on the higher bank." Smith thought the cotton crop might be replanted after the water subsided if there was any seed, but there was none available. "We would suggest that those who have seed to spare make it known at once."[7]

The Galveston Weekly News for June 6, 1866, stated that the steamer *Royal Arch* arrived "from the Trinity" the previous Thursday:

> Her passengers report the Trinity bottom nearly all overflowered [*sic*], only a few places of high ground that are now above water. The sheet of water on both sides of the river varies from 3 to 6 and even 8 miles wide. The plantations overflowed [*sic*] are entirely ruined for the present year, as the crops are destroyed and there is now no time to replant. The cotton crop of the Trinity valley is, therefore, a total loss, with the exception of a small portion of a few plantations beyond the reach of the water.
>
> The Royal Arch lay at Liberty some 24 hours on Monday last, during which time the water rose some four inches, and was still rising, when she left, on Tuesday. The heavy rise reported up at Dallas has not reached Liberty, and when it does, will probably cause still greater damage.[8]

Hall's friend G. W. "Wash" Rose, a well-known steamboat captain, had taken the *Ruthven* upriver on June 1. In an open letter published in *The Galveston Weekly News* on June 27, 1866, the "planters along the [Trinity] river, one and all, wish to tender to Captain Wash Rose, the efficient commander of the steamer Ruthven, their thanks for his kindness on his last trip down, in his backing up at every landing to notify them of the coming flood, whereby they were enabled to save a large amount of stock and property, which would otherwise have been lost." Rose sailed as far up the Trinity as Pine Bluff, 575 miles upriver from Galveston or 119 river miles above Hall's Bluff. According to the newspaper, losses of "[w]ork stock, hogs, cattle, growing crops, fences, etc. will amount to two million dollars to the farmers on this river alone." The thoughtful and courageous Captain Rose returned safely to Galveston on June 17.[9]

The flooding also affected rail traffic. On August 1, 1866, *The Galveston Weekly News* printed a story from *The Liberty Gazette* that stated: "The railroad bridge across the Trinity is, we learn, nearly ready for the cars again. Since the overflow went down, the work of repairing the bridge has been pushed forward with much vigor and spirit. We learn the cars will pass over the bridge next Friday." The bridge had been completed in 1861.[10]

Hall spent Sunday, May 27, writing in his journal and visiting with James Wrigley in the afternoon. The *Royal Arch* brought him buggy cushions and five gallons of kerosene on Monday, and a norther that night made the temperature "quite cold." On Tuesday, May 29, Wrigley began building "a shed" onto the warehouse, and John Redman left on the *Royal Arch* "to visit" New Orleans—Hall was no doubt relieved. Work continued on the warehouse shed with help from "the hands" the following day.

Thursday May 31st 1866. Today I am at work at the warehouse. Col. Wrigley with the hands finished the ground work and laying the floor of the warehouse shed. Hicks & Steve are at work hauling the salt out of the McKim house and piling it upon the platform or floor of the shed. Jimmy & I are still suffering with the itch or some other infernal sores. Weather variable and cool with occasional showers of rain. Thus closes my jottings for the month of May.

Friday June 1st 1866. Today I am at work at the warehouse. Hicks & Steve are still hauling salt & finished removing the same. The steamer Indian No 2. arrived from Galveston bound up the river, after taking on board 100 sacks salt, she proceeded on her voyage. Jimmy & I are still sorely afflicted with the itch. As this is the first day of summer I began to note the stage of the thermometer as I have heretofore kept it. Ed. Jones arrived from Galveston on the steamer Indian No 2. Weather variable and hot. Ther: 86°.

Saturday June 2nd 1866. Today I am at work at the warehouse. Col. Wrigley with the hands let the McKim house down and cut out several doors in order to convert the building into a black smith shop. The steamer Ruthven arrived from Galveston bound up the river and after putting off some freight she left on her voyage. Weather variable and hot, with a rain at night. Ther: 88°.

By Sunday, June 3, Hall suffered from a cough in addition to the itch, and the entire family also had the itch. Social events, however, lightened the days.

Monday June 4th 1866. Today I am at work at the warehouse. Hicks & Steve are hauling sand to fill up the black smith shop. I am still suffering with the cough & itch. At night the little woman had a magnificent oyster supper to which she invited Col. Wrigley & family, Mr & Mrs Trowell, Ed Jones, Mrs. Buckley and various others. The affair passed off very pleasantly and to the general satisfaction of all. Weather variable and hot with occasional showers of rain. Ther: 86°.

By Wednesday, June 6, Hall noted that in the evening he was "confined at home with the fever in addition to all my other ailments." On Friday, June 8, he "took quinine all day and missed the fever. I am however suffering severely with the cough."

Captain Dawson opened the blacksmith shop for "public custom" on Wednesday, June 13, but work on the shop continued through Saturday, June 23. Wrigley next supervised the construction of an additional salt shed and a shop for "wagon work" (Saturday, June 30). The 32,000 shingles from Beaumont, delivered on Saturday, June 9, were used on these buildings.

Margaret was once again doing her own cooking and housework, Winney having left on the first of June.

Thursday June 7th 1866. The forenoon of today, I worked at the warehouse. In the evening I remained at home & painted one shutter, after which I had another fever in addition to my other diseasements. Hicks hauled bricks and sand to the black smith shop. The little woman hired a negro woman by the name of Ann, incumbered with two children for her services as cook in addition to supporting her two children, she is to receive six dollars per month in specie, thus relieving the little woman from cooking. Weather variable and hot. Ther: 88°

Ann was not mentioned again in the journal, and it is not known how long she remained with the Halls.

Hall spent Sunday, June 10, "writing up this journal" and visiting with Ed Jones and Captain Dawson. The *Royal Arch* on Monday, June 11, brought "a barrel of ice to cool the parched tongue" from Galveston. No doubt the ice was more than welcome.

During this time, Hall's entries became very short. He worked at the warehouse, painted shutters, and described his health concerns. The itch and the cough did not improve. He noted the passage of steamboats up and down the river, the passing of friends to and from Galveston or Houston, and visits with friends, especially Captain Dawson and Ed Jones. Bill Hicks and men named Montgomery and Ed worked in the potato and corn patches. His fever returned on Saturday, June 16.

Friday, June 15th 1866. Today I worked at the warehouse. Ed Jones arrived from Houston on the cars, bringing an umbrella & some other things for me. I sent my buggy down to the shop for some repairs. I am still suffering with my cough. Hicks is engaged hauling. Weather cloudy & hot with a hard gale at night. Ther: 89°.

Wednesday June 20th 1866. Today I am at work at the warehouse. Col. Wrigley and the hands are still at work on the shop. Steve's team run away and litterly [sic] *smashed Col. Wrigley's wagon. Hicks had to run my wagon and team in place of Col. Wrigley's, hauling lumber from the cars. The Str. Royal Arch left for Galveston. Weather clear & hot. Ther: 88°.*

Monday, June 25th 1866. Today I worked at the warehouse until dinner loading and making out freight bills for the Str. Royal Arch in order that she may leave for Galveston, which she done in the evening. I drove up town and attended the election for State and County officers. I also attended a session of the City Council. I am still suffering with cough and the itch. Roberta had a fever which lasted nearly all day. Weather clear and hot. Ther: 90°.

Tuesday June 26th 1866. Today I attended a meeting of the City Council at which we passed several sanitary ordinances in order to protect the citizens of Liberty against the small pox, which disease is now prevalent in the city. In the evening George Gordon and Henry P. Angell came over from West Liberty having walked nearly the entire distance and being pretty well broken down. Mr. Gordon stopped with Col. Wrigley and Mr. Angell put up with me. At night I attended a party at Col. Wrigley's residence, which was quite a gay affair. We danced until about 3 O'clock in the morn. Everything passing off to the entire satisfaction of all concerned. The hands are still at work on the salt shed. Weather variable and hot. Ther: 92°.

The party was apparently a major social event and was covered in the local newspaper. T. J. Chambers, editor of *The Liberty Gazette*, attended the "very pleasant party, at Col. Jas. Wrigley's, on the evening of the 28th ult [ultimo, or last]. A large portion of the youth and beauty of the town were present, and all seemed to enjoy themselves finely." The editor's article appeared in *The Liberty Gazette*, July 4, 1866; the disparity in dates may be a misprint.

Wednesday June 27th 1866. Today I done but little work. I am however loafing around generally for want of sleep and rest from my dissipation last night. Mr. Angell is still with me. Hicks is at work on the salt shed. Roberta & Jimmy both had fever. Weather variable and hot with a shower of rain in the evening. Ther: 92°.

By Saturday, June 30, four of the children (Roberta, Jimmy, Fanny, and Florence) were sick with fever, but all of the children improved rapidly except Florence, who remained feverish for another week. Smallpox claimed three lives in town, Hall wrote on Monday, July 9.

Unaware of approaching tragedy, Hall left for Galveston aboard the *Royal Arch* on Tuesday, July 10. At Walnut Bluff, the steamboat "got aground where we remained two hours, after getting off we run down to Pipkins' [*sic*] place and there tied up for the night."

Wednesday July 11th 1866. Today we left Pipkin's [sic] *place, and after a hard and boisterous run, we succeeded in reaching the mouth of the river a distance of 12 miles, where we came to anchor for the night and had magnificent exercise fighting mosquitoes the whole night. Weather cloudy and warm, with rain throughout the day. Ther: 86°.*

After "a boisterous run across the bay," Hall reached Galveston on Thursday, July 12, where he "found" James Wrigley, and they "put up at the Washington Hotel." Hall purchased items to take home, and in the evening he drove out to the beach with Dr. Stanwood, who told Hall about his "domestic difficulties." Hall and Wrigley attended a party at Dr. Stanwood's home that night (Friday, July 13). After attending to business on Saturday (July 14), Hall left Wrigley in Galveston and "had a pleasant run across the bay and up the bayou" to Houston on the *Era No. 3*. Hall must have received a telegram, by means of the railroad telegraph office, urging him to hurry home.

Monday July 16th 1866. Today about dawn I arrived in Houston and immediately left in an omnibus for the depot of the Texas and New Orleans Rail Road, we left the depot on the train at 9. O'clock A.M. for Liberty. I arrived home at 4 O'clock P.M. just in time to witness the death throes of my sweet little daughter Josephine Martha, who departed this life at 5½ O'clock, and now reposes sweetly upon the bosom of her Savior. She died at the tender age of two years seven months and one day. The neighbors generally came in and bestowed upon my stricken family such consolation as they could under our heavy trial. Weather cloudy and hot, with occasional showers of rain. Ther: 90°.

Tuesday July 17th 1866. Today my poor wife is indeed a sorrow stricken and almost heart broken woman, for the loss of our sweet little angel Josephine Martha. I performed the last sad rite for her little remains and had them interred in the burial ground at Liberty there to remain until her God shall call her again to meet him, in the great day of accounts. My sweet little babe, may she rest peacefully on the bosom of her God, and may this sad bereavement be for our future good. Edward Jones left on the cars for Houston. Weather Cloudy and hot, with occasional showers of rain. Ther: 86°.

Wednesday July 18th 1866. Today I drove up town in my buggy and while the [there] *paid the funeral expenses of my sweet little angel Josephine Martha, which amounted to 55$ in gold. I then drove to the warehouse but did not remain long, being in no condition to attend to business. My little woman is still suffering great agony for our sad bereavement. Edward Jones arrived on the cars from Houston and brough*[t] *me a large piece of ice, which is quite refreshing* [in] *this hot weather. Mrs Buckley came over and* *spent the evening with the little woman, giving her all the Consolation in her power. Weather variable and hot. Ther: 90º.*

Hall spent most of Thursday, July 19, at the warehouse, although he took time to pay Dr. Coleman "his medical bill for his attention to my sweet little babe." Mrs. Beale, Nellie's mother, and Mrs. Buckley, the teacher, stayed with Margaret. James Wrigley and his mother-in-law "Grand Ma Gayle" returned from Houston the next day, and Hall noted that Margaret was "fixing up her clothing to visit Houston & Galveston."

Saturday July 21st 1866. Today I drove up town in Company with Col. Wrigley to attend a meeting of the board of aldermen for the City of Liberty and while there was re-elected Mayor of said City for the ensuing year, after which I returned home and drove in the buggy to the Rail Road depot with The little woman, Roberta, Florence, Jimmy and negro woman Louisa [Hicks] *and all their baggage, when we all left on the cars for Houston. Mrs Buckley also went along with us. we arrived in Houston about 4 O'clk and put up with Mrs Perkins. Expenses of the day 20$ specie. Weather changeable and hot, with occasional showers of rain. Ther: 90°.*

On Sunday the family remained with Mrs. Perkins. Margaret "visited church and in the evening went around to see Mrs Ruthven." On Monday, they traveled to Galveston by rail, arriving about seven o'clock that evening, and rented rooms at the Washington Hotel. Mrs. Buckley stayed with the family of Major Bolling, a merchant.

Tuesday July 24th 1866. Today we left the hotel, and moved our quarters to the residence of Capt Peacock, who agreed to board my family during their stay in the Island City. I hired a hack and went with the little woman and children down the beach, we had quite a pleasant drive. The little woman purchased a nice little Italian marble monument to be placed over the grave of my sweet little babe Josephine. Weather clear & hot. Ther: 90°.

Wednesday July 25th 1866. Today we are still in Galveston and stopping at Capt. Peacock's. In the evening I purchased a match horse for Rob for which I paid 250$. I drove out to the beach with Capt. Peacock in order to try my new horse Charley. The [troop] *transport Clinton arrived in port with several cases of Cholera on board. Weather variable & hot. Ther: 91°.*

Thursday July 26th 1866. Today we all left Galveston in route for home, and arrived in Houston about 10½ O'clock A.M. and put up at the Eldorado Hotel. The little woman went out shopping and purchased a few articles. Weather variable and very hot: Ther: 92°.

Friday July 27th 1866. Today we all left Houston, on the Texas & N. Orleans rail road in route for Liberty, and arrived home about 12 O'clock M [meridian, or noon]. *Dr Tarleton came over with me upon a tour of inspection*[.] *Col. Wrigley and family I found all well. I also found the steamer Col. Stell lying at the wharf, but she left in the evening for Galveston. Weather variable and hot. Ther. 92°.*

Saturday July 28th 1866. Today I drove up town in company with Dr. Tarleton and introduced him to the citizens of the place, after which he left on the train for Houston. I spent the evening at the warehouse. Jimmy had a fever. Weather clear and very hot. Ther: 96° being the hottest day of the summer so far.

After a quiet day on Sunday, which Hall spent reading and going to the warehouse, a thunderstorm "came up attended with rain, which cooled the air a little."

Monday July 30th 1866. Today I worked at the warehouse. Dr. Tarleton, wife and child came over on the train from Houston having determined to make Liberty their home. They put up at the hotel. Jimmy missed the fever. Weather variable and hot with occasional showers of rain. Ther: 92°.

Tuesday July 31st 1866. Today I am at work at the warehouse. Dr. C. L. Tarleton, wife and child came to my house to stop until he could make arrangements to keep house. Capt. John W. Redman also came to my house and put up with me, he having arrived on the cars from Sour Lake. I sent my wagon up town after their baggage. Weather variable and hot. Ther: 94° thus closes my notes for July.

All of these people took advantage of Hall's generosity, making the last weeks of his life thoroughly frustrating.

The actions of the Eleventh Legislature, which convened on August 6, 1866, alarmed military commanders, the assistant commissioner of the Freedmen's Bureau, and members of Congress. The decisions of the Eleventh Legislature included: the selection of O. M. Roberts and David G. Burnet, both former secessionists, to serve in the Senate; refusal to ratify the Thirteenth and Fourteenth Amendments; and passage of "black codes" designed to govern black laborers, which appeared to initiate a new form of slavery, although to whites they were meant as a way to stabilize labor relations. These acts indicated that "the former Confederates were back in control and unrepentant."[11]

The Radical Republicans in Congress, who had gained control over the more conservative members, ended Presidential Reconstruction by enacting the First Reconstruction Act on March 2, 1867. This act divided the South into military subdistricts and stated that the currently elected state governments were only provisional. On July 30, 1867, Texas Governor James W. Throckmorton, elected the previous year, was removed from office. Elected officials in fifty-seven counties plus Austin and San Antonio were removed in November, and others were dismissed as late as 1869. The "Iron-Clad Oath" required Southerners to swear that they had never voluntarily given aid to soldiers, supported a hostile government, or borne arms against the United States, thus eliminating former Confederates from holding office.[12]

Another constitutional convention had to be held, and the new state constitution established a more centralized government. The Twelfth Legislature met in February 1870, passed the Fourteenth and Fifteenth Amendments, and elected two U.S. senators. Congressional Reconstruction ended on March 30, 1870, when President Ulysses S. Grant readmitted Texas into the Union, but Radical Republican government continued until January 1874, when Democrat Richard Coke took office as governor.

James Hall would not see any of these events take place.

Wednesday August 1st 1866. Today I was compelled to go up town, in order to try Nat. Holley for an assault & battery committed upon the person of Wm. Thomas, after hearing the evidence I found him guilty & entered a fine of 10$ & costs. Capt John W. Redman is still here. Hicks is at work building a wagon shed. Weather variable and hot. Ther: 90°.

The summer heat was relieved on Thursday, August 2, by an evening thunderstorm that brought "severe & intense rain and wind from the North, which caused the thermometer to run down to 80° & stopped all kind of business."

Friday August 3rd 1866. Today I am at work at the warehouse. Capt Redman is still with me. The little woman drove up town in the buggy after some articles. I am still afflicted with the itch. Hicks is still at work on the wagon shed. Weather cloudy & hot with occasional showers of rain. Ther: 86°.

A quiet weekend followed, with only a meeting of the city council on Saturday and attendance at the funeral of seventeen-year-old Prescott Pickett, son of Colonel E. B. Pickett, on Sunday to interrupt the usual daily events.

Monday August 6th 1866. Today I went up town and held an election for seven trustees or aldermen for the Corporation of the City of Liberty[,] *The time of the old board having expired, At which said election I was again re-elected one of the Aldermen. Capt John W. Redman is still with me. I received from Galveston by way of Houston the little monument purchased by the little woman, and to be erected over the grave of my sweet little babe Josephine Martha. Weather variable and hot. Ther: 96°.*

Tuesday August 7th 1866. Today I am at work at the warehouse. Dr. Tarleton & family also Capt John W. Redman are still with me. Hicks finished covering one side of the roof of the wagon shed. Weather clear and hot. Ther: 95°.

For two quiet days, very little business took place at the warehouse. Bill Hicks fell ill for those two days, a rare occurrence for that indefatigable man.

Friday August 10th 1866. Today I am at work at the warehouse. Col. Wrigley left the warehouse sick and is now confined at his home. Ed Jones and Grandma Gayle arrived on the cars from Houston & Galveston and report the cholera prevailing at the latter City. Capt John W. Redman is still with me. Hicks is better and worked a little on the wagon shed. Weather variable and hot. Ther: 92°.

Ed Jones and Mrs. Gayle traveled by rail to Houston on Saturday, August 4.

Bill Hicks "finished covering in the wagon shed" on Saturday, August 11, and on Monday, August 13, he hauled wood, apparently recovered from his illness.

Tuesday August 14th 1866. Today I worked at the warehouse. Mrs James Wrigley left on the train for Houston. Capt John W. Redman rode out in the country after dinner and remained all night. Hicks is at work on the wagon shed. In the evening I commenced a border leading from the front gate to the house made with glass bottles. I was assisted by Ned Smith. Ed Jones is quite sick. Weather clear and hot. Ther: 92°.

On Wednesday, August 15, Hall spent the morning at the warehouse, and in the evening he continued work on the glass border from the gate to the front steps with Ned Smith. Likewise, Bill Hicks continued work on the wagon shed, and John Redman returned "from his visit to the country" and "put up" with Hall. The following day passed almost the same, except that Bill Hicks finished the wagon shed, and Ed Jones recovered from his illness.

The horse Charley arrived by rail from Galveston on Friday, August 17. Stable and other expenses added up to $31.50. A hard rain fell that evening.

Saturday August 18th 1866. Today I left Liberty on the cars for Houston in Company with Col. Wrigley and his family. We arrived in Houston safe and sound and put up with Mr Perkins, I carried over with me $4000. in gold. Col. Wrigley's son John was sick all the way over. I am sorry to state that I drank too much brandy as medicine, to prevent the cholera which is now prevailing in Houston. Weather cloudy and hot, with occasional showers of rain. Ther: 88°.

Hall and the Wrigley family remained in Houston on Sunday, August 19, "there being no communication between Houston & Galveston on sunday." The next day, however, Hall and Wrigley traveled by rail to Galveston, arriving about half past six that evening, and "took rooms at the Washington Hotel."

Tuesday August 21st 1866. Today I am still in Galveston. I deposited with Messrs. J. C. & S. R. Smith & Co the sum of 3000$ in gold, subject to the order of myself or Col. James Wrigley. In the evening I left Galveston on the Steamer Era No 3. bound for Liberty, having left Col. Wrigley in Galveston[.] *I had a pleasant trip across the bay & up Buffalo bayou, and met many old acquaintances on board of the Steamer. Weather variable & hot: Ther: 84°.*

He did not say what happened to the other $1,000.

Wednesday August 22nd 1866. Today at 7½ O'clock A.M. I arrived at Houston and immediately took a carriage for the rail road depot and arrived in time for the train for Liberty. I arrived in Liberty at 12. O'clock M. and found my family all well. I also found Capt. John W. Redman still living at my house. I hired Ned Smith a freedman to work for me, one month for which I am to pay him 20$. he losing all lost time. [In other words, he would not be paid for days he did not work.] *Weather variable & hot: Ther: 84°.*

Thursday August 23rd 1866. Today I am at work at the warehouse. Capt. John W. Redman is still with me. Roberta is staying over with Grandma

Gayle as Company for her. Hicks & Ned are at work getting wood. Mr. Beard commenced to make a railing to enclose the grave of my sweet little Angel Josephine Martha. Weather cloudy and hot with a hard rain in the evening. Ther: 86°.

While Hall worked at the warehouse, Mr. Beard made and installed the railing for Josephine's grave; Bill Hicks and Ned Smith prepared the ground for sowing turnip seed; and Hall received, by rail, a buggy he had bought for Jimmy during his recent trip to Houston, and for which he paid $22.50 in gold.

Tuesday August 28th 1866. Today I am at work at the warehouse. Capt. John W. Redman is still with me. Hicks is at sewing [sowing] *and brushing in turnip seed. Ned Smith assisted Capt. Dawson in the black smith shop to mend the tongue of Jimmy's little buggy which was broken. I paid Ned Smith on a/c $1.50. Mr & Mrs Tarleton are still boarding with me and upon the whole are the most disagreeable Couple that I ever had any transactions with. Weather cloudy and hot, with a strong north wind blowing. Ther: 80°.*

The Tarleton family and John Redman continued to plague Hall. Perhaps because he could not depend upon Redman, he hired R. B. Sewell to paint the house.[13]

Friday August 31st 1866. Today I am at work at the warehouse. Billy Sewell came over on the cars from Houston in order to paint Col. Wrigley's and my house. Mr. Beard also arrived on the cars. Hicks [is] *still at work hauling white oak blocks* [from nearby woods]. *Capt. John W. Redman is still with me and quite sick. Jimmy had a fever. Roberta again missed the fever and is now well. Weather variable and hot. Ther: 89°. Thus closes my notes for the month of August and as it also closes the summer months, I shall cease noting the state of the thermometer until next summer should I be spared to live.*

He noted on Saturday, September 1, that Redman remained "quite sick" and that the Tarletons were still there. On Sunday, Captain Dawson and his wife "spent the day" with Margaret.

Monday September 3rd 1866. Today I am at work at the warehouse. Jimmy missed the fever. Billy Sewell commenced painting my house. Mrs. Jim Wrigley, Ida and Corinne arrived on the cars from Houston all well. Capt. John W. Redman is still with me. My boarders Dr. Tarleton and his wife had quite a family broil, which was very unpleasant to all who had no interest in the quarrel & yet [were] *compelled to witness it. Weather, variable and hot.*

Tuesday September 4th 1866. Today I am at work at the warehouse. Billy Sewell is still at work painting my house. Fanny had a chill & fever. Capt. John W. Redman is still with me. I am sorry to record that I was compelled to have a slight altercation with my boarder Mrs Tarleton, in order to protect my children from insult and abuse, all of which was very unpleasant to me & which I am determined to obviate by requiring her to seek other quarters. Weather cloudy and hot, with a storm attended with rain in the evening.

Wednesday September 5th 1866. Today I am at work at the warehouse. Billy Sewell is at work painting the chimneys to my house. Capt. Redman is still with me. Mr. Beard made a tongue for Jimmy's little buggy. Hicks is engaged [in] *hauling wood. My relations with my boarder, Mrs Tarleton are still quite unpleasant. Weather, variable and hot.*

Thursday September 6th 1866. Today I am at work at the warehouse. Ed Jones left on the cars for Houston in order to procure some painting materials for Col. Wrigley's house. Hicks is at work hauling fire wood. Dr. Tarleton & wife are now making preparations to leave my house & may God speed them. Capt. John W. Redman is still with me. Weather, cloudy and hot, with occasional showers of rain.

Friday September 7th 1866. Today I am at work at the warehouse. Hicks is engaged in hauling rails for Capt. Dawson & worked for him all day. Capt. Redman is still with me also Dr. Tarleton & wife, who make haste very slowly to leave. Weather, cloudy and hot, with occasional showers of rain throughout the day and hard rain at night.

Saturday September 8th 1866. Today I am at work at the warehouse. In the evening I drove up town in my buggy with my horse Charley working in order to try him. The boys finished chopping white oak blocks. Hicks went to [the] *Mill and upon his return, he had a hard chill & fever. Capt. Redman left on his pony and rode out in the Country, and remained all night. Dr Tarleton and wife are still here. Weather cloudy and hot, with occasional showers of rain and a severe storm at night attended with a flood of rain.*

Sunday September 9th 1866. Today I remained at home, reading. Capt. Redman is still absent on his visit. Dr. Tarleton & family are still here. Weather cloudy and hot, with occasional showers of rain throughout the entire day.

Monday, September 10th 1866. Today I remained at the warehouse during the forenoon. In the evening I drove up town and while there settled in full with J. D. Skinner [a merchant] *up to this date. I also purchased a few articles for the little woman. Capt. Redman returned from his visit to the Country in a state of intoxication, and was rather quarrelsome & abusive. Hicks & Ned are at work getting fire wood. Weather cloudy and hot, with occasional showers of rain.*

Thus ends the journal of James Madison Hall, who died of cholera on November 17, 1866, and was buried at the city cemetery in Liberty beside his daughter, Josephine Martha. The two lie there today in a beautiful, tree-shaded location overlooking the Trinity River.

Afterword

The Galveston Weekly News for Friday, November 30, 1866, reported the presence of cholera in Liberty. "*The Liberty Gazette* says the physicians say that the cholera is in that place. Three deaths occurred there last week, two of which were pronounced cholera. It is not thought that the disease can spread there at this season of the year." The same paper announced the death of "Major J. M. Hall, an old citizen of Texas, at Liberty, of cholera on Saturday evening last." The journal of William B. Duncan corroborates the date of November 17.

The Liberty City Council held a "called session" on November 21, 1866. Part of the business of the meeting was dedicated to passing a resolution expressing regret for the death of Mayor Hall "after a brief illness." Present at the meeting were Thomas W. Key, mayor *pro tem.*; P. K. Smith, secretary; and members "Baldwin, Ballio [Baillio], and Skinner." An election was scheduled for Saturday, December 1, to elect a member to fill Hall's unexpired term.

Hall's tombstone sits next to little Josephine Martha's in the Liberty cemetery. Both are white marble. Inscribed on Hall's tombstone are his birth and death dates. However, his date of death reads September 12, 1866, two days after the last entry in the journal. Contemporary accounts corroborate November 17, 1866. Unanswered questions remain: did Hall begin another journal, now lost, to continue his notes; was he too busy or too ill to continue the journal; did he fall ill, recover, and then pass away from cholera; why is the death date incorrect on the tombstone? James Madison Hall, so open and honest in his journal, has left us with a mystery.

After Hall's death, Margaret (1840-1878) returned to Houston County and within a few years she married Confederate veteran Frank Stewart. He had joined Company B, Thirteenth Regiment, Texas Cavalry, organized by Captain John T. Smith and commanded by Colonel John H. Burnett on February 22, 1862. The company first saw action in Arkansas. Dismounted on September 28, 1862, the company was transferred to an infantry brigade led by Colonel Overton Young. General Thomas N. Waul took over Colonel Young's brigade in 1864 during a reorganization of troops, when Waul was assigned to Walker's Division. The company fought in several skirmishes in Arkansas and Louisiana, as well as in the battles of Mansfield and Pleasant Hill, both part of the Red River Campaign.

In 1870, Stewart (age thirty-one) was a farmer with real estate valued at $8,320 and personal property worth $300. Living with Margaret and Frank were Florence Hall (age ten), Madison Hall (age four), and Fanny Fitzsimmons (age nineteen, born in Louisiana).[1] Madison lived until 1874. It is not known what became of Fanny Fitzsimmons.

Margaret and Frank Stewart had three children. Ed F. Stewart was born in 1872, followed by Louis O. Stewart in June 1873. Louis married Donna Phillips on November 19, 1900. Hall family records indicate that a child named Sam S. Stewart died on November 20, 1876.

Florence Hall married James Christian prior to 1878. He was born in Georgia and killed about 1879. They had two children, Maggie, born about 1878, and Lina, born in 1879. According to the 1880 census, Florence and her two daughters lived with widower Frank Stewart. Florence later remarried and is believed to have moved to the Dallas area.[2]

Joshua and Mahala Hall continued to live in Houston County. A few years after the war ended, freedmen French Taylor, Bob Denby, and Alf Warfield asked Joshua Hall if they could establish a cemetery on Hall's land. He agreed and donated land for a cemetery about a mile from his house. The earliest marked grave is that of Mary A. "Nellie" Sharp. African-American and white families are buried there. A count in 1997 revealed twenty-nine marked and 105 unmarked graves.

Roberta Hall (1852-1915) married John Henry Downes, Jr. (1844-?), a nephew of James Hall's friend Lodowick E. Downes, before 1880, but the marriage did not last. She married Marcus M. Halyard about 1886. (Halyard was born in 1850 and was living with his sons in the 1920 census.) The Halyard children consisted of twins, Marcus A. and Margaret, born in 1892, and Leander (called "Joe") born in 1894. The Halyards left Houston County about 1902 and for a time they lived in San Patricio County, where they were enumerated in 1910. They eventually moved to Gilmer, in Upshur County, where Berta and Marcus are buried at the Willow Oak Cemetery.[3]

Horace Oscar Hall (1854-1934), nicknamed "Toby," was born at Elkhart Creek Plantation in Houston County. He married Florene Kirkpatrick about 1879, and they had seven children. Horace Hall owned a farm near the city limits of Crockett, where he died at almost eighty years of age. He was buried at Glenwood Cemetery in Crockett.[4]

Samuel Houston Sharp, Sr. (1839-1885), had been born in San Augustine, Texas. He married Mary Alexandrien Lemaire, called "Nellie" (1843-1876), on July 11, 1861. Although Sam and Nellie had six children, James knew only the eldest, James Hall Sharp, whom he called "the little Major" (1863-1936). Their later children were an infant lost through miscarriage in 1864, Samuel Houston Sharp (1867-1921), Margaret Elizabeth (1869-1935), Ida Mae (1871-1964), Berta Mary (1873-1955), and Willie (1876-1885). After the Civil War, Sam Sharp held positions as farmer, storekeeper, and bookkeeper. He served as justice of the peace for Precinct 5, Houston County, in 1871. His beloved wife Nellie died five years later and was buried in the Hall family cemetery. Sam did not remarry, and he is buried beside her.

James Hall's eldest daughter Margaret married John A. McLemore (1833-1906). In 1860, the Alabama-born McLemore, age twenty-seven, was a merchant's clerk in Crockett. He owned real estate valued at $3,000 and personal property worth $2,000. His wife, "M. H. McLemore" (age sixteen) was a housewife born in Texas. They had a four-month-old son, E. L. McLemore. "A. C. Hall" (age thirty-three) lived with them.

McLemore served as a captain in Company I, Twenty-Eigth Texas Cavalry Regiment, organized by Colonel Horace Randal on August 1, 1862, and dismounted in September 1862. The regiment was assigned to Walker's Division in December 1862 and saw action primarily in Arkansas and Louisiana. The division participated in Mansfield, Pleasant Hill, and Jenkins' Ferry, all part of the Red River Campaign. The Twenty-Eighth Texas Cavalry surrendered at Austin in May 1865. McLemore served throughout the war.[5]

In 1870, the McLemores lived in Crockett. John's occupation was given as farmer. He owned real estate worth $1,000 and personal property valued at $1,000. He was thirty-six when the census was taken on June 12, 1870. "M. H." (Margaret Helen), his wife, was twenty-six. Their children were Annie P. (age two) and Ella (age four). "C. A. Hall" (age forty-six) lived with them. She owned real estate valued at $2,000, but she did not declare a value for personal property.

By 1887, Cornelia (James' first wife) lived in Waco with John and Margaret McLemore. In 1900, John A. McLemore was a grocer living in Waco. His wife Margaret H. and daughter Harriett Ella (born in 1866, age thirty-four) lived with him. The 1890 telephone directory for Waco lists Cornelia's home address on South 3rd Street, which would have been the McLemore home. Her occupation was given as "widow of James M." Cornelia lived with the McLemores until her death in 1894. She is buried in Oakwood Cemetery in Waco.

Margaret and John McLemore had seven children. Only sons James Edgar and John Cullen, and daughter Ella, reached adulthood. The aging McLemore applied for a Confederate pension, but was denied. After his death on September 18, 1906, Margaret lived with her son John in Dallas in 1910. She applied for a Confederate widow's pension while living with her son-in-law (Chris B. Callan) and daughter Ella in Dallas (1910 and 1916), which was approved. She remained with them through the 1920 census. Margaret died of Bright's Disease on November 22, 1920, in Austin. She is buried beside her mother at Oakwood Cemetery in Waco.[6]

The author was unable to locate any post-war information about Bill Hicks in the census records for 1870 and 1880 in Houston and surrounding counties, nor in Liberty County. There are many unmarked graves in cemeteries in Houston County, and it is likely that he is buried there at an unknown location.

Bill Tubbs appears in the Liberty County census for 1870. He was fifty-one years old, born in South Carolina, and owned personal property valued at $150. Louisa Tubbs, age fifty-five, also born in South Carolina, was keeping house. Nathan Tubbs (age fifteen) was a farm laborer. Fannie Tubbs (age ten), Anne Tubbs (age six), and William Tubbs (age one), all born in Texas, were enumerated in the same household.

The 1880 census listed a Bill Tubbs, age sixty, with his birthplace as Virginia, as well as that of his parents. Assuming this is the same individual, he was a farm laborer working for Scipio LaCour.

During the Civil War, James Wrigley (1822-1896) served first with the Ninth (Nichols') Texas Infantry Regiment for six months. After the Ninth dissolved, he enlisted as a captain in Company B of Thomas N. Waul's Second Battalion of the Texas Legion and rose to the rank of lieutenant colonel. After the war, he returned to his business as a commission merchant in the cotton trade. He was a city councilman for Liberty in 1857, 1865, 1876-1879, and a mayor in 1850-1851, 1858, and 1882.

In 1870, James Wrigley (age forty-seven) gave his occupation as merchant liaison. Besides his wife Ann (age forty-one), the household included John (age thirteen), Ida (age eleven), and Annie (age six). Ann Gayle (age sixty-two) was retired. Wrigley listed real estate worth $2,500 (under Ann's name) and personal property valued at $250. In 1880, John Wrigley (age twenty-five) was deputy county clerk, and his mother Ann, sister Annie (age sixteen), and grandmother Ann Gayle (age seventy-three) remained in the household.

Around 1886, James and Ann Wrigley moved to Alvarado in Johnson County. There he served as mayor from April 1892 until April 1896. He remained active as a Freemason and an Oddfellow. *The Liberty Vindicator* for Friday, May 22, 1896, reported that he died at his home in Alvarado the previous Saturday night (May 16). He was described as "a good man, jovial, kind, gentle as a woman, big-hearted. He was a brave soldier and gallant officer in the late Confederate army and commanded a regiment in Waul's legion in the terrible struggle of the siege of Vicksburg." A subsequent article stated that he died "after an illness of only a few short moments." In April, Wrigley had fallen onto his side "in getting off of the train" when returning home from a meeting of the Knights Templar at Cleburne. On the day of his death, he had come home from town, complaining of pain in his side, and went to bed. He died shortly afterward. James Wrigley was buried with Masonic honors at Alvarado. Ann Wrigley (born in 1829) remained in Alvarado until her death on November 24, 1904.[7]

After the war, Charles Lund moved to Galveston, where he opened a store on Market Street. However, in April 1866, he offered the business for sale "on account of departure." It is not clear whether he left and returned shortly thereafter, or found a business partner. By November 1866, Lund and Joseph Turner, "Commission Merchants, Wholesale Dealers in Groceries and General Merchandise" operated a store on The Strand. They sold "Groceries, Western Produce, Tobacco and Liquors" and accepted consignments of "Cotton, Wool, Hides, Merchandise, etc." In 1870, Lund and his family lived in Galveston, with his occupation given as office clerk. Wife Mary and a daughter named Nelly (age ten) lived in the home. On July 13, they lived at one address, and on July 15, they were enumerated at a different address, indicating they had moved to a new home. By 1880, Lund had passed away, and Mary Lund was living in Galveston with her daughter Nelly.[8]

Around 1890, Ed and Lelia (Wrigley) Jones moved to San Angelo in Tom Green County. He applied for a Confederate pension on September 7, 1911, which was approved on March 1, 1912.[9]

Watson Dugat Williams, half-brother of Eugenie Stanwood Mouton, became editor of *The Star State* and served a term as mayor of Liberty (1875-1876). He married Laura Bryan on December 11, 1865, as noted by Hall. Williams is buried in the Bryan-Neyland Cemetery in Liberty. Ben C. Stuart, in his "Texas Steamboat Days" article used herein as a reference, states that W. Dugat Williams and J. W. Whitfield, "pilots," compiled the list of Trinity River landings in 1867-1868.

In 1880, William A. Stewart, a widower, was still listed in the Crockett census. His daughters Ella (single, age twenty-two), Willie (widowed, age twenty), and Mollie (single, age seventeen) lived at home. All had been born in Texas. Stewart represented Houston County in the Sixteenth Texas Legislature of 1879.

In 1870, Benjamin F. Cameron (possibly age twenty-four), born in Alabama, was a dry goods clerk. His wife Adelia A. (age twenty-one), born in Texas, kept house. A child named Bennie (age one) and Mary E. Wrigley (age fourteen) lived in the household. His real estate was worth $2,500 and personal property was valued at $1,000. In the 1880 census, Benjamin F. Cameron (age thirty-nine), was identified as a farmer and county clerk in Liberty. Also in the household were Adelia (age thirty-one), Mattie (age eight), Frank W. (age five), Nina (age three), and Charley (age one month).

According to *The Liberty Vindicator* (December 9, 1887), Colonel B. F. Cameron "Worthy Master of Liberty Lodge #48 was representative to Grand Lodge in Houston, and was later made District Deputy of 51st District." As Worthy Master of the Liberty Lodge, he reported the death of James Wrigley in 1896. Cameron represented the Thirty-Sixth District in the Texas House of Representatives during the 1895-1896 session.[10]

Notes

Notes for Introduction

[1.] Esther Hall Biggers, "Joshua James Hall," in *History of Houston County, Texas 1687-1979*, comp. and ed. Eliza H. Bishop and The History Book Committee of the Houston County Historical Commission (Tulsa: Heritage Publishing Company, 1979), 384; Robert L. Hall, "Introduction," typescript accompanying the copy of James Madison Hall's journal, courtesy of The Sam Houston Regional Library and Research Center, Liberty, Texas; Hall family genealogical records, courtesy of Vickie P. Everhart; Armistead Albert Aldrich, *The History of Houston County, Texas* (San Antonio: The Naylor Co., 1943), 155-158.

[2.] Aldrich, *The History of Houston County, Texas*, 152-154. A. A. Aldrich served as an attorney, county judge, and representative to the Twenty-Seventh Texas Legislature, and as a trustee for Austin College. See also: Eliza H. Bishop, "Houston County," in *The New Handbook of Texas*, ed. Ron Tyler, et al., 6 vols. (Austin: Texas State Historical Association, 1996), 3:728-730.

[3.] Eliza H. Bishop, "Halls [*sic*] Bluff, Texas," in *The New Handbook of Texas*, 3:421.

[4.] Aldrich, *The History of Houston County, Texas*, 133-134.

[5.] John L. Hall (1809-1857) raised a company of men, including James Madison Hall, to serve in the Mexican War. Afterwards, he returned home to Crockett. In 1850, John L. Hall (age forty) was enumerated as a hotel keeper, born in Maryland, with real estate valued at $47,700. His wife Lavinia L. (age thirty-one) had been born in Louisiana. Their children, Nancy (age five) and Silvester (age two), had both been born in Houston County. Captain Hall's hotel in downtown Crockett burned in 1871. 1850 U.S. Census; Aldrich, *The History of Houston County, Texas*, 44, 156-157; Joshua James Hall diary, Reel 33 of 44, Records of Ante-Bellum Plantations from the Revolution through the Civil War, Series G, Part 1, University Publications America, Frederick, Md., Microfilm B, 3762; James Madison Hall diary, Reel 34 of 44, Records of Ante-Bellum Plantations from the Revolution through the Civil War, Series G, Part 1, University Publications America, Frederick, Md., Microfilm B, 3762, courtesy of the M. D. Anderson Library, University of Houston, Houston, Texas. The physical journals of Joshua J. Hall and James M. Hall ("Hall, James Madison, Family Papers, 1807, 1813, 1840-1980") are located at The Dolph Briscoe Center for American History, University of Texas at Austin.

[6.] Charles D. Spurlin, *Texas Volunteers in the Mexican War* (Austin: Eakin Press, 1998), 54-55, 91, 170 (from National Archives Microcopy No. 278); Robert L. Hall, "Introduction," typescript; Discharge letter, signed by Captain John L. Hall and Colonel George T. Wood, issued to Sergeant James Madison Hall, October 2, 1846, Microfilm B, 3762.

[7.] *The Crockett Printer*, December 6, 1853.

[8.] Frederick Law Olmsted, *A Journey through Texas* (Austin: University of Texas Press, 1986), 83-85; originally published in 1857.

[9.] *Texas Almanac* (1858), 69.

[10.] Affidavit from H. O. (Horace Oscar or "Toby") Hall regarding marriage of Mahala L. Hall and Joshua J. Hall, dated October 31, 1914, filed on November 2, 1914, recorded in Vol. 145, p. 534, Deed Records, Jefferson County, Texas, notarized by Geo. W. Crook, Houston County, Texas, courtesy of Eliza H. Bishop, Houston County Historical Commission, Crockett, Texas, 2005.

11. Isaac Peacock was buried at Glenwood Cemetery at Crockett. His tombstone states that he was born in Kent County, Maryland, on February 2, 1822, and died on March 11, 1859. *The Dallas Herald*, March 9, 1859, courtesy of Vickie P. Everhart; Aldrich, *The History of Houston County, Texas*, 156; *The Houston Weekly Telegraph*, March 23, 1859; Widow's Application for a Pension, July 3, 1916, No. 33011, courtesy of Texas State Library and Archives Commission, Austin, Texas.

12. Widow's Application for a Pension, July 3, 1916, No. 33011.

13. *The Houston Weekly Telegraph*, March 23, April 13, June 15, and November 9, 1859.

14. T. R. Fehrenbach, *Lone Star: A History of Texas and the Texans* (New York: Collier Books, 1980), 338.

15. Hall did not state who was in charge of the farm. He hired young Frank Stewart for the remainder of 1861, but did not give a specific reason for Stewart's employment, although it is possible that he was hired to manage the farm. John Harwell operated the gristmill. However, both men left to enter the Confederate military. Presumably Joshua Hall then supervised whatever work was done on the property since many of the slaves who worked for Hall on the farm moved to Liberty to work for him there.

16. *The Liberty Gazette*, November 28, 1866.

Notes for Chapter 1

1. In the 1860 U.S. Census, taken in August, Hall was listed as the head of household (age forty), a farmer with real estate worth $33,200 and personal property valued at $6,200. "M. A." (Margaret, age twenty) was described as a housewife. Sam Sharp and John Harwell also lived in the household. Hall's farm on Elkhart Creek lay between that of J. H. Leaverton and J. W. Brent. Gaines Pennington, John Williams, and W. H. Beasly (also spelled Beazley or Beasley) were neighbors. Hall owned seven slaves. 1860 U.S. Census; Schedule 2—Slave Inhabitants in Beat No. 12, Houston County, August 4 and 6, 1860, Page No. 34, 1860 U.S. Census.

2. Sam Sharp (age twenty-one) was listed as a farmer, born in Texas, who owned personal property valued at $800. John C. Varnadore remained in Crockett in the 1870 U.S. Census, but sometime after that moved to Hot Springs, Arkansas. By 1891, he returned to Crockett and was engaged in real estate. 1860 U.S. Census; 1870 U.S. Census; Bebe Beasley Ulrich, "Newspapers 1853-1896," *Houston County Collection Volume I, Crockett* (Crockett, Tex.: Privately Printed, 1984), 58.

3. Reuben (age forty-four) and Frances (age thirty-five) Matthews were the parents of six children. In 1860, they owned fourteen slaves and three "slave houses." He had also served as a county commissioner. 1860 U.S. Census; Schedule 2—Slave Inhabitants in Beat No. 12, Houston County, August 4 and 6, 1860, Page No. 34, 1860 U.S. Census; *The Crockett Printer*, December 6, 1853, in Armistead Albert Aldrich, *The History of Houston County, Texas* (San Antonio: The Naylor Company, 1943), 44.

[4] Karen Gerhardt Britton Fort, *Bale o'Cotton* (College Station: Texas A&M University Press, 1992, reprint 2015), 30-39.

[5] In the 1850 U.S. Census, Sarah Peacock's age is given as twenty-eight. In the 1860 U.S. Census, her age is listed as forty-five. The author has no explanation for this discrepancy.

[6] Eskelle V. and Eddie Vaughn Keen Garrison, "The Keen Clan," in *History of Houston County, Texas 1687-1979,* comp. and ed. History Book Committee of Houston County Historical Commission (Tulsa: Heritage Publishing Company, 1979), 430; Thomas Nelms Mainer, *Houston County in the Civil War* (Crockett, Tex.: Publications Development Company of Texas, 1981), 95-96; 1860 U.S. Census.

[7] 1860 U.S. Census. Stewart's place of birth was listed as Georgia; however, the 1870 U.S. Census states that his place of birth was Alabama.

[8] 1860 U.S. Census.

[9] Joshua James Hall diary, Reel 33 of 44, Records of Ante-Bellum Plantations from the Revolution through the Civil War, Series G, Part 1, University Publications America, Frederick, Md., Microfilm B, 3762; James Madison Hall diary, Reel 34 of 44, Records of Ante-Bellum Plantations from the Revolution through the Civil War, Series G, Part 1, University Publications America, Frederick, Md., Microfilm B, 3762, courtesy of the M. D. Anderson Library, University of Houston, Houston, Texas.

[10] By the 1870 U.S. Census, the Downes family had increased to nine children, and Downes' occupation was that of farmer, indicating he had retired from the mercantile business. L. E. Downes died at age sixty-three and was buried at Old Glenwood Cemetery in Crockett. Eliza H. Bishop, "Lodwick [*sic*] E. Downes," in *History of Houston County, Texas 1687-1979*, 334; Aldrich, *The History of Houston County, Texas*, 30-34; 1860 U.S. Census; 1870 U.S. Census; http://awt.ancestry.com/AncestryWorld Tree Project: 10964, "Lodowick Elbert Downes," [accessed March 31, 2005].

[11] *The Crockett Printer*, reprinted in *The Houston Weekly Telegraph*, December 28, 1859.

[12] W. T. Block, *Cotton Bales, Keelboats and Sternwheelers: A History of the Sabine River and Trinity River Cotton Trades, 1837-1900* (Woodville, Tex.: Dogwood Press, 1995), 164, 165; Keith Guthrie, *Texas Forgotten Ports III* (Austin: Eakin Press, 1995), 85-89.

[13] *The Houston Weekly Telegraph*, February 28, and March 6, 1860; *The Dallas Herald*, May 2, 1860.

[14] *The New York Illustrated News*, January 10, 1863.

[15] Lonn Taylor, "Rails, Rocks, and Pickets: Traditional Farmstead Fencing in Texas," in *Built in Texas*, ed. Francis Edward Abernethy (Denton: University of North Texas Press, 1979), 178, 181.

[16] A search of census records revealed several men named Isaac Tanner, with sons, in and around Houston County. It is possible that Tanner moved around, changing employment, during the census period and was enumerated more than once. The Isaac Tanner hired by Hall could not be positively identified. 1860 U.S. Census.

[17] *The Crockett Printer*, December 6, 1853; Aldrich, *The History of Houston County, Texas,* 44, 175-177; 1860 U.S. Census; *The Houston Weekly Telegraph*, March 9, 1859 (reprinted from *The Crockett Printer*).

18. 1860 U.S. Census; Aldrich, *The History of Houston County, Texas*, 156, 191; Charles D. Spurlin, *Texas Volunteers in the Mexican War* (Austin: Eakin Press, 1998), 186; Mainer, *Houston County in the Civil War*, 67, 69-70; Donald S. Frazier, *Blood & Treasure: Confederate Empire in the Southwest* (College Station: Texas A&M University Press, 1995), 233. For an image of Isaac Adair, see Frazier, *Blood & Treasure*, 233.

19. The news story, dated March 22, 1860, appeared in *The Houston Weekly Telegraph* on March 27, 1860. The article originated in one of the Crockett newspapers.

20. 1860 U.S. Census; Aldrich, *The History of Houston County, Texas*, 36, 142-144.

21. 1860 U.S. Census; Aldrich, *The History of Houston County, Texas*, 139-140.

22. Dan had been born in Louisiana and was ill for eight days before his death. 1860 Mortality Schedule for Houston County—Slaves, compiled by Kimberly Wells, 1860 Mortality Schedule: Houston County, Texas, T1134 Reel 54, TXGenWeb Census, 1998-2005, The USGenWeb Census Project. Green Hicks (age two) had been born in Texas. He had been ill for ten days before his death. Angelina (age twenty-two), also born in Texas, had been ill for twenty-three days before her death. 1860 Mortality Schedule for Houston County—Slaves.

23. The Telegraph Mills post office was discontinued in 1859, "and a neighboring office established under the name of Elkhart. The Telegraph, Houston, and the Telegraph Mills, Houston County are too easily confounded." From *The Crockett Printer*, reported in *The Houston Weekly Telegraph*, August 31, 1859.

24. 1860 U.S. Census; Spurlin, *Texas Volunteers in the Mexican War*, 170.

25. *The Houston Weekly Telegraph,* April 27, 1859.

26. Guy and his younger brother William J. Stokes came to Texas during the winter of 1842-1843 along with Captain Thomas Ingles Smith. William R. Howe, from Lauderdale County, Tennessee, had settled on Chambers Creek in 1839, where he built a home. Related to Howe by marriage, the Stokes brothers settled between Chambers and Onion Creeks, near the present town of Italy. In 1850 and 1852, Guy Stokes served as "overseer" for a road building project, and in 1854, after the death of William Howe, he became the guardian of Howe's three children. 1850 U.S. Census; 1860 U.S. Census; US GenWeb Project, TX GenWeb Project, "History and Biographical Sketch of the William R. Howe Family" by Granville D. Edwards, 2004 [accessed May 6, 2015]; Minutes of the Ellis County Commissioner's Court 1850-1853, Order Book 1, Extracted by Barbara Knox, Monday and Tuesday, Nov. 18 and 19, 1850 and Special Term of Court, Monday, Nov. 15, 1852, Pct. No. 2, www.rootsweb.ancestry.com/~txellis/emin.htm; Ellis County TX GenWeb, Vol. A, Probate Minutes, Some Early Guardianships, Extracted by Barbara Knox, 1998-2004, www.rootsweb.ancestry.com/~txellis/ctrecords/ellisgdn/htm.

27. 1860 U.S. Census; Mainer, *Houston County in the Civil War*, 46, 97.

28. Aldrich, *The History of Houston County, Texas*, 50, 199-202.

29. 1860 U.S. Census; Mainer, *Houston County in the Civil War*, 90, 95-96; Muster Roll for Texas State Troops, "Harwell, John S., Pvt.," Texas State Archives, Texas State Library and Archives Commission, Austin, Texas.

30. John Storck and Walter Dorwin Teague, *Flour For Man's Bread: A History of Milling* (Minneapolis: University of Minnesota Press, 1952), 102-105. Illustrations by Harold Rydell are noteworthy.

[31] Mason Maddox, miller, Colvin Run Mill Historic Site, Great Falls, Virginia, correspondence with the author, August 26, 2005; Henry Baumgartner, "Water-powered gristmill takes its place in history as an engineering landmark," ASME NEWS Online, April 2001, 3 pages [accessed on August 26, 2005].

[32] Walter L. Buenger, "Texas and the Riddle of Secession," *Southwestern Historical Quarterly*, LXXXVII (Oct. 1983), 151-182; Randolph B. Campbell, *An Empire for Slavery: The Peculiar Institution in Texas 1821-1865* (Baton Rouge: Louisiana State University Press, 1989), 224-225, 227-228; Donald E. Reynolds, "Texas Troubles," in *The New Handbook of Texas*, ed. Ron Tyler, et al., 6 vols. (Austin: Texas State Historical Association, 1996), 6:439.

[33] *The Houston Weekly Telegraph*, October 26, 1859.

[34] 1860 U.S. Census; *The Galveston Weekly News*, April 25, 1866.

[35] 1860 U.S. Census; *The Houston Weekly Telegraph*, February 8, 1860.

[36] *The Texas State Gazette* (Austin), June 16, 1860; TX GenWeb/Houston County, Texas—*The Crockett Printer* [accessed November 15, 2004]; *The Houston Weekly Telegraph*, June 12 and June 26, 1860.

[37] *The Crockett Printer*, June 13, 1860; TX GenWeb/Houston County, Texas—*The Crockett Printer* [accessed November 15, 2004].

[38] Aldrich, *The History of Houston County, Texas*, 51-52, 54; *The Houston Weekly Telegraph*, February 8, April 3, June 5, June 26, 1860, and February 26, 1861.

[39] Muster Roll, National Archives Microcopy No. 323, Roll 250, courtesy of Hill College History Complex, Hillsboro, Texas; TX GenWeb/Houston County, Texas—*The Crockett Printer* [accessed November 15, 2004].

[40] *The Houston Weekly Telegraph*, June 22, 1859; Block, *Cotton Bales, Keelboats, and Sternwheelers*, 164; Guthrie, *Texas Forgotten Ports III*, 67.

[41] Donald R. Walker, "Texas State Penitentiary at Huntsville," in *The New Handbook of Texas*, 6:430-432; James L. Nichols, "Civil War Industry," in *The New Handbook of Texas*, 2:127; *Austin State Gazette*, July 6, 1861; Charles W. Ramsdell, "The Texas State Military Board, 1862-1865," *Southwestern Historical Quarterly*, XXVII, no. 4 (April 1924), 253-275; *The Galveston Weekly News*, May 21,1862, September 10, 1862, and November 18, 1863; Ralph A. Wooster, *Texas and Texans in the Civil War* (Austin: Eakin Press, 1995), 125; Clayton E. Jewett, *Texas in the Confederacy: An Experiment in Nation Building* (Columbia: University of Missouri Press, 2002), 148-149.

[42] 1860 U.S. Census; 1880 U.S. Census.

[43] 1860 U.S. Census.

[44] 1860 U.S. Census; Muster Roll, Texas State Library and Archives Commission; Mrs. Thomas J. Hayman, "Beazley Family," in *History of Houston County 1687-1979*, 253-254.

[45] 1860 U.S. Census; *The Liberty Gazette*, February 26, and March 6, 1855; Miriam Partlow, *Liberty, Liberty County, and the Atascosito District* (Austin: The Pemberton Press/Jenkins Publishing Co., 1974), 275, 287, 353.

[46] 1860 U.S. Census.

[47] Aline Rothe, "Marianna, Texas," in *The Handbook of Texas*, ed. Walter Prescott Webb and H. Bailey Carroll, 2 vols. (Austin: Texas State Historical Association, 1952), 2:143; Block, *Cotton Bales, Keelboats and Sternwheelers*, 165; Ben C. Stuart,

"Texas Steamboat Days," typescript (October 11, 1919), 43, 85, courtesy of Rosenberg Library, Galveston, Texas; Guthrie, *Texas Forgotten Ports III*, 32, 33-39.

[48.] *The Liberty Gazette*, November 17, 1856.

[49.] U.S. Navy, *Dictionary of American Naval Fighting Ships, Vol. II* (Washington, D.C.: Navy Department, Office of the Chief of Naval Operations, Naval History Division), Appendix II, Confederate Forces Afloat, Annex III, Texas Marine Department, Confederate States Army, 1963), 493; Frederick Way, Jr., *Way's Packet Directory, 1848-1994* (Athens, Ohio: Ohio University Press, 1983, revised edition 1994), No. 0026, p. 3; William M. Lytle and Forrest R. Holdcamper, *Merchant Steam Vessels of the United States, 1790-1868* (Staten Island, N.Y.: The Steamship Historical Society of America, Inc., 1952, revised edition 1975 with later supplements), 2.

After the *Ruthven* sank, her steam-powered machinery was sold to mills and cotton gins, and the cabin was salvaged and converted into a "residence." Block, *Cotton Bales, Keelboats and Sternwheelers*, 215-216; Ben C. Stuart, "Texas Steamboat Days," 41, 55, 62, 73, 87.

In 1997, the Southwest Underwater Archeological Society and the Texas Historical Commission documented the remains of the *Ruthven*. Measurements revealed that the vessel was 127 feet long, 30 feet wide, and 4 feet 8 inches deep. One secret of the steamer's lengthy service was an inch-thick layer of planking attached to the hull, which protected the hull from damage by obstructions in the river. Adam I. Kane, *The Western River Steamboat* (College Station: Texas A&M University Press, 2004), 39, 107.

[50.] 1850 U.S. Census; 1860 U.S. Census; David G. McComb, *Houston: A History* (Austin: University of Texas Press, 1981), 24, 36; *The Houston Weekly Telegraph*, January 19, 1859, and April 17, 1860.

[51.] *The Houston Weekly Telegraph*, February 2, 1859.

Notes for Chapter 2

[1.] *The Houston Weekly Telegraph* advertisement dated September 26, 1856, reprinted in the *Telegraph* on January 19, 1859; notice relating to Ruthven printed on June 12, 1860.

[2.] Ann Darsey, "Dailey Family," in *Crossroads to Progress II* "Grapeland: Queen City of the Sand Flats, 1872-1987" (Grapeland, Tex.: Grapeland Community Council, 1988), 187-188.

[3.] Lacy and Cunningham, 1860 U.S. Census.

[4.] Brevet Major General Twiggs (1790-1862) was dismissed from the U.S. Army on March 1, 1861, and on May 1, he received a dishonorable discharge from President Buchanan for traitorous conduct. Although Twiggs accepted a Confederate commission as major general, with command of Louisiana, on May 22, 1861, his health failed, and he died on July 15, 1862. J. J. Bowden, *The Exodus of Federal Forces from Texas 1861* (Austin: Eakin Press, 1986), 2-3, 43, 49-63, 121 (note 1), 133 (note 44). The Texas commissioners sent by the Committee on Public Safety were Thomas J. Devine, Samuel A. Maverick, James H. Rogers, and Philip N.

Luckett. Rogers, however, had been sent to Louisiana to obtain military weapons and supplies and was not present in San Antonio when Twiggs surrendered.

5. Bowden, *The Exodus of Federal Forces from Texas 1861*, 62-63.

6. Llerena Friend, *Sam Houston: The Great Designer* (Austin: University of Texas Press, 1954), 321-354; Ralph A. Wooster, *Texas and Texans in the Civil War* (Austin: Eakin Press, 1995), 22.

7. 1850 U.S. Census; *The Liberty Gazette*, May 15, 1858; Advertisement dated October 20, 1856, printed in *The Liberty Gazette*, October 12, 1860; Muster Roll for Texas State Troops, Liberty County, "Wrigley, James, Capt.," Texas State Archives, Texas State Library and Archives Commission, Austin, Texas; Miriam Partlow, *Liberty, Liberty County, and the Atascosito District* (Austin: The Pemberton Press/ Jenkins Publishing Co., 1974), 193, 275, 287, 353. Although loved as a dear friend by Hall, James Wrigley was not popular with everyone, especially the Hardin family of Liberty County. See Camilla Davis Trammell, *Seven Pines: Its Occupants and Their Letters, 1825-1872* (Dallas: Southern Methodist University Press, 1986), 119, 143, 150-152.

8. *The Liberty Gazette*, June 22, 1860; 1860 U.S. Census.

9. *The Houston Weekly Telegraph*, October 5, 1859.

10. Dr. Thomas A. Stanwood (age forty-four in 1860), born in Connecticut, owned real estate worth $3,000 and personal property valued at $1,000. His wife "M. J." (Margaretta, age forty-one) had been born in Louisiana. Their daughter Sarah Eugenia was eighteen in 1860. Margaretta Dugat had previously been married to Judge John A. Williams, with whom she had three children. The judge died in 1840, and she married Dr. Stanwood that same year. Her son Watson Dugat Williams was a prominent citizen of Liberty. Margaretta died on January 9, 1862, and in late October, Dr. Stanwood married a nineteen-year-old widow at Washington-on-the-Brazos. Dr. Stanwood served as a Liberty city councilman (1844-1846) and as mayor (1849). During the war he treated sick soldiers at a hospital in Liberty. 1860 U.S. Census; Trammell, *Seven Pines*, 122-123, 153, 167, 172; Partlow, *Liberty, Liberty County, and the Atascosito District*, 94, 266, 353.

Dr. Ben B. Fatheree (age thirty-four in 1860) was a physician born in Mississippi. He owned personal property valued at $500 and was living at the home of James Wrigley in 1860. His wife had operated a "School for Young Ladies and Girls" during the 1850s, but she had died by 1860. 1860 U.S. Census; *The Liberty Gazette*, November 17, 1856.

11. Muster Roll, Liberty County, "E. L. Jones, 2nd Jr. Lieut.," Texas State Library and Archives Commission. The Muster Roll reads Company B, but the pension application states Company F (Adjutant General's Office, Washington, D.C., September 21, 1911). Trammell, *Seven Pines*, 147, 151; W. T. Block, *Cotton Bales, Keelboats, and Sternwheelers: A History of the Sabine River and Trinity River Cotton Trades, 1837-1900* (Woodville, Tex.: Dogwood Press, 1995), 170, 172, 238 (note 35). Stuart also names Ed. L. Jones in his list of "old time river men." Ben C. Stuart, "Texas Steamboat Days," typescript (October 11, 1919), 96, courtesy of the Rosenberg Library, Galveston, Texas. Soldier's Application for Pension, September 16, 1911 (approved on March 1, 1912); No. 20630, courtesy of the Texas State Library and Archives Commission, Austin, Texas.

[12] *The Liberty Gazette*, January 11, 1861.

[13] Clayton E. Jewett, *Texas in the Confederacy: An Experiment in Nation Building* (Columbia: University of Missouri Press, 2002), 113; Wooster, *Texas and Texans in the Civil War*, 25, 27; J. G. Randall and David Donald, *The Civil War and Reconstruction*, 2nd ed. (Boston: D. C. Heath and Company, 1961), 177, 249-252.

[14] Bowden, *The Exodus of Federal Forces from Texas 1861*, 100-104; Edward T. Cotham, Jr., *Battle on the Bay: The Civil War Struggle for Galveston* (Austin: University of Texas Press, 1998), 21-22.

[15] Bowden, *The Exodus of Federal Forces from Texas 1861*, 97-118; Brownson Malsch, *Indianola: The Mother of Western Texas* (Austin: State House Press, 1988), 149-151.

[16] H. P. N. Gammel, compiler and arranger, "Laws of the State of Texas passed October 24, 1866," *Laws of Texas 1822-1897*, Vol. 5 (Austin: The Gammel Book Company, 1898), 162-167.

[17] Stuart, "Texas Steamboat Days," 41, 73, 94; Block, *Cotton Bales, Keelboats, and Sternwheelers*, 173; Keith Guthrie, *Texas Forgotten Ports, Vol. III* (Austin: Eakin Press, 1995), 6, 8, 22-23, 26-27, 87; 1880 U.S. Census.

[18] The street was named for Judge Billups Gayle, Ann Wrigley's father, who died in 1853. *The Liberty Gazette*, December 22, 1856.

[19] 1860 U.S. Census; Armistead Albert Aldrich, *The History of Houston County, Texas* (San Antonio: The Naylor Company, 1943), 21-22; L. W. Kemp, "Jowers, W. G. W.," in *The Handbook of Texas*, ed. Walter Prescott Webb and H. Bailey Carroll, 2 vols. (Austin: The Texas State Historical Association, 1952; Fourth Printing, 1976), 1:931; Georgia Kemp Caraway, "Jowers, William George Washington," in *The New Handbook of Texas*, ed. Ron Tyler, et al., 6 vols. (Austin: Texas State Historical Association, 1996), 3:1008-1009; *The Galveston Weekly News*, August 5, 1866.

[20] Harold D. Woodman, *King Cotton and His Retainers: Financing & Marketing the Cotton Crop of the South, 1800-1925* (Lexington: University of Kentucky Press, 1968), 269-294.

[21] Muster Roll for Waul's Texas Legion, Texas State Archives, Texas State Library and Archives Commission, Austin, Texas; Thomas W. Cutrer, "Waul's Texas Legion," in *The New Handbook of Texas*, 6:852; Ralph A. Wooster, *Lone Star Regiments in Gray* (Austin: Eakin Press, 2002), 99-106.

[22] Colonel Harold B. Simpson, *Hood's Texas Brigade: Lee's Grenadier Guard* (Dallas: Alcor Publishing Company, 1983), 14-15; J. B. Polley, *Hood's Texas Brigade* (Dayton, Ohio: Morningside Bookshop, reprint, 1976; originally published in 1910), 304.

[23] Jewett, *Texas in the Confederacy*, 50-54.

[24] Gary Kronk, correspondence with the author, March 2, 2006; see also, Gary Kronk, *Cometography*, Cambridge University Press, 1999.

[25] Chas. W. Ramsdell, "The Texas State Military Board, 1862-1865," *Southwestern Historical Quarterly*, XXVII, No. 4 (April 1924), 256-257; Wooster, *Texas and Texans in the Civil War*, 44-46; T. R. Fehrenbach, *Lone Star: A History of Texas and the Texans* (New York: Collier Books, 1985), 353-365.

[26] Wooster, *Texas and Texans in the Civil War*, 31, 32; Jewett, *Texas in the Confederacy*, 116; Fehrenbach, *Lone Star*, 354.

[27.] Donald S. Frazier, *Cottonclads! The Battle of Galveston and the Defense of the Texas Coast* (Fort Worth: Ryan Place Publishers, 1996), 50-51; Wooster, *Texas and Texans in the Civil War*, 65, 198; Cotham, *Battle on the Bay*, 107-109; David G. McComb, *Galveston: A History* (Austin: University of Texas Press, 1986), 76.

[28.] "Ochiltree, Thomas Peck," in *The New Handbook of Texas*, 4:1102-1103.

[29.] Order No. 34, Military Department of Texas, Galveston, Texas, October 11, 1861, Brigadier General P. O. Hébert, in *The War of the Rebellion: A Compilation of the Official Records of the Union and Confederate Armies*, Series I, Volume IV (Washington: Government Printing Office, 1882; reprint, Historical Times, Inc., 1985), 117, hereafter referred to as *Official Records*, ebooks.library.cornell.edu/m/moawar/waro/html [accessed throughout 2016].

[30.] Cotham, *Battle on the Bay*, 61-64; McComb, *Galveston: A History*, 72-77; Alwyn Barr, "Texas Coastal Defense, 1861-1865," in *Lone Star Blue and Gray*, ed. Ralph A. Wooster (Austin: Texas State Historical Association, 1995), 151-174 (no maps).

[31.] Wooster, *Texas and Texans in the Civil War*, 44-45.

[32.] Stuart, "Texas Steamboat Days," 93; Block, *Cotton Bales, Keelboats, and Sternwheelers*, 173; 1860 U.S. Census.

[33.] 1860 U.S. Census; Partlow, *Liberty, Liberty County, and the Atascosito District*, 268; Trammell, *Seven Pines*, 123, 150, 229.

[34.] Joseph N. Dark, *The Liberty Gazette*, July 4, 1866; Trammell, *Seven Pines*, 149, 233-34; Partlow, *Liberty, Liberty County, and the Atascosito District*, 183, 213, 274; B. F. Sterling: *The Liberty Gazette*, October 12, 1860, and January 25, 1861; "Sterling, Ross Shaw," in *The New Handbook of Texas*, 6:91-92; William F. Hardin: Trammell, *Seven Pines*, 143.

[35.] *Official Records*, Series I, Vol. IV, 117.

[36.] *The Liberty Gazette*, October 12, 1860.

[37.] Wooster, *Texas and Texans in the Civil War*, 31, 51; Kenneth W. Hobbs, "Terry, Benjamin Franklin," in *The New Handbook of Texas*, 6:265; Ralph A. Wooster, "Introduction," *Lone Star Blue and Gray*, xi-xii.

[38.] Alwyn Barr, "Texas Coastal Defense, 1861-1865," *The Southwestern Historical Quarterly*, XLV, No. 1 (July 1961), 6-7, 8 (entire article, pages 1-31, with maps).

[39.] Frazier, *Cottonclads!*, 27, 42; Barr, "Texas Coastal Defense, 1861-1865," in *Lone Star Blue and Gray*, 153-154; Cotham, *Battle on the Bay*, 38-40, 50-56, 63-64.

Notes for Chapter 3

[1.] P. O. Hébert, Brigadier General, to Hon. J. P. Benjamin, Secretary of War, October 24, 1861. *The War of the Rebellion: A Compilation of the Official Records of the Union and Confederate Armies*, Series I, Vol. IV, 126-127, hereafter referred to as *Official Records*. ebooks.library.cornell.edu/m/moawar/waro/html [accessed throughout 2016].

[2.] Ben C. Stuart stated that W. Dugat Williams and J. W. Whitfield, "pilots," compiled a list of Trinity River landings in 1867-1868; "Texas Steamboat Days," typescript (October 11, 1919), 84, 94, courtesy of the Rosenberg Library, Galveston, Texas. *The Liberty Gazette*: September 14, 1860, and January 25, 1861. Miriam

Partlow, *Liberty, Liberty County, and the Atascosito District* (Austin: The Pemberton Press/Jenkins Publishing Co., 1974), 209-210, 266, 353. W. T. Block, *Cotton Bales, Keelboats and Sternwheelers: A History of the Sabine River and Trinity River Cotton Trades, 1837-1900* (Woodville, Tex.: Dogwood Press, 1995), 173. Block states that the "table of distances" was written in 1869 and published in the *Galveston Daily News* on April 23, 1893; 164, 237 (note 11). Camilla Davis Trammell, *Seven Pines: Its Occupants and Their Letters, 1825-1872* (Dallas: Southern Methodist University Press, 1987), 122-123.

3. 1850 U.S. Census; 1860 U.S. Census; Partlow, *Liberty, Liberty County, and the* Atascosito District, 287, 291, 353; Trammell, *Seven Pines*, 16, 143.

4. 1860 U.S. Census.

5. Margaret Swett Henson, "Chambers, Thomas Jefferson," in *The New Handbook of Texas*, ed. Ron Tyler, et al., 6 vols. (Austin: Texas State Historical Association, 1996), 2:30-31.

6. Stuart, "Texas Steamboat Days," 85; Keith Guthrie, *Texas Forgotten Ports, Vol. III* (Austin: Eakin Press, 1995), 8.

7. 1860 U.S. Census.

8. Data courtesy of the Sam Houston Regional Library and Research Center.

9. Barbara H. Fisher, "Pickett, Edward Bradford," in *The New Handbook of Texas*, 5:190; Partlow, *Liberty, Liberty County, and the Atascosito District*, 274, 353. He and his brother James J. Pickett, also an attorney, practiced law together; *The Liberty Gazette*, October 12, 1860.

10. *Official Records*, Series I, Volume IX, 715-716, 735-736; Edward T. Cotham, Jr., *Battle on the Bay: The Civil War Struggle for Galveston* (Austin: University of Texas Press, 1998), 54.

11. Chas. W. Ramsdell, "The Texas State Military Board, 1862-1865," *Southwestern Historical Quarterly*, XXVII, No. 4 (April 1924), 256-257.

12. *Official Records*, Series I, Vol. IX, 710-713; James L. Nichols, *The Confederate Quartermaster in the Trans-Mississippi* (Austin: University of Texas Press, 1964), 17-27; Chas. W. Ramsdell, "The Texas State Military Board, 1862-1865," 261-267; Clayton E. Jewett, *Texas in the Confederacy: An Experiment in Nation Building* (Columbia: University of Missouri Press, 2002), 148-152.

13. *Official Records*, Series I, Vol. IV, 139-140; Edward T. Cotham, Jr., *Battle on the Bay*, 37-41.

14. David G. McComb, *Galveston: A History* (Austin: University of Texas Press, 1986), 74; Cotham, *Battle on the Bay*, 50-56; Alwyn Barr, "Texas Coastal Defense, 1861-1865," in *Lone Star Blue and Gray*, ed. Ralph A.Wooster (Austin: Texas State Historical Association, 1995), 159.

15. Mayo Clinic website, www.mayoclinic.org [accessed November 29, 2012].

16. *The Liberty Gazette*, May 14, 1855; 1860 U.S. Census; Partlow, *Liberty, Liberty County, and the Atascosito District*, 213, 353.

17. Partlow, *Liberty, Liberty County, and the Atascosito District*, 353.

18. Cotham, *Battle on the Bay*, 50-56.

19. Cotham, *Battle on the Bay*, 56; Thomas W. Cutrer, "Hébert, Paul Octave," in *The New Handbook of Texas*, 3:539; *Official Records*, Series I, Vol. IX, 733-734.

[20] Bill of Sale/Title Transfer, Watson A. Neyland Collection IV, Sam Houston Regional Library and Research Center, Liberty, Texas.

[21] Mrs. Ben E. Pickett, "Tarkington Prairie, Texas," in *The New Handbook of Texas*, 6:204.

[22] Partlow, *Liberty, Liberty County, and the Atascosito District*, 256; *The Galveston Weekly News*, March 6, 1860; 1860 U.S. Census.

[23] 1860 U.S. Census. John H. Smith owned real estate valued at $1,000 and personal property worth twenty-five dollars.

[24] Harold D. Woodman, *King Cotton and His Retainers: Financing & Marketing the Cotton Crop of the South, 1800-1925* (Lexington: University of Kentucky Press, 1968), 236.

[25] Dr. William A. Murchison (1809-1866) was born in Fayetteville, North Carolina. He lived in the Grapeland-Elkhart-Dailey (Daly's) area. Courtesy of the Texas State Library and Archives Commission, Austin, Texas.

[26] Cotham, *Battle on the Bay*, 57-72.

[27] 1860 U.S. Census; Pamela Ashworth Puryear and Nath Winfield, Jr., *Sandbars and Sternwheelers: Steam Navigation on the Brazos* (College Station: Texas A&M University Press, 1976), 117; *The Liberty Gazette*, June 18, 1855.

[28] *Official Records*, Series I, Volume IV, 151.

[29] Camilla "Mimmie" Hardin to her brother William F. "Bee" Hardin, November 22, 1862, Trammell, *Seven Pines*, 174,184.

[30] R. Henderson Shuffler, "Decimus et Ultimus Barziza," *Southwestern Historical Quarterly*, LXVI, No. 4 (April 1963), 501-512.

[31] For illustrations of the carding, spinning, and weaving process by Charles Shaw, see Elizabeth Silverthorne, *Plantation Life in Texas* (College Station: Texas A&M University Press, 1986), 100-103.

[32] *The Liberty Gazette*, December 22, 1856, and July 4, 1866; Diana J. Kleiner, "Liberty County," in *The New Handbook of Texas*, 4:188-190; Partlow, *Liberty, Liberty County, and the Atascosito District*, 269-270, 353.

[33] George Shumway, Edward Durell, and Howard C. Frey, *Conestoga Wagon 1750-1850*, 2nd ed. (York, Pa.: George Shumway and Early American Industries Association, Inc., 1966), 197.

Notes for Chapter 4

[1] Eliza H. Bishop, "Shiloh, Texas," in *The New Handbook of Texas.* ed, Ron Tyler, et al., 6 vols. (Austin: Texas State Historical Association, 1996), 5:1028.

[2] Joshua James Hall diary, Reel 33 of 44, Records of Ante-Bellum Plantations from the Revolution through the Civil War, Series G, Part 1, Microfilm B, 3762, M. D. Anderson Library, University of Houston, Houston, Texas.

[3] Elizabeth Silverthorne, *Plantation Life in Texas* (College Station: Texas A&M University Press, 1986), 96-104; Paula Mitchell Marks, *Hands to the Spindle* (College Station: Texas A&M University Press, 1996), 11, 100.

[4] David G. McComb, *Galveston: A History* (Austin: University of Texas Press, 1986), 47.

5. Additional postmasters in Crockett, who were friends of Hall, were Thomas P. Collins (1846 and 1864), Joseph A. Wright (1856), William Wortham (1861), W. E. Haden (1862), and Sylvester V. Hall (1865), http://www.rootsweb.com/~txpost/houston.html [accessed December 17, 2001].

6. 1860 U.S. Census; Hall family records.

7. *The Crockett Printer*, December 6, 1853; Armistead Albert Aldrich, *The History of Houston County, Texas* (San Antonio: The Naylor Company, 1943), 44, 175-177; 1860 U.S. Census; *The Houston Weekly Telegraph*, March 9, 1859 (reprinted from *The Crockett Printer*.)

8. 1860 U.S. Census; 1880 U.S. Census; Aldrich, *The History of Houston County, Texas*, 24; Texas State Library and Archives Commission.

9. 1860 U.S. Census.

10. Ibid.

11. Miriam Partlow, *Liberty, Liberty County, and the Atascocito District* (Austin: The Pemberton Press/Jenkins Publishing Co., 1974), 350-352; 1860 U.S. Census.

12. Lewis F. Fisher, *C. H. Guenther & Son at 150 Years: The Legacy of a Texas Milling Pioneer* (San Antonio: Maverick Publishing Company, 2001), 9-10.

13. "Malaria," World Health Organization Fact Sheet No. 94, http://www.who.int/mediacentre/factsheets/ [accessed August 5, 2005].

14. David P. Smith, "Conscription and Conflict on the Texas Frontier, 1863-1865," in *Lone Star Blue and Gray*, ed. Ralph A. Wooster (Austin: Texas State Historical Association, 1995), 275-287; Ralph A. Wooster, *Texas and Texans in the Civil War* (Austin: Eakin Press, 1995), 102-103.

15. A *vara* is about thirty-three and one-third inches. "*Vara*," *The New Handbook of Texas*, 6:710.

16. Aldrich, *The History of Houston County, Texas*, 159; Thomas Nelms Mainer, *Houston County in the Civil War* (Crockett, Tex.: Publications Development Co. of Texas, 1981), 77-78, 97; "Gould's Battalion: Sketch of Its History by a Member," from the *Houston County Courier*, Vol. 2, No. 25, July 24, 1891, http://www.rootsweb.ancestry.com/~txhousto/military/goulds_txbat_6thtxcav.htm [accessed September 28, 2016].

17. W. T. Block, *Cotton Bales, Keelboats and Sternwheelers: A History of the Sabine River and Trinity River Cotton Trades, 1837-1900* (Woodville, Tex.: Dogwood Press, 1995), 164, 165; Keith Guthrie, *Texas Forgotten Ports, Vol. III* (Austin: Eakin Press, 1995), 85, 86.

18. 1850 U.S. Census; Block, *Cotton Bales, Keelboats and Sternwheelers*, 216-217; *The Houston Weekly Telegraph*, June 5, 1860; *Confederate Pensions* (Baltimore, Md.: Genealogical Publishing Company, 1970), 5:275 (Pension No. 3,518 ["List of Pensioners on the Roll, January 1, 1883, As Called for by Senate Resolution of December 8, 1882"]. Isaac Peacock was the man killed by Hall in 1859 (see Introduction).

19. 1870 U.S. Census.

20. The greatest wheat production at this time occurred in the counties along the Red River and in North Central Texas, while some wheat was being grown in what became known as the Blackland Prairie of Central Texas. Clayton E. Jewett, *Texas in the Confederacy: An Experiment in Nation Building* (Columbia: University of Missouri Press, 2002), 46.

Notes for Chapter 5

[1] Clayton E. Jewett, *Texas in the Confederacy* (Columbia: University of Missouri Press, 2002), 116, 120-124; David P. Smith, "Conscription and Conflict on the Texas Frontier, 1863-1865," in *Lone Star Blue and Gray*, ed. Ralph A. Wooster (Austin: Texas State Historical Association, 1995), 275-287.

[2] Smith, "Conscription and Conflict on the Texas Frontier, 1863-1865," in *Lone Star Blue and Gray*, 276-277; Chas. W. Ramsdell, "The Texas State Military Board, 1862-1865," *Southwestern Historical Quarterly*, XXVII, No. 4 (April 1924), 253-275; Jewett, *Texas in the Confederacy*, 121.

[3] Smith, "Conscription and Conflict on the Texas Frontier, 1863-1865," in *Lone Star Blue and Gray*, 277-279; Jewett, *Texas in the Confederacy*, 128, 130; H. P. N. Gammel, comp., *The Laws of Texas 1822-1897*, 10 vols. (Austin: The Gammel Book Company, 1898), 5:677-679, https://texashistory.unt.edu/explore/collections/GLT/#description [accessed August 3, 2016].

[4] Jewett, *Texas in the Confederacy*, 130; T. R. Fehrenbach, *Lone Star: A History of Texas and the Texans* (New York: Collier Books, 1985), 361; Ralph A. Wooster and Robert Wooster, "'Rarin' for a Fight': Texans in the Confederate Army," in *Lone Star Blue and Gray*, 56-57.

[5] Jewett, *Texas in the Confederacy*, 144-145; Ralph A. Wooster, *Texas and Texans in the Civil War* (Austin: Eakin Press, 1995), 74.

[6] Jewett, *Texas in the Confederacy*, 136-137; Gammel, *The Laws of Texas 1822-1897*, 5:698-699.

[7] Jewett, *Texas in the Confederacy*, 134, 136-137; Smith, "Conscription and Conflict on the Texas Frontier, 1863-1865," in *Lone Star Blue and Gray*, 279; Gammel, *The Laws of Texas 1822-1897*, 5:698-699.

[8] Smith, "Conscription and Conflict on the Texas Frontier, 1863-1865," in *Lone Star Blue and Gray*, 279-280; Wooster, *Texas and Texans in the Civil War*, 105-106; Fehrenbach, *Lone Star*, 366.

[9] Gammel, *The Laws of Texas 1822-1897*, 5:677-679.

[10] Smith, "Conscription and Conflict on the Texas Frontier, 1863-1865," in *Lone Star Blue and Gray*, 280; Wooster, *Texas and Texans in the Civil War*, 106.

[11] Smith, "Conscription and Conflict on the Texas Frontier, 1863-1865," in *Lone Star Blue and Gray*, 281-282.

[12] Marshall is approximately 106 miles from Crockett.

[13] Telephone interview between the author and Daniel Seifu, miller, at Homestead Heritage Craft Village, Waco, Texas, August 10, 2016.

[14] Douglas Hale, "Lane, Walter Paye," in *The New Handbook of Texas*, ed. Ron Tyler, et al., 6 vols. (Austin: Texas State Historical Association, 1996), 4:62-63. For more on Lane's Rangers, see Ralph A. Wooster, *Lone Star Regiments in Gray* (Austin: Eakin Press, 2002), 155, 174-176, 179, 181, 183, 321.

[15] Thomas W. Cutrer, "Nunn, David Alexander," in *The New Handbook of Texas*, 4:1077; Thomas Nelms Mainer, *Houston County in the Civil War* (Crockett, Tex.: Publications Development Company of Texas, 1981), 43-47, 52; Armistead Albert Aldrich, *The History of Houston County, Texas* (San Antonio: The Naylor Co., 1943), 182-183.

[16] After the Civil War, some of Cortina's followers resumed their bandit raids, requiring U.S. Army presence in South Texas. John Salmon Ford, *Rip Ford's Texas*, ed. Stephen B. Oates (Austin: University of Texas Press, 1987), xxxix, 262-264, 276, 351, 364, 371, 376, 383, 388-393, 408; Stephen B. Oates, "John S. 'Rip' Ford: Prudent Cavalryman, C.S.A.," in *Lone Star Blue and Gray,* 313-335.

[17] James L. Nichols, *The Confederate Quartermaster in the Trans-Mississippi* (Austin: University of Texas Press, 1964), 43-52, 104-105.

[18] Miriam Partlow, *Liberty, Liberty County, and the Atascosito District* (Austin: The Pemberton Press/Jenkins Publishing Co., 1974), 214.

[19] Palestine is a little more than thirty miles from Crockett, or about eighteen miles from Hall's farm.

[20] 1850 U.S. Census; 1860 U.S. Census.

[21] Ben C. Stuart, "Texas Steamboat Days," typescript (October 11, 1919), 84, courtesy of the Rosenberg Library, Galveston, Texas; Mark Odintz, "Magnolia, Texas," in *The New Handbook of Texas*, 4:460-461.

[22] Howard N. Martin, "Alabama-Coushatta Indians," in *The New Handbook of Texas*, 1:77-81.

[23] Howard N. Martin, "Beazley, William Herbert," in *The New Handbook of Texas*, 1:450-451; Ralph A. Wooster and Robert Wooster, "'Rarin' for a Fight': Texans in the Confederate Army," in *Lone Star Blue and Gray*, 56; Partlow, *Liberty, Liberty County, and the Atascosito District*, 214.

[24] Stuart, "Texas Steamboat Days," 92; W. T. Block, *Cotton Bales, Keelboats and Sternwheelers: A History of the Sabine River and Trinity River Cotton Trades, 1837-1900* (Woodville, Tex.: Dogwood Press, 1995), 172; Muster Roll, Jefferson County, Texas State Library and Archives Commission; Partlow, *Liberty, Liberty County, and the Atascosito District*, 213, 287, 352; *The Liberty Vindicator*, May 22 and June 5, 1896.

[25] 1860 U.S. Census; Block, *Cotton Bales, Keelboats and Sternwheelers*, 171-172; Captain Thomas Stubblefield was murdered by a passenger on the *Ida Rees* in March 1870; *Galveston Tri-Weekly News*, March 9, 1870. Ben C. Stuart states that Captain Stubblefield was "shot and killed by the steamers [*sic*] bar keeper . . ." on the *Ida Rees*; Stuart, "Texas Steamboat Days," 72.

[26] The revised tax law allowed farmers to keep "all corn under 200 bushels, to substitute salt pork for cured bacon, and to receive credit for losses due to enemy action or accident." Nichols, *The Confederate Quartermaster in the Trans-Mississippi*, 45. See Nichols, *The Confederate Quartermaster in the Trans-Mississippi*, Chapter 3, "The Tax-in-Kind in the Trans-Mississippi," which provides details, 43-52.

[27] Hall family records; Charles Christopher Jackson, "Connell, John," in *The New Handbook of Texas*, 2:271.

[28] Dr. Abner King was a Georgian. When he and his family moved to Texas, a Mr. Rentfrow joined them to remain close to the family. This may be the Mr. "Renfro" who was mentioned by Hall on January 26, 1860. Renfro had come to the house to make arrangements with Hall to rent "the lower field" for growing cotton and corn. A John Rentfro, age twenty-five, born in Georgia, is listed in the 1860 U.S. Census as living in the Elkhart Post Office Precinct, but so is Henry Rentfro, age fifty-one, born in North Carolina. No conclusion can be drawn regarding which of the men Hall

referenced. http://benotforgot-journal.blogspot.com/1970/09/dr-abner-g-king.html [accessed on August 10, 2016]. In the 1870 U.S. Census, King was enumerated in Houston County, age forty-two, born in Georgia. His wife and six children were also listed. He did not appear on the 1880 U.S. Census.

29. Telephone interview between the author and Jane Pigeon, weaver, Conner Prairie Living History Museum, February 7, 2007 (Connor Prairie Interactive History Park, 2016), Fishers, Indiana; Edward F. Worst, *Foot-Power Loom Weaving* (Milwaukee, Wis.: The Bruce Publishing Company, 1918; Twelfth Printing, 1952), 27-34.

30. Jewett, *Texas in the Confederacy*, 168-170; Ella Lonn, *Salt as a Factor in the Confederacy*, reprint (University, Ala.: University of Alabama Press, 1965), 13-18.

31. Wooster, *Texas and Texans in the Civil War*, 123; Lonn, *Salt as a Factor in the Confederacy*, 19-34.

32. Bill Winsor, *Texas in the Confederacy: Military Installations, Economy and People* (Hillsboro, Tex.: Hill Junior College Press, 1978), 50-51, 53-54; Gammel, *The Laws of Texas 1822-1897*, 5:752; Lonn, *Salt as a Factor in the Confederacy*, 35-53.

33. 1860 U.S. Census.

34. Gammel, *The Laws of Texas 1822-1897*, 5:484-485; Jewett, *Texas in the Confederacy*, 165-166.

35. Ramsdell, "The Texas State Military Board, 1862-1865," 255-261; Wooster, *Texas and Texans in the Civil War*, 98-99.

36. Ramsdell, "The Texas State Military Board, 1862-1865," 266-267.

37. Jewett, *Texas in the Confederacy*, 174, 175, 186-187, 192-193, 201-203; Ramsdell, "The Texas State Military Board, 1862-1865," 270-271.

38. Jewett, *Texas in the Confederacy*, 177, 178, 188-190; Wooster, *Texas and Texans in the Civil War*, 106-107; Ramsdell, "The Texas State Military Board, 1862-1865," 270-271; Nichols, *The Confederate Quartermaster in the Trans-Mississippi*, 53-82.

39. Ramsdell, "The Texas State Military Board, 1862-1865," 258; Jewett, *Texas in the Confederacy*, 187-188.

40. Ramsdell, "The Texas State Military Board, 1862-1865," 271; Fehrenbach, *Lone Star*, 366-367; Jewett, *Texas in the Confederacy*, 190-196; Ronnie C. Tyler, "Cotton on the Border, 1861-1865," in *Lone Star Blue and Gray*, 225.

41. Jewett, *Texas in the Confederacy*, 188-190; Wooster, *Texas and Texans in the Civil War*, 98, 106-108.

42. Wooster, *Texas and Texans in the Civil War*, 106; Nichols, *The Confederate Quartermaster in the Trans-Mississippi*, 53-82; Ramsdell, "The Texas State Military Board, 1862-1865," 253-275; Jewett, *Texas in the Confederacy*, 194.

43. Jewett, *Texas in the Confederacy*, 165; Gammel, *The Laws of Texas 1822-1897*, 5:680; Ramsdell, "The Texas State Military Board, 1862-1865," 269-275.

44. Jewett, *Texas in the Confederacy*, 189.

45. Gammel, *The Laws of Texas 1822-1897*, 5:816-818. This law was intended to "identify and distribute cloth and thread" from the penitentiary for indigent families; permitted tax payments "in produce"; set up records for distribution of cloth and produce to indigent families; and repealed the war tax of January 1, 1862, and indigent family act of March 6, 1863. This Act was approved on November 15, 1864.

[46.] J. G. Randall and David Donald, *The Civil War and Reconstruction*, 2nd ed. (Boston: D. C. Heath and Company, 1961), 256-258.

[47.] Randall and Donald, *The Civil War and Reconstruction*, 259-260.

[48.] Ibid., 260-261.

[49.] Ibid., 260-264.

[50.] Wooster, *Lone Star Regiments in Gray*, 149, 151, 155.

[51.] Ibid., 151, 154, 156, 205, 327.

[52.] Ibid., 142, 153-159, 178-179, 182-183, 190, 191.

Notes for Chapter 6

[1.] John Salmon Ford, *Rip Ford's Texas*, ed. Stephen B. Oates (Austin: University of Texas Press, 1987), 389.

[2.] J. G. Randall and David Donald, *The Civil War and Reconstruction*, 2nd ed. (Boston: D. C. Heath and Company, 1961), 522, 525-527; Col. Harold B. Simpson, "Hood's Texas Brigade at Appomattox," in *Lone Star Blue and Gray*, ed. Ralph A. Wooster (Austin: Texas State Historical Association, 1995), 337-347.

[3.] T. R. Fehrenbach, *Lone Star: A History of Texas and the Texans* (New York: Collier Books, 1985), 393-395; Ford, *Rip Ford's Texas*, 397.

[4.] Ford, *Rip Ford's Texas*, 389-393; Ralph A. Wooster, *Texas and Texans in the Civil War* (Austin: Eakin Press, 1995), 180-181.

[5.] David G. McComb, *Galveston: A History* (Austin: University of Texas Press, 1986), 81.

[6.] Wooster, *Texas and Texans in the Civil War*, 179-180; Brad R. Clampitt, "The Breakup: The Collapse of the Confederate Trans-Mississippi Army in Texas, 1865," *Southwestern Historical Quarterly*, 108 (April 2005), 499-534; Karen Gerhardt, "A Most Miserable Hole: Camp Ford, C.S.A.," *North and South Magazine*, Vol. 1, No. 5 (April 1998): 48-55.

[7.] The diary and letters of Captain William B. Duncan provide details about Spaight's Battalion throughout the war. Duncan was a Freemason and a friend of both Hall and Wrigley. William B. Duncan diary, Liberty County, Texas, transcribed from the original owned by Mrs. Julia Duncan Welder, Liberty, Texas, San Jacinto Museum of History, Houston, Texas, 1940, courtesy of Sam Houston Regional Library and Research Center, Liberty, Texas; Wooster, *Texas and Texans in the Civil War*, 72; Alwyn Barr, "Texas Coastal Defense, 1861-1865," in *Lone Star Blue and Gray*, 161, 165; Andrew Forest Muir, "Dick Dowling and the Battle of Sabine Pass," in *Lone Star Blue and Gray*, 187.

[8.] 1860 U.S. Census.

[9.] Gerald L. Holder, "Danville, Texas," in *The New Handbook of Texas*, ed. Ron Tyler, et al., 6 vols. (Austin: Texas State Historical Association, 1996), 2:509.

[10.] *The Liberty Gazette*, June 22, 1860; *The Galveston Weekly News*, June 20, August 22, and September 26, 1866.

[11.] David G. McComb, *Houston: A History* (Austin: University of Texas Press, 1981), 54-55; Miriam Partlow, *Liberty, Liberty County, and the Atascosito District* (Austin: The Pemberton Press/Jenkins Publishing Co., 1974), 215.

[12] Barry A. Crouch, *The Freedmen's Bureau and Black Texans* (Austin: University of Texas Press, 1992), 13, 16.

[13] Camilla D. Trammell, "Hardin, Benjamin Franklin," in *The New Handbook of Texas*, 3:453. For more on the Hardin family, see Camilla Davis Trammell, *Seven Pines: Its Occupants and Their Letters, 1825-1872* (Dallas: Southern Methodist University Press, 1987).

[14] Trammell, *Seven Pines*, 66, 67; 1860 U.S. Census; *The Liberty Gazette*, October 12, 1860, January 11, 1861, and July 4, 1866; Partlow, *Liberty, Liberty County, and the Atascosito District*, 352, 353.

[15] Kenneth M. Stampp, *The Era of Reconstruction 1865-1877* (New York: Vintage Books, 1965), 42-43, 62; Fehrenbach, *Lone Star*, 396.

[16] Randall and Donald, *The Civil War and Reconstruction*, 558.

[17] Ibid., 559, 560, 601-603.

[18] Stampp, *The Era of Reconstruction 1865-1877*, 62-64; Fehrenbach, *Lone Star*, 396, 398; Crouch, *The Freedmen's Bureau and Black Texans*, 17.

[19] Crouch, *The Freedmen's Bureau and Black Texans*, 2-3; Randall and Donald, *The Civil War and Reconstruction*, 576-578; Stampp, *The Era of Reconstruction 1865-1877*, 135-136.

[20] Crouch, *The Freedmen's Bureau and Black Texans*, 12-40.

[21] Harold D. Woodman, *King Cotton and His Retainers: Financing & Marketing the Cotton Crop of the South, 1800-1925* (Lexington: University of Kentucky Press, 1968), 227, 236.

[22] Woodman, *King Cotton and His Retainers*, 246-253.

[23] Ben C. Stuart, "Texas Steamboat Days," typescript (October 11, 1919), 73, 98, courtesy of Rosenberg Library, Galveston, Texas; W. T. Block, *Cotton Bales, Keelboats and Sternwheelers: A History of the Sabine River and Trinity River Cotton Trades*, 1837-1900 (Woodville, Tex.: Dogwood Press, 1995), 182-183, 226, 227; Pamela Ashworth Puryear and Nath Winfield, Jr., *Sandbars and Sternwheelers: Steam Navigation on the Brazos* (College Station: Texas A&M University Press, 1976), 99-100.

[24] Frequent references to Ed. L. Jones, A. B. Trowell, James Wrigley, and B. F. Sterling appear in Trammell, *Seven Pines*. See Chapter 2, note 11, for references relating to Ed L. Jones.

[25] See Trammell, *Seven Pines*, Chapter 3, note 2, for references relating to W. D. Williams.

[26] William B. Duncan diary, Liberty County, Texas, transcribed from the original owned by Mrs. Julia Duncan Welder, Liberty, Texas, San Jacinto Museum of History, Houston, Texas, 1940, courtesy of Sam Houston Regional Library and Research Center, Liberty, Texas.

Notes for Chapter 7

[1] *The Liberty Gazette*, December 22, 1856, and July 4, 1866.

[2] 1860 U.S. Census.

3. Carl H. Moneyhon, "Reconstruction," in *The New Handbook of Texas*, ed. Ron Tyler, et al., 6 vols. (Austin: Texas State Historical Association, 1996), 5:474-481, quotation, 476.

4. *The Liberty Gazette*, July (no date), 1866, and May 8, 1867; Miriam Partlow, *Liberty, Liberty County, and the Atascosito District* (Austin: The Pemberton Press/ Jenkins Publishing Co., 1974), 353.

5. Silvier Pierre Baillio was a city councilman (1866-1867). Partlow, *Liberty, Liberty County, and the Atascocito District*, 353.

6. *Frederick* Way, Jr., *Way's Packet Directory, 1848-1994* (Athens, Ohio: Ohio University Press, 1983, revised 1994), No. 1230, p. 104; W. T. Block, *Cotton Bales, Keelboats and Sternwheelers: A History of the Sabine River and Trinity River Cotton Trades, 1837-1900* (Woodville, Tex.: Dogwood Press, 1995), 165, 205, 212, 213; Ben C. Stuart, "Texas Steamboat Days," typescript (October 11, 1919), 73, courtesy of Rosenberg Library, Galveston, Texas; *The Galveston Weekly News*, May 9, 1866; *The Galveston Weekly News*, February 1 and March 28, 1867; *The Civil War Naval Chronology 1861-1865* (U.S. Navy, Naval History Division, Navy Department, Washington, D.C., 1972), 6:214; *Dictionary of American Naval Fighting Ships, Vol. II* (U.S. Navy Department, Office of the Chief of Naval Operations, Naval History Division, Washington, D.C.; Appendix II, Confederate Forces Afloat, Annex III, Texas Marine Department, Confederate States Army, 1963), 510.

7. *The Galveston Weekly News*, May 23, 1866.

8. *The Galveston Weekly News*, June 6, 1866.

9. Block, *Cotton Bales, Keelboats and Sternwheelers*, 172; Stuart, "Texas Steamboat Days," 74, 86, 93; *The Galveston Weekly News*, June 27, 1866.

10. *The Liberty Gazette*, January 11, 1861.

11. Moneyhon, "Reconstruction," in *The New Handbook of Texas*, 5:477.

12. J. G. Randall and David Donald, *The Civil War and Reconstruction*, 2nd Edition (Boston: D. C. Heath and Company, 1961), 553 (footnote 6).

13. R. B. Sewell advertised his work as a painter in *The Liberty Gazette*, pointing out the new "enamel finish." He referred readers to the parlors he had painted for James Hall, James Wrigley, and T. J. Chambers, the editor of the newspaper. *The Liberty Gazette*, November (?), 1866, in Partlow, *Liberty, Liberty County, and the Atascocito District*, 274.

Notes for the Afterword

1. 1860 U.S. Census; Thomas Nelms Mainer, *Houston County in the Civil War* (Crockett, Tex.: Publications Development Company of Texas, 1981), 77-79; 1870 U.S. Census.

2. 1870 U.S. Census; 1880 U.S. Census; Marriages, Groom Index, 1882-1917, transcribed by Mary Turner Kinard; Correspondence from Robert L. Hall to Dennis Frazier, August 13, 1962, describing and listing Hall family relationships; Ida Mae (Sharp) Halyard, September 13, 1962, deposition. On September 13, 1962, Ida Mae (Sharp) Halyard, a daughter of Sam and Nellie Sharp, stated in a deposition the history of her immediate family. The deposition was sworn to by Dennis C. Frazier,

a Notary Public in Houston County, on that date. This deposition has been an important document in telling the story of the Hall and Sharp families. A copy of the deposition was kindly provided to me by Vickie P. Everhart, a descendant of Sam and Nellie Sharp, on April 12, 2005.

3. Halyard, 1962 deposition; Genealogical data, courtesy of Vickie P. Everhart and the Hall family. Ida Halyard's husband was the nephew of Marcus M. Halyard, Roberta Hall's second husband.

4. Obituary, *The Crockett Courier*, p. 14, No. 13, April 12, 1934, courtesy of Vickie P. Everhart; Halyard, 1962 deposition; Genealogical data, courtesy of Vickie P. Everhart and the Hall family. Correspondence from Robert L. Hall to Dennis Frazier, August 13, 1962; Affidavit from H. O. Hall regarding marriage of Mahala L. Hall and J. J. Hall, dated October 31, 1914, filed on November 2, 1914, recorded in Vol. 145, p. 534, Deed Records, Jefferson Co., Texas, notarized by Geo. W. Crook, Houston County, Texas, courtesy of Eliza H. Bishop, Houston County Historical Commission, Crockett, Texas, 2005.

5. Widow's Application for a Pension, July 3, 1916, No. 33011, courtesy of Texas State Library and Archives Commission, Austin, Texas; 1860 U.S. Census; 1870 U.S. Census; 1900 U.S. Census.

6. Courtesy of Mrs. Angelia Moore; Widow's Application for a Pension, July 3, 1916, No. 33011.

7. 1850 U.S. Census; *The Liberty Vindicator*, Friday, May 22 and Friday, June 5, 1896; Southeast Texas Family History Collection/Wrigley-Gayle Families, Sam Houston Regional Library and Research Center, Liberty, Texas; Alvarado, Texas, Public Library.

8. 1860 U.S. Census; 1880 U.S. Census for Galveston.

9. Camilla Davis Trammell, *Seven Pines: Its Occupants and Their Letters, 1825-1872* (Dallas: Southern Methodist University Press, 1987), 147, 151; Muster Roll, Texas State Library and Archives Commission (the muster roll reads Company B, but the pension application states Company F); W. T. Block, *Cotton Bales, Keelboats and Sternwheelers: A History of the Sabine River and Trinity River Cotton Trades, 1837-1900* (Woodville, Tex.: Dogwood Press, 1995), 170, 172, 238 (footnote 35). Stuart also names Ed. L. Jones in his list of "old time river men"; Ben C. Stuart, "Texas Steamboat Days," typescript (October11, 1919), 96, courtesy of Rosenberg Library, Galveston, Texas.

10. Soldier's Application for Pension, September 16, 1911, No. 20630, courtesy of Texas State Library and Archives Commission, Austin, Texas.

Index

CPSIA information can be obtained
at www.ICGtesting.com
Printed in the USA
LVOW01s0755120317
526844LV00006B/7/P